EXTREME HAUNTINGS

Britain's Most Terrifying Ghosts

EXTREME HAUNTINGS

Britain's Most Terrifying Ghosts

PAUL ADAMS & EDDIE BRAZIL
Foreword by Guy N. Smith

The
History
Press

For Colin Wilson.

First published 2013

The History Press
The Mill, Brimscombe Port
Stroud, Gloucestershire, GL5 2QG
www.thehistorypress.co.uk

British Library Cataloguing in Publication Data.
A catalogue record for this book is available from the British Library.

ISBN 978 0 7524 6535 7

Typesetting and origination by The History Press
Printed in Great Britain
Manufacturing managed by Jellyfish Solutions Ltd

From the Collins English Dictionary

Extreme [adj.] Being of a high or of the highest degree or intensity.
Haunt [verb] To visit (a person or place) in the form of a ghost.

From the Authors

Extreme Haunting [noun] An intense and or prolonged encounter with the paranormal, often involving apparitions, physical violence, and intense fear...

CONTENTS

ACKNOWLEDGEMENTS

Several people have assisted with the writing and production of this book, and we would like to take this opportunity to thank the following: Guy N. Smith, the master of British horror, for writing the foreword; Peter Underwood, for the use of illustrations and for generously providing information from his files; Bowen Pearse, Paul Cawthorne and Alan Murdie, who helped with information on the late Andrew Green and also assisted with photographs; Paul Screeton, who shared information on his investigation into the Hexham Head mystery; Darren W. Ritson and Michael Hallowell, for information and feedback on our examination of the South Shields Poltergeist case; Sean Tudor and Richard Bramall, who assisted with photographs of haunted roads; Michael Briant for recollecting his experiences at Wookey Hole and Chris Goodchild of Wookey Hole Ltd who provided illustrations; Damien O'Dell for information on the haunting of Flitwick Manor and William King for helping with photographs; Guy Playfair for providing the photograph of Maurice Grosse; and last but by no means least, our editor Matilda Richards at The History Press. On the home fronts we would also like to thank Sue and Rebecca Brazil, and Aban, Idris, Isa and Sakina Adams, for their patience and support.

In connection with photographs, we have made every attempt to clear copyright information on the illustrations used in this book and apologise if any have been inadvertently omitted. If you feel your copyright has been infringed, please contact the publisher and we would be pleased to amend the credits in any future edition.

FOREWORD

by Guy N. Smith

I have known Paul Adams as a personal friend and a researcher of the paranormal for several years. Whilst he claims that there are no 'experts' on the subject, in my opinion he comes pretty close. Paul has several published works to his credit: *The Borley Rectory Companion* (2009) and *Shadows in the Nave* (2011), both co-written with Eddie Brazil. This year saw his first solo book *Ghosts and Gallows* and now we have another collaboration with Brazil. All this in a space of just three years and I have no doubt that there will be more.

This book leaves me with a sense of unease, far more so than any spooky novel or film has ever done. One of the reasons is that the happenings are true, or purported to be, and that these mysterious events are not solved which would put the mind at rest.

Most disconcerting of all for myself is the episode of the Hexham Heads, about which I had read elsewhere. What exactly were they and do such creatures as werewolves exist? Strangely, last year the press reported the finding of a rectangular tablet, engraved with a star and strange writing, buried in Hopwas Wood, Staffordshire, unearthed by investigators from the West Midlands Ghost Club. Nobody knows what this find represents or how old it is. This ancient woodland is reputed to be haunted so one cannot help wondering if the tablet is associated with the paranormal. The events following the discovery of the Hexham Heads, and now this latest find, send shivers up my spine. I certainly would not care to be in possession of either of them.

Extreme Hauntings has revived memories of a couple of my own strange experiences. The first took place around 1956 adjacent to the old Snow Hill Station in Birmingham. On my way home from work early one foggy November evening (we had *real* fog in those days), I decided to make a call at the adjoining gent's toilet. A man preceded me; I didn't take much notice of him, just one of many thronging the street. It was only when I entered that I became aware that the interior was empty, there was not another soul in sight.

I had not imagined this figure in the fog and he had definitely entered those toilets.

My second experience also occurred on a fogbound November afternoon, this time in 1972. My wife and I had only been married a couple of months and our first home was a large, two-floor flat in Lichfield.

On the day in question my wife had gone to visit her mother and I was alone in the flat. I was working at my desk when suddenly I heard heavy footsteps directly above me in the main bedroom.

Nobody could have gone up there without passing in full view of my desk. The only other vague possibility was that some agile and reckless person might have shinned up the drainpipe, but even then they would surely have attracted my attention through the window.

Basically, the only route to the upper floor was via the stairs. I mounted these stealthily, burst open the bedroom door and shouted, 'All right, let's have you!' There was nobody in the room, nor in the adjoining rooms. I checked everywhere, under beds, inside fitted cupboards, behind doors. Nothing.

This was certainly scary and on my wife's return she looked at me and asked, 'Are you alright? You look like you've seen a ghost!'

Well, I believe I had certainly heard one. A few weeks later we moved from that flat to a house – and not just because we needed more space.

Extreme Hauntings brings back that sense of fear of the unknown. A truly fascinating read… but I prefer to read it during the daylight hours!

Guy N. Smith
Shropshire, 2013

INTRODUCTION

This book is a survey of true paranormal cases spanning a period of nearly 250 years, from the beginning of the second half of the eighteenth century through to the opening years of the New Millennium. These supernatural dramas, just over thirty in number, play out in a disparate variety of settings: a Tudor manor house, a rural Victorian rectory, an Edinburgh townhouse, lonely woods and highways, council houses, a Northumberland flour mill, a seaside theatre. The players cover the widest range of British society: titled gentry, the affluent and the working class, country vicars, journalists, ordinary suburban families. The ghosts and psychical phenomena that spans the years and binds them all together is something that we have termed 'extreme hauntings', i.e. spontaneous paranormal experiences that are characterised by their intense and often disturbing nature.

This intensity can be represented in many ways: the longevity of the haunting, as at the notorious Borley Rectory; strange and disturbing apparitions, such as the ghosts of Willington Mill; extraordinary violence and physical destruction, chillingly demonstrated by the poltergeist cases of Enfield and South Shields; strange forces associated with ancient relics, like the Seton sacrum bone and the buried Celtic heads at Hexham. All of these cases and many others like them await the reader in the pages that follow.

In Britain, we are fortunate that our country, evocatively described by the novelist and historian Peter Ackroyd as 'a land engulfed by mist and twilight', has an extraordinarily rich supernatural heritage that we as writers and researchers have been able to draw upon, although, interestingly enough, the majority of our cases are of twentieth-century origin, proof that the most turbulent and eventful period in human history has seemingly given rise to the most frightening and extreme of our native ghosts. Fittingly, this haunted land is the birthplace of organised psychical research and investigation, and this strong and pioneering ghost-hunting tradition traces a long and distinguished lineage through the work of organisations such as The Ghost Club, the Society for

Psychical Research, Harry Price's old National Laboratory of Psychical Research and its successor, the University of London Council for Psychical Investigation, to the Unitarian Society for Psychical Studies and the Association for the Scientific Study of Anomalous Phenomena (ASSAP), through to the many regional and local paranormal groups active in the country today, to whom the contents of this book will undoubtedly be of interest.

Those who become more than superficially involved in the investigation of the paranormal soon find themselves walking a tightrope that crosses a yawning canyon of conflict and opposites: critical study verses sensationalism and media exploitation, scientific method and scepticism as opposed to uncritical belief and acceptance, practical experimentation and research compared with unfounded theory and speculation. It must also be said that there are no 'experts' where the paranormal is concerned: there are many well-informed, knowledgeable and experienced researchers and investigators, but despite 130 years of organised investigation and study (since the founding of the Society for Psychical Research in 1882), both in this country and abroad, the mystery remains – we still do not know why houses become haunted, why there appear to be different 'types' of ghost, how a poltergeist can levitate and throw an object across a room, or how mediums and psychics can seemingly communicate with the dead; or even if survival after death is a reality, or simply the ultimate item on the wish-list of humanity. There is also the issue of scepticism and the backlash against the belief of and research into the subject of the paranormal by the scientific mainstream.

Much of the criticism levelled against the reality of paranormal phenomena gains support from the lack of ability on the part of ghost hunters and psychical researchers to recreate psychic phenomena as repeatable experiments under laboratory conditions. This scepticism achieved a semi-professional status in the mid-1970s with the foundation, by American secularist and humanist writer Paul Kurtz, of CSICOP, the Committee for the Scientific Investigation of Claims of the Paranormal, known today as the Committee for Skeptical Enquiry, or CSI. In the early 1980s, the torch was also taken up by retired stage magician and illusionist, James 'The Amazing' Randi, known for his controversial 'One Million Dollar Challenge' and summary dismissal as 'flim-flam' of a wide range of alleged supernormal phenomena, from the Geller effect, psychic healing and mediumship, through to astrology, ghosts, hauntings and possessions. In 1996, Randi set up his own CSICOP-inspired body, the James Randi Educational Foundation, that continues to promote, as the late American psychical researcher D. Scott Rogo once described it, the former entertainer's 'holy war against psychics and parapsychologists', that has now entered its fourth crusading decade.

A factor that compounds the problem of repeatable experimentation for ghost hunters and psychical researchers is something that writer Colin Wilson, in his book *Afterlife*, has described as 'James' Law' (after William James, the American psychologist), i.e. no paranormal phenomenon is ever 100 per cent convincing. This can lead over time to a sensation of frustration on the part of dedicated researchers and those genuinely interested in finding the truth and solving the mysteries behind the enigmatic psi-universe, who gradually loose the feelings of youthful enthusiasm and excitement that in the beginning, contact with the world of ghosts and hauntings through books and literature, can create.

Which brings us to the reasons behind the compilation of the present work. In this project, we have attempted to produce the kind of book that, if we were able to wind back the clock (through more years than we both would care to admit), would be the kind of book that we would want to pull off the shelf and read. In it we have tried to include a broad range of cases: there are some personal favourites, some well-known ghosts, as well as rarities from the vast psychic literature of this country, plus personal experiences and new hauntings. The cases are grouped in sections in date order, and for each of our extreme hauntings we have included preliminary comments plus individual bibliographies for further research and study.

Will the mysteries ever be solved? Possibly, one day, but when that will be is a mystery in itself. In the meantime, we hope that you enjoy our book of 'extreme' ghosts and poltergeists. If seasoned ghost hunters who are kind enough to look through another addition to the steadily increasing body of paranormal literature come away with a renewed sense of enthusiasm for this, the most challenging of disciplines, and if those new to parapsychology and the supernatural find it stimulating enough to take the first steps on the road to practical investigation, we will have succeeded in our aims in writing it. But, before you begin the journey, perhaps it is advisable to sign off with an interesting quotation by the late British science-fiction writer and futurist thinker, Arthur C. Clarke, who often paraphrased the biologist J.B.S. Haldane, when asked about his views on hauntings and the paranormal: 'The universe is not only stranger than we imagine, it's stranger than we *can* imagine.'

Paul Adams & Eddie Brazil
Luton & Hazlemere, 2013

Chapter One

MILESTONES OF THE PARANORMAL

A Collection of Classic Hauntings

The Many Ghosts of Berkeley Square (1800s)

One of the most famous haunted houses in London, the 'Electric Horror' of Berkeley Square has secured its place as one of Britain's most enigmatic hauntings. The case remains unsolved.

If this survey of extreme hauntings was being compiled at the beginning of the twentieth century, one case that would feature high up on the list is what was undoubtedly regarded for many years as the most haunted house in London, a ghost story 'firmly believed by society dandies and East End costermongers alike'. In his book *Haunted Houses*, a forerunner to today's popular gazetteer guides and issued by Chapman and Hall in 1907, author Charles G. Harper observed that '[t]he famous "haunted house in Berkeley Square" was long one of those things that no country cousin coming up from the provinces to London on sight-seeing bent, ever willingly missed', so perhaps it is fitting that we begin the present work here with a classic British haunting that has been in existence for well over 200 years.

The Bridlington-born designer and landscape architect William Kent laid out the plans for Berkeley Square in the mid-1700s. Many of the original Georgian buildings have now been replaced, but the famous plane trees planted at the time of the French Revolution and familiar to both visitors and Londoners alike, are now among the oldest trees in central London, and some of the original atmosphere of the area's former days are rekindled in the lyrics of Eric Maschwitz's romantic song 'A Nightingale Sang in Berkeley Square', written shortly before the outbreak of war in 1939.

Over the years, this particular part of Mayfair has seen many distinguished residents: Horace Walpole (1717-1797), the art historian and Whig politician, lived at No.11; Sarah Sophia Child became the Countess of Jersey when she married George Villiers, the 5th Earl of Jersey, in the drawing room of 38 Berkeley Square in 1804, and died in the same house in 1867; Robert Clive of India committed suicide in his rooms at No.48 on 22 November 1774; while as a child, the very young Winston Spencer-Churchill lived for a time at No.48. Another British Prime Minister, George Canning, who held office for the shortest period in history (119 days in 1827), owned for some years a five-storey Georgian terraced mansion containing some fine Adam fireplaces on the south-west side of Berkeley Square: this building still stands and has been described in the past as having 'at least one room of which the atmosphere is supernaturally fatal to body and mind' and whose walls 'when touched, are found saturated with electric horror': this is No.50, home of the 'Ghost of Berkeley Square'.

The origins of this famous Mayfair haunting are obscure. Many of the alleged incidents of paranormal activity are anecdotal in nature but most of the reported happenings that were to lay the foundations for the building's sinister reputation date from the first half of the nineteenth century, in a block of years beginning with the death of George Canning and ending sometime in the mid-1800s; following on from this, a late-Victorian period involving some attempts at investigation together with reports of additional experiences seemingly brought the 'horror' of Berkeley Square to an end

No.50 Berkeley Square, photographed in the 1970s. At one time, stories of strange happenings and inexplicable deaths gave it the reputation as being the most haunted house in London. *(Chris Underwood)*

in the late 1880s. Accounts of ghostly phenomena at No.50 after this time are almost non-existent, although an isolated incident was reported as having taken place in 1937, the same year that the property was occupied by Maggs Brothers Ltd, a long-established firm of antiquarian booksellers whose notable acquisitions include two copies of the Gutenberg Bible and the preserved penis of Napoleon Bonaparte. Maggs continue to operate from No.50 today and they have consistently denied experiencing anything out of the ordinary during their long period of residence.

Accounts of the many ghosts said to have been seen here over the years are varied and like many haunted houses across Britain, one particular room has become the focus of much of the phenomena said to have taken place. In this particular case, the 'haunted room' is located on the top floor, with a single sash window looking out onto the square.

Several writers with an interest in the supernormal have looked at the Berkeley Square case and found evidence of unusual happenings taking place in this particular area of the building. Spiritualist author Jessie Adelaide Middleton compiled three collections of paranormal material covering hauntings, prophetic dreams and vampirism in the years leading up to the First World War. *The Grey Ghost Book* appeared in 1912 and was followed by a sequel, *Another Grey Ghost Book* (1914) and, two years later, a final instalment, *The White Ghost Book* (1916). In the first of these, Middleton recounts one reported ghost said to haunt No.50, the sad and lonely spirit of a small Scottish child. According to the author, the haunted room at the top of the house was used as the little girl's nursery, and it was here that the poor child was frightened to death, or possibly even tortured by a sadistic nanny. After her death, the girl's 'pathetic little wraith' dressed in a kilt or Scotch plaid frock is said to have been seen in the upper part of the building, sobbing and wringing its hands in grief. The apparition was so unsettling that the house was abandoned and for many years the building remained empty and untenanted. According to Middleton, who entered into correspondence with a relative of a former occupier of No.50, Berkeley Square, this haunting appeared to date from the latter part of the 1700s, not long after the house had been built.

During her research into the haunting, Middleton uncovered a further two anecdotal accounts, again involving the mysterious room under the attics. One of these, the ghost of a suicide, is that of a young woman named Adela or Adeline, who jumped to her death from the top-floor window into the street below in order to escape being raped by a 'wicked uncle', also her guardian, who lived with her in the same house. This 'screaming girl' apparition is said to have re-enacted its fatal fall on occasion and has been seen clinging to the window ledge before dropping away and vanishing. This has an interesting parallel with a similar apparition alleged to have appeared at the window of the sinister Blue Room at Borley Rectory, the 'most haunted house in England' that we will visit in a later part of the present survey. How mainstream this particular aspect of the Berkeley Square haunting became is unclear, but due to the notoriety of the case during the nineteenth century, the possibility that it inspired its counterpart at the lonely Essex rectory (alleged to have taken place shortly after the house was built in the early 1860s) is distinctly possible.

In a similar vein to a much later aspect of the Borley case is another facet of the haunting of No.50 Berkeley Square, namely the appearance of supernatural writing on the walls of the building. Details are scant and the phenomenon is most likely an anecdotal offshoot from the spirit-writing craze that formed part of the early years of Modern Spiritualism in Britain in the mid-1800s. Physical mediums, such as 'Dr' Henry Slade, an American quack physician, claimed to be able to contact and obtain communication from the spirits of the departed who left messages written in chalk on simple slate boards and Slade, who arrived in England in July 1876, was one of the greatest exponents of this particular ability. Other astonishing physical phenomena were said to take place in Slade's presence, including poltergeist-type knocking and the materialisation of solid spirit hands, but he was caught fraudulently using specially prepared slates in London in October 1876 and narrowly escaped a sentence of three months' hard labour by fleeing to the Continent. The drop-leaf table owned and used by Henry Slade later became part of the psychic museum at the National Laboratory of Psychical Research in South Kensington and Slade himself, who died penniless in an asylum in Michigan in 1905, is today one of the controversial celebrity personalities allegedly materialised by the modern physical medium David Thompson and his Sydney-based Circle of the Silver Cord. At Berkeley Square, a tenant of the building is said to have waited for a certain spirit message to appear on the wall of the haunted room, but despite much supernatural correspondence, the correct message never arrived and the unhappy Spiritualist later died insane and went on to haunt the building himself.

Despite being located in what soon became a highly regarded residential district of London, one fact that becomes clear is that for long periods of time throughout the 1800s, No.50 Berkeley Square remained tenantless and unfurnished. Perhaps then it is unsurprising that the unlit and empty building gained a reputation for being a haunted house, but the fact that this reputation appears to have been established as early as the beginning of the nineteenth century, not long after the house was built, makes it likely that there was a real reason rather than simply local rumour or gossip, and that this may well have been incidents of a paranormal nature.

The English ghost hunter Harry Price (1881-1948), whose unique career in psychical research we will encounter several times during the course of this book, like many researchers of his generation, became interested in the history of the haunting, and was of the opinion that at least some aspects of the alleged phenomena could be put down to genuine poltergeist activity. Today, only one building in Berkeley Square is used as a private dwelling, but Price, who was born in Holborn and knew London well, was able to interview several residents, one of whom recalled hearing about a series of incidents that took place in the early 1840s, when No.50 was closed and empty. At night time, on several occasions, local people were disturbed by loud noises from within the house as of heavy items of furniture or packing cases being dragged across bare floorboards, accompanied on occasion by the violent ringing of the servant bells. As well as auditory phenomena, these disturbances were also accompanied by the materialisation or transportation of solid physical objects, a common aspect of poltergeist hauntings also found in spiritualist séances, that have become known as 'apports'. Small objects such as stones and pebbles, books and even a pair of metal spurs, would clatter down onto the pavement in front of the building, as though they had been dropped or thrown out of the windows. Price was told that on a number of occasions, the house was searched immediately following the disturbances but the entire building was found to be deserted and empty – nothing that could conceivably cause the mysterious noises was present inside, although the bells in the butler's pantry were seen in motion following at least one incident – and following one night of mysterious activity, all the windows in the front elevation of the house facing the street were discovered to be broken. Harry Price, an experienced investigator, considered this to be 'good Poltergeist stuff running true to type', but another explanation, and one considered by Jessie Middleton in *The Grey Ghost Book*, is that these periods of nocturnal 'phenomena' were actually created purposefully by a coining gang in order to scare away inquisitive neighbours and mask their illegal activities. As most researchers today consider the presence of an adolescent child to be necessary for true poltergeist phenomena to take place in a given environment, perhaps this period of haunting at No.50 can be put down to such a bold and clever ploy, but this would only explain one period of what can be considered to be a protracted and persistent haunting, and there exists other evidence, both for and against, genuine psychical activity at Berkeley Square.

The 'poltergeist' disturbances that so intrigued Harry Price took place during the ownership of the Hon. Miss Curzon, who bought the house in 1827 following the death of George Canning in an apartment at Chiswick House on 8 August. Miss Curzon lived intermittently at Berkeley Square until her own death at the age of ninety in 1859, following which the house was let by the executors of her estate to a London gentleman named Myers, who carried out extensive refurbishment of the building in preparation for his forthcoming wedding. Unfortunately, the bride called off the wedding at the very last moment, and the jilted Mr Myers appears to have descended rapidly into the life of a recluse, 'a curiously Dickensian character, part Scrooge, part Miss Haversham', living alone, apart from a man-servant, in the 'haunted' room at the top of the house, shunning company and, like a precursor to Stoker's *Dracula*, sleeping by day and wandering the rooms candle in hand, vampire-like, at night. In 1873, the eccentric Myers was taken to court by Westminster Council for the non-payment of rates on his now dilapidated and once fine residence, and he appears to have died not long after, a mysterious figure who appears to have contributed much to the mythology of the case.

It was around this period of time – the 1870s – that the haunting of Berkeley Square received a certain amount of publicity in the journals and periodicals of the day, particularly *Notes and Queries*, an academic correspondence magazine founded in 1849 with an emphasis on the discussion of history and folklore. In November 1872, during the last years of Myers' tenancy, *Notes and Queries* published a request for information from a reader, asking for details of the alleged haunting, an enquiry that elicited a response from George Lyttelton, the 4th Baron Lyttelton, of Hagley Hall in Worcestershire. 'It is quite true that there is a house in Berkeley Square said to be haunted, and long unoccupied on that account,' Lord Lyttelton confirmed. 'There are strange stories about it, into which this deponent cannot enter.' Although he was less than forthcoming with information, the 4th Baron's opinion was based on personal experience, as he was one investigator into the mystery who had in fact set foot inside the house. During the intermittent occupation by Miss Curzon, Lord Lyttelton had entered into a wager to spend a night in the haunted room and appears to have bribed the resident caretaker to be allowed access inside. Unlike the specialist gadgetry of organised paranormal researchers of today, Lyttelton's ghost-hunting kit comprised of a pair of loaded blunderbusses (see also the investigations of Captain Luttrell at Hinton Ampner on p.178) whose ammunition was made up of a mixture of buckshot and silver sixpences, the coins representing a long-held belief in European folklore of the power of silver to ward off and kill evil spirits. During his night-time vigil, Lord Lyttelton claimed to have seen a strange black shape that seemed to leap out from the shadows and promptly fired one of his weapons in its direction. Despite hearing something fall to the floor, a quickly struck match revealed no trace of the fallen phantom, and in the cold light of morning, all that remained of the amateur ghost hunter's adventures was a section of sundered floor boarding.

Perhaps the unknown horror that allegedly menaced Lord Lyttelton was the same mysterious 'something' that forms the basis of probably the most famous supernormal experience said to have taken place at No.50 Berkeley Square, this time during the 1870s following the death of the reclusive Mr Myers. According to the story, two penniless sailors passing by the house one evening while looking for a place to shelter, saw its empty and dilapidated condition and decided to risk breaking in. After forcing open a basement window, the two men made their way through the building and decided to spend the night in one of the top-floor rooms that faced onto the Square. After settling down, the two men became aware of mysterious banging noises and footsteps, which gradually began to rise up through the building and approach the room where they were resting. Heavy footfalls came up to the closed door and then halted, following which the door handle turned and, almost in the manner of a short story by horror master H.P. Lovecraft, a hideous, shapeless mass slid into the room and surged towards them. One sailor managed to escape past the apparition and ran screaming out of the house, where he was confronted by a passing policeman. When the constable, who accompanied the rating back to Berkeley Square, arrived at No.50, he found the building deserted and the second seaman dead, impaled on the spiked railings adjacent to the front entrance, as though he had fallen or been pushed through an open window while trying to flee from the house. Unfortunately for the psychical researcher, despite its notoriety, no report or newspaper article confirming this startling happening has been forthcoming, and this Lovecraftian addition to the haunting of Berkeley Square is most likely an embellished tale that may, or may not, have some grain of truth at its centre.

Many of the old houses in Charles Street, which runs from the south-west side of Berkeley Square, still stand and it was into a flat in one of these building that Mrs Mary Balfour, a Scottish clairvoyant, moved in the early weeks of 1937. Later the same year, in the period between Christmas and New Year, Mrs Balfour was called to the kitchen window at the rear of the apartment by her maid, who pointed out a man that both women could see standing in one of the windows of a house diagonally opposite. The back additions of the houses in Charles Street overlooked the rear of several properties in the neighbouring square and in what turned out to be one of the back rooms for No.50 was a man dressed in what was clearly an eighteenth-century costume complete with a silver-coloured coat, breeches and a periwig. The figure, whose face was somewhat drawn and pale in appearance, stood unmoving and the Scotswoman felt a distinct aura of melancholy about his person. Assuming it was a New Year reveller in fancy dress who 'either had a hangover or some personal trouble', Mrs Balfour chastised her servant for staring and the two women moved away; later, when she went back into the kitchen, the sad-looking figure was no longer there. 'It was only afterwards that I discovered that the house was number fifty,' Mary Balfour, who had originally moved to London from the Highlands, now aged eighty, told a reporter many years later in 1969, 'Believe it or not, I had not until that time heard of the reputation of the house.'

Over the years, the 'horror' of Berkeley Square has proved inspirational to a number of artists and writers. In 1859, the English politician and novelist Edward Bulwer-Lytton, the 1st Baron Lytton, author of *Godolphin* (1833) and *The Last Days of Pompeii* (1834), wrote a much admired short ghost story, 'The Haunted and the Haunters', which first appeared in *Blackwood's Magazine*. Although no name is given, Bulwer-Lytton's 'haunted house in the midst of London', home of the sinister 'Shadow', is undoubtedly based on the Berkeley Square case, while there is no ambiguity concerning another piece of Victorian literature, Rudyard Kipling's 1884 poem 'Tomlinson', which begins with the sinister lines: 'Now Tomlinson gave up the ghost in his house in Berkeley Square, And a spirit came to his bedside and gripped him by the hair…'. Respected ghost hunters researching the case have also visited the house in search of clues to supernormal happenings: as well as Harry Price, they include Peter Underwood in 1970 and Frank Smyth in 1981. On each occasion, the occupiers have fielded questions with ease and reported no unusual happenings, particularly in the notorious 'haunted room', where staff at Maggs Brothers watched for falling incendiaries during the Second World War, and which has been used as a book store and office for many years.

If the truth behind the first of our extreme hauntings is lost in the mists of time, then the next case is almost the complete opposite, and represents a compelling body of evidence for the workings of a paranormal universe at present totally unexplainable by modern science…

Consult: Charles G. Harper, *Haunted Houses* (Chapman & Hall, London, 1907); Jessie A. Middleton, *The Grey Ghost Book* (Eveleigh Nash, London, 1912); Harry Price, *Poltergeist Over England* (Country Life Ltd, London, 1945); Peter Underwood, *Haunted London* (George G. Harrap Ltd, London, 1973).

Willington Mill: Doorway to the Unknown (1835-41)

The haunting of a mill house on the north bank of the River Tyne during the first half of the nineteenth century is now regarded as one of the most important cases from the early years of organised psychical research. The reported phenomena, experienced over a period of several years by a number of independent witnesses, include poltergeist effects, paranormal sounds, and the appearance of strange animal-like apparitions.

The former village of Willington Quay, now part of a corridor of urbanised and developed land along the banks of the River Tyne heading eastwards towards the open sea at the coastal towns of North and South Shields, lies five miles north-west of the centre of Newcastle. Often remembered today for its association with the engineer George Stephenson, builder of the famous 'Rocket', in the latter years of the eighteenth century a watermill was located here on a small river known as Willington Gut which flows through the north bank of the Tyne, and at a point where, in the late 1830s, the newly built Newcastle and North Shields railway line would cross the water on an impressive multi-arched viaduct. In 1800, the old mill was demolished and replaced with a modern steam mill as part of a new flour business formed in a partnership between the original mill owner, William Brown, and two other local men, Joseph Procter and Joseph Unthank. As part of the development, a four-storey mill house was built close to the factory buildings as a residence for the mill staff, and this was quickly occupied as the new business got underway. In these pioneering days of change and development, happening as they did midway through the century of social and manufacturing upheaval brought about by the Industrial Revolution, it is inconceivable that the thoughts of these Northumberland businessmen would have at any point turned to bear on the twilight world of ghosts and the supernatural: yet the newly built Willington Mill was soon to become the focus of a wealth of bizarre and frightening paranormal activity that today ranks it as being one of the most haunted buildings in Britain.

The march of progress no doubt would have also dispelled any superstitious belief in a number of local tales which perhaps still clung to the area around Willington Quay at that time, namely tales of witchcraft, possibly involving a midwife from nearby Newcastle named Mrs Pepper. In 1665, a local witch-hunt saw the Newcastle woman on trial, accused by Sir Francis Riddle, the local mayor, of sorcery: luckily for Mrs Pepper she was acquitted and there is some suggestion that she was in fact the 'notorious witch' for whom a cottage was built by a man named Oxon at Willington the same year. Ghost stories involving curses and the appearance of a mysterious female apparition became common knowledge in this part of the village, and around 1780, this cottage originally belonging to the 'Willington Witch' was demolished by William Brown to make way for the first of the two flour mills to be built on the site.

Joseph Procter and Joseph Unthank, both Quakers, were related by marriage: in 1791, Joseph Unthank had married Margaret Richardson, the sister of Procter's wife, Elizabeth. Following their marriage, the Unthanks had moved to Whitby on the North Yorkshire coast, but Margaret Unthank, originally from North Shields, grew unhappy with her new home and the couple made a decision to return to Tyneside, where Joseph Unthank's brother-in-law proposed a business venture involving William Brown and his mill on the Willington Gut. Following the building of the new Willington Mill, the Brown family moved into the newly constructed mill house and lived there until 1806, during which time the business thrived. The following year, perhaps tiring of the albeit successful three-way partnership, William Brown sold his share of the business and moved out of Willington Mill, now able financially to set up an independent business of his own in North Shields and nearby Sunderland. With the departure of the Browns, Joseph and Margaret Unthank together with their children made the mill house their home, and went on to live in the immediate shadow of the imposing seven-storey factory buildings that surrounded the property on two sides for an unbroken period of twenty-five years; finally leaving Willington in 1831. By this time, Joseph Procter had died (in 1813) and his young son, also called Joseph, had taken his place in the family business alongside Joseph Unthank's own son, Edmund.

Joseph Unthank, one of the original founders of the business, died in 1842 and the Procters continued to live on in the mill house for a further five years before finally leaving Willington Mill in 1847 and moving to Camp Villa at North Shields. The flour business continued on for nearly twenty years until 1865 when Joseph Proctor Jr, now the sole proprietor, decided to close the mill permanently; Joseph died ten years later on 6 November 1875. The mill premises were partly dismantled, including the mill house which, after being divided into flats, was demolished, and the buildings used for warehousing. Today, the site of the former Willington Mill forms part of a modern industrial estate and the one surviving factory building from the time of Joseph Procter and Joseph Unthank, now much altered, is used by the Bridon Ropes Company, an amalgamation of several businesses that have operated on the site since the early 1920s.

The early Victorian success story of Willington Mill would have been consigned to the pages of provincial history if it had not been for what amounted to a protracted haunting of, at times, astonishing intensity and variety that affected the original mill house residence on the bank of Willington Gut for many years. Much of what is known about the case comes from a document described as the 'Procter Diary', an allegedly contemporary account of the disturbances compiled by Joseph Procter Jr and later edited for publication (in 1892 in the *Journal* of the Society for Psychical Research) by Procter's son, Edmund. The case also received publicity during Joseph Procter's lifetime when it was included in the book *The Night Side of Nature* (1852), a seminal collection of true paranormal encounters compiled by the Victorian novelist and pioneering psychic investigator Catherine Crowe, a spiritualist investigator who, until

Willington Mill, Tyneside: The haunted house of the Procter family, where bizarre apparitions including phantom animals and the figure of an eyeless woman were seen by several people over a period of many years. *(Bridon Ropes Ltd)*

recent years, has been one of the unsung heroes of organised psychical research. Later researchers who have investigated the case include Harry Price (1945), Alan Gauld (1979), Andrew MacKenzie (1982), and Colin Wilson (1985). The first full-length study of the case was undertaken by two local researchers, Michael Hallowell and Darren Ritson, and published as *The Haunting of Willington Mill* in 2011.

The Procter narrative covers a period of time lasting just over five and a half years, beginning in early 1835 and ending in the middle of August 1841. However, there are gaps in the chronology and Edmund Procter notes that manifestations continued to occur in the haunted mill house right up until the time the family left Willington in 1847; while Hallowell and Ritson suggest that the haunting spanned a much longer period and may in fact have begun almost immediately after the building was constructed at the beginning of the 1800s, with the phenomena possibly being the reason behind the departure of William Brown and his family in 1806. Whatever the true duration of the events, even a cursory glance through the 'Procter Diary' will show that this respectable and enterprising Quaker household appeared to be living not only at the beginning of the new Victorian age of social and political change, but also on the threshold of a chilling and unseen world completely beyond our present-day knowledge and understanding. Unleashed inside the mill house and its immediate environs was a relentless onslaught of sinister and inexplicable phenomena that included the sound of voices and heavy footsteps, raps, knocks and rustling noises, the appearance of apparitions and quasi-animal forms, bell-ringing, the physical movement of objects, disembodied heads and faces, as well as coughing, moaning and tapping sounds.

One particular room in the upper part of the house located directly above the children's nursery appeared to be the focus of many of the extraordinary happenings. In the early weeks of January 1835, the Procter's nursemaid became frightened by strange noises as she sat each evening in the nursery: despite the room overhead being unfurnished and unoccupied, heavy footsteps that at times made the sashes in the nursery window shake, paced the floor above; the phenomenon would last for ten minutes at a time and then fade away. Soon Elizabeth Procter and other members of staff became aware of the sounds, 'a step as of a man with a strong shoe or boot going towards the window and returning'. Knocks and raps 'as of a mallet on a block of wood' began to affect the household at night; on one particular occasion, Joseph Procter heard a tapping sound coming from the direction of a child's crib and felt the vibrations of invisible blows on the woodwork.

The strange noises were not restricted to the interior of the mill house at Willington. On several occasions, Joseph Procter and a number of the servants claimed to have heard the sound of someone following them down the gravel path outside at night: on each occasion there was no person visible to account for the noises. The mill foreman, Thomas Mann, a trusted employee who at the time had been working for the Procters for just over two years, also claimed to have heard strange noises at night. On one occasion, in the early hours of the morning, as he went to fill a coal barrow to fuel the mill's boiler, he heard a loud creaking and grinding noise which he immediately recognised as being the familiar sound of a wheeled horse-drawn cistern, used to water the mill horses, which normally stood in a particular location in the yard outside. Assuming that the cistern was being stolen, Mann rushed out into the yard, upon which the sounds instantly ceased, and the foreman was amazed to see the closed yard locked and empty, and the heavy cistern (which would have taken several people to move by hand) standing in its usual place apparently undisturbed. Despite searching the mill yard thoroughly with a lantern, Mann could find no physical cause for the sounds, which he subsequently regarded as being of supernatural origin.

Soon apparitions began to be seen at Willington Mill. A neighbour of the Procters passing by the mill house saw what he described as a transparent white figure that he took to be of a woman, standing at one of the upper-floor windows. A short time afterwards, Elizabeth Procter's sister, Mrs Christiana Wright, who lived at Mansfield, came to stay and was given accommodation in the foreman's house which stood a short distance from the mill house itself, separated by a small kitchen garden and a narrow road. One evening at around half past nine, Mrs Mann went out to a coal bunker and, happening to look across towards the mill house, was amazed to see a glowing transparent figure like 'a priest in a white surplice' floating at the same window. She went to fetch her husband and ultimately Thomas Mann, together with his daughter and Mrs Wright, all collectively saw the apparition, which lasted nearly a quarter of an hour before gradually fading away from the top downwards. It was a dark, moonless night and by this time the Procters had retired and there were no lights showing in any other parts of the building. The mill foreman was able to view the figure from a close vantage point in the cottage garden and all three witnesses described it as being suspended in the air, seemingly around 3ft above the floor of the room, while as it walked and alternated between periods of movement and rest, the apparition appeared to pass through the window itself and obscure the sash and blind behind it.

Strange noises and footsteps continued to afflict the occupants of the mill house. Not long after the sighting of the priest-like figure at the window, Jane Carr, another of Elizabeth Proctor's married sisters, was disturbed at night by knocks and footsteps passing close to her bed, as well as a mysterious winding or ticking noise (a phenomenon often encountered in séances for physical mediumship) which lasted for ten minutes before fading away. The family also began to be disturbed in their beds at night. Elizabeth Procter, her nursemaid Miss Pollard, as well as Elizabeth's sister Jane, all experienced the shaking and moving of their besteads, as though someone were underneath and trying to push them up into the air. The Procter children were affected as well as the adults in the house: footsteps as of an invisible person prowled around their beds at night, a loud 'clattering or jingling' sound was heard coming from the nursery closet, while the crib of the Procter's young son (also called Joseph) was shaken and on one occasion was seemingly raised up off the floor several times; while all the time the house at Willington Mill seemed to be alive with strange and unexplained sounds and noises: thumps and knocks, an eerie moaning and a sound 'like a child sucking', indiscernible voices and speech, a whistling noise, and once a voice calling out 'Chuck, chuck' from the foot of young Joseph Procter's crib as though someone or something was standing in the darkness, rocking the bed as it spoke…

By the beginning of 1840, the Procters had officially been chronicling the haunting for over five years. Despite the length of time, the phenomena showed no signs of abating and in fact, some of the most remarkable and disturbing events at Willington Mill were yet to occur. One night early in February 1840, shortly before twelve o'clock, Jane Carr and the Procters cook, Mary Young, 'a most respectable and intelligent woman', were awakened by a loud thumping sound on the landing outside their bedroom door. By this time frightened by many of her experiences in the mill house, Mrs Carr now refused to sleep alone and the two women shared an old-fashioned four-poster bed whose drawn curtains, together with a rushlight left burning on a nearby dressing-table, afforded some comfort against the many unusual happenings that were taking place. As they lay in the half-light, both women heard the door bolt slide back and the sound of the bedroom door opening, after which footsteps began moving about the room together with the sound of the night light being snuffed out (the diary is ambiguous as to whether or not the light was actually extinguished). Soon the curtains around the bed were being rustled and the terrified Mary Young saw what she later described as a 'dark shadow' on the curtain around the four-poster:

On getting to the bed-board where Jane C. lay, a loud thump as with a fist was heard on it; something was then felt to press on the counterpane on M. Young's side of the bed, the bed curtain being pushed in but nothing more seen. Whatever the visitor might be was then heard to go out, seeming to leave the door open.

A short while after, the two women mustered enough courage to check the bed chamber and found the door bolted from the inside as they had left it on retiring and nothing inside the room that could conceivably have caused the chilling effects that they had both collectively experienced. Despite the unnerving experience, Mrs Carr continued to stay on at the mill house, although this 'night of horror' at Willington Mill was one that she remembered for the rest of her life.

Later the same month, Mrs Carr was sleeping in the same room, this time with her young niece Jane Procter, who at the time was aged around four and a half. The following morning, the child told her parents of a strange experience the previous night that would have shaken any adult, and no doubt made Elizabeth Procter's sister glad that on this particular occasion she had slept through until dawn. Through a gap in the bed curtains, the child saw low down near the floor by the washstand, what appeared to be the head of an old woman with 'something down the sides of her face and passed across the lower part of it', looking in at her, while the hands that were spread out in front had two fingers on each 'extended and touching each other'. The apparition was clearly visible despite the darkness, almost as though it had brought its own illumination with it. Afraid, the girl hid her head under the covers and thankfully went to sleep and was not disturbed for the rest of the night. However, a day or so later, the same child ran to her parents one evening around dusk in a frightened state to say that while coming down the stairs from the upper part of the house, she had seen a similar head resting by itself on the landing…

As the weeks passed, beating sounds, rustlings, strange vibrations and the curious sound of a bell ringing like no hand bell known to be present in the building, continued to afflict the Proctor household during the night. Despite the startling aural and physical phenomena, perhaps one of the most bizarre and disturbing aspects of the entire haunting of Willington Mill is the appearance of strange animal-like apparitions, both outside and within the troubled house, that were seen and experienced by several members of the family and their staff. During the winter of 1841, another of Elizabeth Procter's married sisters, Mrs Hargrave, saw what she later described as a large white cat moving through the vegetable garden at the back of the mill house. The creature was larger than an ordinary domestic animal with a long white snout instead of a nose and, as she watched, it passed through the closed garden gate and crossed to the doorway of the furnace room in the factory building opposite, where one of the most surreal incidents in any reported British haunting took place: as the cat-like animal approached the factory it appeared to pass through the closed door into the room inside, where it was seen by Joseph Procter who was inside checking on the furnace – as he watched, the creature crossed to the open furnace door and walked straight into the fiery interior and was lost to sight. Not long afterwards, Mrs Hargrave noticed the same apparition inside the mill house, where it again walked through a closed bedroom door and disappeared. Edmund Procter was also scared by the appearance of what appears to be an identical creature around the same time.

One Saturday afternoon in November 1841, Joseph Procter came into the nursery to find his children looking under chairs and behind the furniture in a state of excitement. A few minutes before, his son Joseph had claimed that a 'monkey' had suddenly appeared from nowhere and jumped across the room at him, pulling at his boot strap and tickling his foot. The animal had apparently been invisible to his siblings and had disappeared as mysteriously as it had arrived. Elsewhere inside the house, other mysterious apparitions of a similar nature were less easy to identify, and as at Berkeley Square, there is a Lovecraftian element to several of the reported creatures seen inside the mill house at this time: on one occasion, a formless object that resembled a white towel was seen to suddenly 'burst into life' and run down the main staircase, while a 'white face' that hopped away when challenged was also seen on the stairs leading up into the attics, again by the child Joseph together with his brother, Henry Procter. Another unidentifiable form, 'like a white pocket-handkerchief knotted at the four corners' was seen dancing about outside the house by an aunt of Thomas Davidson, a local craftsman and fiancé of the Procter's cook, Mary Young: the object at times rose as high as the first-floor windows of the house before disappearing.

Not surprisingly, given the duration and intensity of the haunting, the Procter ghosts became well known amongst the locals and villagers living in and around the quiet hamlet of Willington Quay. Workers at the steam mill heard about the strange sights and happenings inside the house and some villagers had experiences of their own: Thomas Davidson, the future husband of Mary Young, saw a white cat-like animal 'as large as a sheep' while waiting for her one evening in the roadway outside the mill house, and some of Joseph Procter's own employees at the mill also spoke about a strange apparition like a white donkey, that they had seen in the vegetable garden and in the furnace room of the mill. A local farmer named Davison heard about the haunting and ultimately proved to be the catalyst for one of the most celebrated incidents connected with the case. Davison had known for several years a doctor named Edward Drury who worked in a practice in Church Street, Sunderland. Drury, despite being a sceptic, had become interested in the accounts of the Wesley poltergeist at Epworth in Lincolnshire in the early 1700s (see *Shadows in the Nave*, The History Press, 2011) and when he was told about the haunting at Willington, decided to investigate the matter for himself. Having written to Joseph Procter, the two men agreed that the doctor would spend the night of 3 July 1840, alone apart from an elderly servant, in the mill house, the family being away on holiday in Carlisle at the time.

Edward Drury arrived at Willington Mill around eight o'clock in the evening. At the mill house he found that Joseph Procter had unexpectedly decided to return by himself to spend the night, and there was soon to be a second visitor at the haunted house: a local chemist, Thomas Hudson, had heard about the Sunderland doctor's ghost hunt and had decided to invite himself along. The two men were shown around the house by Joseph Procter, after which they all sat down to supper. In order to impress on his host that no practical jokes or trickery would be tolerated, Drury had brought a brace of pistols with him, with the plan to allow one of the guns to 'accidentally' fall on the floor before the vigil began as a clear warning that he did not suffer fools gladly. However, after speaking with Procter over their meal, he became convinced that the mill owner was being honest about his experiences and the display of strength went unperformed. Just before eleven o'clock, Drury and Hudson went upstairs and settled themselves on one of the landings directly opposite the door leading into the bedroom over the nursery where much of the eerie phenomena had occurred. After an hour or so, both men became aware of a pattering sound like bare footfalls on the floorboards, and shortly afterwards there were a series of percussive knocks or raps which sounded as though they were coming from beneath the floor where they were sitting. The ghost hunters also heard rustling noises, as if someone in silk garments was walking up the staircase towards them, and a coughing sound which appeared to come from within the 'haunted room' itself.

Despite being the instigator of the investigation, after nearly two hours sitting unmoving in the cold and shadowy stairwell, Dr Drury checked his watch and, finding it was a quarter to one in the morning, decided to abandon the vigil and go to bed. Hudson, however, felt strong enough to see the business through until the morning and wished his companion a good night. As Drury got up, he glanced down the hallway and saw a door leading into a closet opposite where they were sitting silently open and a woman dressed in grey emerge and begin walking along the passageway towards them. The figure's gaze appeared to be directed towards the floor and one hand was pressed to its chest 'as if in pain'. Drury looked to see if his companion had also seen the apparition but Hudson had succumbed to tiredness and had fallen asleep. Now seized with fright, the Sunderland doctor, with a shout, made to grab at the woman, but the figure was suddenly no longer there and Drury collapsed in a faint on top of his fellow ghost hunter and had to be carried downstairs 'in an agony of fear and terror' which lasted for some three hours and of which he later had no recollection. The shock of the experience had a profound effect on the sceptical Drury and on 13 July 1840 he wrote to Joseph Procter giving a full account of his experiences at Willington that night.

Edward Drury was not the only person during the history of the haunting to see the apparition of a grey lady at Willington Mill. Another investigator, William Howitt, who also visited the house and spent a night there, interviewed a number of Joseph Procter's staff, and was told that several of the children had also reported the appearance of a woman in a grey dress. 'She is sometimes seen sitting wrapped in a sort of mantle, with her head depressed, and her hands crossed on her lap,' Howitt noted in his book *Visits to Remarkable Places*, published in 1840, the same year as Dr Drury's unnerving experience, and he goes on to say: 'The most terrible fact is that she is *without eyes* [our italics]'. Even given the many frightening happenings that are alleged to have taken place in the mill house at Willington over the years, this particular ghost is perhaps the most disturbing of all. The Spiritualist writer William (W.T.) Stead, who we will encounter again later in our survey, discussed the haunting in his book *Real Ghost Stories* (1897), and his is the most chilling of all the descriptions of the famous 'Willington Ghost': 'On one occasion one of the little girls came to Mrs Davidson [formerly Mary Young] and said, "There is a lady sitting on the bed in mamma's bedroom. She had eyeholes, but no eyes; and she looked so hard at me."' The same apparition 'with something tied over her head' was also seen by one of the Procter children to come out of the wall in the bedroom and stand in front of the looking glass: an eyeless ghost looking at itself in a mirror...

Following the departure of the Procters, the mill house was split into two tenements and the works foreman Thomas Mann and his family lived there with another of the mill employees for a period of twenty years. During this time there appear to have been sparing instances of occasional noises and possibly the sighting on at least one occasion of a ghostly figure, but by this time the main body of the haunting had drawn to a close. Today the location is much altered and there is nothing left of the old Procter house for the curious to see. Despite much speculation by various commentators, the origins and reasons behind the haunting of Willington Mill remain a mystery. In his book *Afterlife* (1985), Colin Wilson has drawn parallels with the happenings at Willington Gut and the experiences of the Fox family at Hydesville in 1848, where strange knocks and rappings were the catalyst that ushered in the age of Modern Spiritualism, and other investigators have suggested that a haunting by discarnate entities lies behind much of the bizarre happenings recorded in the Procter narrative. Working with two clairvoyant mediums, Tony Stockwell and Philip Solomon, researchers Michael Hallowell and Darren Ritson have claimed that two murders took place in the mill house during the early 1800s, not long after the mill house was built, and that these violent events are at the root of the haunting. As well as survival, more Fortean-related phenomena such as 'zooforms' (shape-shifting entities) and 'window areas' have also been connected with both the bizarre animal-like apparitions and the location and intensity of the haunting as a whole. A less fantastical and also highly relevant aspect are 'the personal, and possibly sexual, dynamics that existed between a close-knit group during a period of dramatic and stressful social change in the north of England', that researcher Tom Ruffles has suggested have a great bearing on this fascinating case.

Despite the speculation, the haunting of Willington Mill remains a fascinating paranormal enigma, one that William Howitt summed up in his almost poetic description of the Procter house as he first saw it in the late 1830s, and which Catherine Crowe later reproduced in her subsequent *The Night Side of Nature*. Howitt wrote:

> The house is not an old house, as will appear; it was built about the year 1800. It has no particularly spectral look about it. Seeing it in passing, or within, ignorant of its real character, one should by no means say that it was a place likely to have the reputation of being haunted. Yet looking down from the railway, and seeing it and the mill lying in a deep hole, one might imagine various strange noises likely to be heard in such a place in the night, from vessels on the river, from winds sweeping and howling down the gully in which it stands, from engines in the neighbourhood connected with coal mines, one of which, I could not tell where, was making, at the time I was there, a wild sighing noise, as I stood on the hill above. There is not any passage, however, known of under the house, by which subterraneous noises could be heard, nor are they merely noises that are heard; distinct apparitions are declared to be seen…

Consult: Catherine Crowe, *The Night Side of Nature* (G. Routledge & Co., London, 1852); Michael J. Hallowell & Darren W. Ritson, *The Haunting of Willington Mill: The Truth Behind England's Most Enigmatic Ghost Story* (The History Press, Stroud, 2011); William Howitt, *Visits to Remarkable Places* (Longmans, London, 1840); Andrew MacKenzie, *Hauntings and Apparitions* (Heinemann, London, 1982); Harry Price, *Poltergeist Over England* (Country Life Ltd, London, 1945); William T. Stead, *Real Ghost Stories* (Grant Richards, London, 1897); Colin Wilson, *Afterlife: An Investigation of the Evidence for Life after Death* (George G. Harrap Ltd, London, 1985).

The Woman in Black (1882-93)

One of the most famous Victorian hauntings, the 'Morton' ghost at Cheltenham, involving the appearance of a silent woman dressed in black seen by a number of people during the course of several years, has become one of the most highly regarded of spontaneous cases. It dates from the early years of the formation of the Society for Psychical Research and was investigated by one of the society's founding members.

The latter half of the twentieth century is often considered in ghost hunting terms to be the era of the Poltergeist. Today, poltergeist phenomena is the most frequently reported case of haunting, and it is reckoned that within ten miles of where you are reading this book, some form of poltergeist activity is taking place. In recent years, accounts of poltergeist hauntings, such as the Enfield, Cardiff and South Shields cases, have epitomized this all too modern of paranormal experience, with their disturbing accounts of violent, illogical and sometimes malevolent psychic phenomena. Perhaps the behaviour of poltergeists in some way reflects the turmoil, irrationality and frustration of modern-day living, and in that may lie a clue to their nature. By contrast, the traditional ghost tales of phantom ladies and spectral monks seem, from our twenty-first-century perspective, to be more at home in the genteel Victorian era of mysterious country houses, gas-lit terraces and eerie ruins and churchyards, with their customary floating white-sheeted wraiths: certainly a more romantic notion of a ghost story, but one which should not be dismissed too hastily as unworthy of serious paranormal research.

One case that embodies this classic Victorian idea of a ghost story occurred in the last quarter of the nineteenth century in the town of Cheltenham in the West of England. At the time the haunting, known initially as the 'Morton case', was investigated by Frederick W.H. Myers, one of the founders of the then fledgling Society for Psychical Research, and is considered one of the best-documented hauntings in the SPR archives. However, the veracity of the story still divides the ghost-hunting establishment, not only because of differing interpretations of the alleged phenomena put forward by paranormal researchers who have investigated the case, but also because the haunting contains one of the most astonishing and controversial accounts of the sighting of a ghost ever reported.

In April 1882, retired Army captain Frederick William Despard, aged fifty-three, his forty-six-year-old wife Harriet, together with their seven children, Freda, aged twenty, then recently married to a Herbert Kinlock, Rosina, aged nineteen, Edith, aged eighteen, Lillian, aged fifteen, Henry, aged sixteen, Mable, aged thirteen, and six-year-old Wilfred, took up residence at 'Garden Reach', a substantial detached house in its own grounds, on the corner of All Saints Road and Pitville Circus Road in the northern part of the town. The Despards were a typical Victorian upper middle-class family, much travelled, and attended by the usual compliment of servants: a cook, coachman, gardener and parlour maid. Rosina Despard, the main witness to the phenomena and its principle chronicler, would later qualify as a doctor. Their new home was an elegant, eighteen-roomed residence laid out over four floors. A semi-circular carriage drive swept up to a grand entrance portico, while at the rear, a balustraded terrace ran the full length of the back of the house, overlooking an extensive garden with its adjacent orchard.

Despite the grandeur of their new home, the Despards were in fact only tenants. The house had been built in 1860 and its first owner was Henry Swinhoe, an Anglo-Indian solicitor from Calcutta. He had married Elisabeth Francis Higgins on 6 February 1851 in India, and they eventually raised a family of five children. However, Elisabeth died aged thirty-five on 11 August 1866 and four years later, Henry Swinhoe married again. His second wife was Imogen Hutchins of Clifton, Bristol, but their relationship was marred by frequent quarrels, apparently over the upbringing of Swinhoe's children as well as the possession of the former Mrs Swinhoe's jewellery, for which Henry had a secret hiding place fashioned under

The building once known as 'Donore', haunt of the mysterious woman in black, now converted into flats. *(Eddie Brazil)*

the drawing-room floor. The situation was not helped by Henry Swinhoe's gradual descent into alcoholism. Grief turned to drink after Elisabeth's death and soon Imogen herself became a drunkard. Henry and Imogen Swinhoe separated early in 1876: Imogen returned to Bristol while Henry lived on at Garden Reach for only a few months before dying on 14 July. Imogen outlived her husband by just over two years. She died at Clifton on 23 September 1878, but was in fact buried at the Holy Trinity Church in Portland Street, Cheltenham, a short distance from her former home. Following Henry Swinhoe's death, the house remained empty until 1879 when, renamed 'Pitville Hall', it was bought by Benjamin Littlewood from nearby Shurdington, a village on the south-western outskirts of Cheltenham. His ownership was short-lived as he died only a month after moving in, on 5 August 1879, curiously, as it seems, in the same room where Henry Swinhoe passed away, and where the first Mrs Swinhoe's jewellery had originally been concealed. His widow soon moved to a smaller house in the same road. Pitville Hall was to remain unoccupied for two and a half years, a period during which the property began to acquire a sinister reputation.

On several occasions, the figure of a woman dressed in black was seen in the grounds of the empty house. A gardener working in a local residence claimed that he often saw a figure walking in the front driveway. However, empty houses, especially those with a scandal attached to them, can soon become the focus of local gossip, and 'hauntings' become established if both the background and the building lend themselves to the fact. The story of the alcoholic, quarrelling Swinhoes would have provided suitable emotion and drama, while the deaths of both husband and wife under unhappy circumstances, together with the presence of the large house standing tenantless for several years, undoubtedly made the old Swinhoe house a place to avoid while walking through that particular part of Cheltenham at night. But the ghosts at Pitville Hall were more than simple stories, as the new incoming family were soon to find out. Two months after the Despards established their new household, now renamed 'Donore', at the end of April 1882, Rosina Despard saw the apparition for the first time.

One evening after retiring to her room, Rosina was disturbed by the sound of someone in the passageway outside her bedroom. Thinking that it was her mother, an invalid who did not enjoy the best of health, she went to the door and opened it. Out on the darkened landing she saw by the flickering light of her candle the figure of a woman dressed in dark-coloured clothes standing at the head of the stairs. After a few moments, the figure descended the staircase and Rosina followed, wondering who it could be. It was then that her candle spluttered out, plunging the landing into darkness, and she was forced to grope her way back to her room. Curiously, Rosina did not mention her encounter with the figure to any of her family, something that may seem a little strange. For her to come across a stranger wandering the stairs and landings in the dead of night would surely have warranted a comment at the Despard breakfast table the next morning? However, at this distance of time we are not privy to the dynamics of this particular family at the time: if Rosina was aware of the stories attached to the house and realised she had seen an apparition, the subject of ghosts may well have been an unmentionable one for various reasons, the most likely one being the necessity of keeping staff at the house who may have given their notice if stories of a ghostly woman became common knowledge below stairs.

The Cheltenham ghost: the haunted staircase. *(Eddie Brazil)*

Over the next two years, from April 1882, throughout 1883 and into most of 1884, Rosina Despard saw the same silent, black-clad figure around half a dozen times: at first at longer intervals and afterwards at shorter ones, yet she mentioned these strange appearances to no one, apart from a female friend. Rosina kept written records of the appearances of the apparition from the very beginning in the form of letters to her confidant, Miss Catherine M. Campbell, although the letters do not mention whether these incidents were confined solely to the house. It would appear likely, given the many later reports of the apparition moving around the grounds and the garden, that she did encounter it outside the building as well. What is clear is that she told no other member of the Despard family of her experiences and confided solely in her friend Miss Campbell, who also told no one. However, Rosina was not the only person during this two-year period to see the eerie figure of the woman in black.

During the summer of 1882, Rosina's married sister, Freda Kinlock, was coming down the stairs at about 6.30 p.m. on a bright evening when she saw what she took to be a Sister of Mercy cross the hallway and pass into the drawing room. Enquiring after the lady as the Despard family sat down to dinner, she was told there was no such person in the house. A servant was sent to look for the stranger but the drawing room was empty. Although Freda persisted that she had seen a figure in black, the matter was left to rest. In December 1883, the figure was seen by Rosina's young brother, Wilfred, and another little boy as they both played on the garden terrace. The woman entered the drawing room and stood close to the window, prompting the two boys to run in to see why the woman was weeping so bitterly. They found no one in the drawing room, and afterwards the Despard's parlour maid told them that no one had been admitted to the house at that time.

Unaccountable footsteps were also heard throughout the house, not only by Rosina, but also by her sisters and the servants. On the night of 2 August 1883, Edith, Lillian and Mable Despard, together with the cook, heard the sound of footfalls pass and re-pass their respective bedrooms on the top landing. The cook reported that she had heard the footsteps before, and had also seen the figure of a woman on the stairs late at night. The footsteps were described as soft and rather slow, though decided and even, and on hearing the steps, neither the Despard sisters nor their servants would dare venture out on to the landing to investigate. Yet it was Rosina Despard who continued to see the dark figure. Several times she followed the woman downstairs into the drawing room, where she remained a variable time standing to the right-hand side of the bow window. From the drawing room, she would go along the ground-floor passage to the garden door, where she always disappeared.

Up until this time, Rosina Despard had been simply an observer. However, early in 1884 she attempted the first of a number of experiments with the apparition. On 29 January, she tried to speak to the figure for the first time:

> I opened the drawing-room door softly and went in, standing just by it. She came in past me and walked to the sofa and stood still there, so I went up to her and asked her if I could help her. She moved, and I thought she was going to speak, but she only gave a slight gasp and moved towards the door. Just by the door I spoke to her again, but she seemed as if she was quite unable to speak. She walked into the hall, and then by the side door she seemed to disappear as before.

The Cheltenham haunting reached its peak between July and August 1884 when appearances of the apparition were at their maximum. If Rosina Despard's account is to be believed, on 21 July an incident took place that could well be one of the most astonishing and controversial appearances of an apparition in the whole history of psychical research. At around nine o'clock in the evening, Rosina joined her father and sisters in the drawing room and settled down to read:

> I saw the figure come in at the open door, cross the room and take up a position close behind the couch were I was. I was astonished that no one else in the room saw her, as she was so very distinct to me. My youngest brother, who had before seen her [Wilfred Despard on the terrace with his friend], was not in the room. She stood behind the couch for about half an hour, and then as usual walked to the door. I went after her, on the excuse of getting a book, and saw her pass along the hall, until she came to the garden door, where she disappeared. I spoke to her as she passed the foot of the stairs, but she did not answer, although as before she stopped and seemed as though about to speak.

The continued appearance of the figure for over thirty minutes is practically unique and beats the reported appearance of the ghost nun by Geoffrey Croom-Hollingsworth and Roy Potter in the former garden of Borley Rectory during one of their nocturnal vigils in the mid-1970s by an incredible quarter of an hour (see *The Borley Rectory Companion*, The History Press, 2009, pp.123-25). Yet it is this observation by Rosina Despard on 21 July 1884 which has since divided many paranormal researchers over the genuineness of the entire haunting, and it is easy to see why. To witness the appearance of a fully formed, solid human figure in normal conditions in the company of other people for thirty minutes is nothing short of astonishing. It also begs the question: what did Rosina witness on that day? Was it a ghost, a figment of her imagination, or, as some commentators have since suggested, a real living person?

Nevertheless, the woman in black continued to be seen. Ten days after the above incident, Edith Despard informed her sister that someone had passed by her on the stairs during the night, her description of the figure being that which was now all too familiar to Rosina herself. A day after her sister's experience, Rosina Despard was awakened around two o'clock in the morning by the sound of footsteps on the landing outside her bedroom door. Upon investigating, she found the apparition standing at the head of the staircase where it remained for some minutes before descending to the hallway below. Rosina followed the figure and found it standing in the passageway, and here follows what must be a unique occurrence in ghost-hunting history. As Rosina opened the drawing-room door, the figure walked past her into the room and took up her customary place beside the bow window. The apparition stayed there for a few minutes before following her usual path out and along to the rear door, where she disappeared as before. Surely this is the only recorded incidence of a ghost hunter opening a door for a ghost?

During the first week of August 1884, Rosina made the decision to reveal her experiences both to her parents and to the Despard family as a whole. On 5 August, she spoke to Frederick and Harriet Despard about the apparition and presumably her sisters as well. Captain Despard was 'much astonished' about his daughter's tale, especially as he had not heard or experienced anything himself, as was his wife. For the head of the Despard household to remain unaware of what his children and their servants had heard and seen in the house for over a period of two years is really quite remarkable. Nonetheless, Frederick Despard evidently took Rosina's claims seriously and made enquiries with the landlord as to whether anything unusual was known about the house's previous history. At the time nothing was forthcoming, but some-time later, after the principle period of phenomena had ceased, the Despards did hear second-hand stories of a haunting associated with the house.

On 6 August 1884, the day after Rosina Despard's revelations to her parents, the appearance of the ghostly woman was corroborated by someone outside of the house-hold. At this time, Freda Kinlock was in mourning for the recent death of her baby son and was staying at Donore with the family. An immediate neighbour, General Annesley, knew this fact although he did not know Rosina Despard's sister by sight. Sometime during the day he sent his son across to the house to enquire about the lady whom he had seen crying in the orchard which was visible from the road outside. He described her to his son and later to the Despards as a tall lady in black wearing a bonnet with a long veil, standing in a manner of great grief with a handkerchief held up to her face. Needless to say, the description did not fit that of Mrs Kinlock, who also had not been in the orchard that day.

Between 1887 and 1889, the apparition was seldom seen and it is clear that by this time the haunting itself was beginning to wind down. Up until 1886, the figure was solid and lifelike, and as we have seen was often mistaken for that of a living person. During its final appearances to the Despards it began to become 'less distinct'. In her report, Rosina Despard states that the woman in black was not seen after 1889; the footsteps lasted slightly beyond this time, but gradually they too ceased. The Cheltenham haunt-ing had come to an end – or had it?

In 1893, the Despard family moved out of Donore and two years later Rosina qualified as a doctor with a third class honours in medicine, obstetrics and forensics. Following her departure from Cheltenham she lived in various locations in the south of England. After a period as Assistant Medical Officer at Holloway Sanatorium, she retired to the Isle of Wight, where she died on 8 December 1930, aged sixty-seven. As for her former home, it stood empty for five years with its reputation as a haunted house becoming ever more firmly sealed. In 1898, it was renamed 'Inholmes' and opened as a preparatory school for boys. However, the presence of the woman in

black seems to have persisted during this
period for it was reported that the apparition of a woman was encountered on
the stairs and in the corridors, and even
in the boys' dormitories, always leaving
the house from the garden door and
drifting away down the front driveway. In
time the maids left in terror and the place
was again closed.

In 1910, the house was taken over
by nuns of the Ursuline Order. There
appear to be no reports of the sighting
of the ghost from this period, and the
Order left the building in 1912. The
following year it re-opened as a training college for nannies, and from 1935
until 1970 it became the property of
the Diocese of Gloucester as a diocesan
house. In 1969, a clergyman who was
staying there for a residential weekend
and at the time was alone in the house,
woke at around a quarter to eleven one
night to find the room he was sleeping

An impression of the phantom woman in black,
seen by several members of the Despard family
at Cheltenham in the 1880s. *(Psychic Press Ltd)*

in bitterly cold and the bedclothes being pulled away from him towards the end of
the bed. His experience concluded with a grey shape passing across the room, which
disappeared through the wall behind him. After the departure of the ecclesiastical
authorities, the house once again remained empty until it was purchased in 1973 by
a housing association for conversion into flats, and it is in this capacity that it remains
today, a silent witness to one of Britain's most remarkable ghost stories.

Since the days of the Despards at Cheltenham, there have been persistent reports
of the figure of a black-clad woman being seen not only in the immediate area, but
also in a house called Cotswold Lodge, now demolished, which at one time stood on
the opposite side of the road. Today a block of flats occupies the site. On two separate
occasions, in 1958 and 1961, a woman in a long dress was seen in the building at night
time, the first instance by the then owner and on the second occasion by two visitors
who both saw the figure standing in the doorway of the room in which they were
sleeping. As with the accounts given by Rosina Despard, here the appearance of the
apparition was announced by the sound of footsteps in the corridor, and one of the
witnesses saw that the figure held a handkerchief up to its face in the manner of the
woman in black over seventy years previously.

Is it possible to explain the Cheltenham ghost? Following the first full-length account of the haunting, published by Bernard Abdy Collins in 1948, several paranormal researchers have put forward their own views on the case. Andrew Mackenzie, in his *Hauntings and Apparitions* (1982), is generally supportive of the paranormality of the case, whilst veteran British ghost hunter, Peter Underwood, in his 1977 book *Hauntings*, takes a more sceptical and somewhat controversial view, suggesting that the house in Pitville Circus Road was never haunted and what Rosina Despard saw there over the years was not a ghost but in fact a real person.

It is easy to be sympathetic to Underwood's view regarding certain aspects of the alleged haunting: Rosina's claim to have observed, whilst in the company of her father and sisters, the apparition of the woman in black for up to thirty minutes, a sighting seemingly unprecedented in the history of psychical research, and certainly an incident to raise the eyebrows of many a sceptic; would a genuine ghost need to have a door opened so it could enter a room as Rosina claimed to have occurred in August 1884?; there is also the question of why Rosina keep her silence for two and a half years over what she had seen and heard inside her Cheltenham home. Underwood contends that she was fully aware that the woman in black was not a ghost, but was in fact her father's mistress, concealed in a secret room at the top of the house, perhaps even with the approval of his own wife. Mrs Despard has been described as a 'great invalid', so it cannot be considered to be outside the bounds of possibility that the captain might seek intimate companionship with another.

Catherine Campbell, Rosina Despard's friend and to whom she wrote detailing her strange experiences, was asked to present the letters to the Society for Psychical Research, but she ultimately declined, citing 'so many allusions to personal matters' amongst the correspondence. This decision has been used by commentators both for and against genuine supernormal phenomena at Denore. On the one hand it has been suggested that the letters revealed Rosina's surreptitious knowledge of her father's secret liaison, while an alternative viewpoint (given by long-standing SPR member Eric Dingwall) is that the Despard-Campbell letters in fact showed that the writers were lovers and unwilling to have their relationship revealed in such a way. However, if Captain Despard was entertaining a mistress, it surely would have been far simpler and less dangerous to install her in a small dwelling house in a neighbouring district where they could conveniently indulge in their clandestine relationship, rather than bring her right into the middle of the family home where, with all the best will in the world, she would undoubtedly have been discovered at some stage. To consider that this woman was living under the very noses of a large family, undetected and unsuspected, for at least *seven* years is simply incredible, and if the woman in black was indeed the captain's mistress, then she possessed the superhuman ability, if we are to accept Rosina Despard's testimony, to suddenly and completely disappear, pass through cords stretched purposefully across the staircase leaving them intact and unbroken, and materialise within rooms when the doors were closed.

It must also be considered that the apparition was witnessed by up to seventeen people, both before and after the Despards took up residence in Pitville Circus Road. Do we know the identity of the woman in black? For Rosina Despard, the ghost was that of the unfortunate Imogen Swinhoe, returned to haunt the house where she had spent so many unhappy years, and where her spirit may possibly still linger.

The Cheltenham case is one of psychical research's more curious, and certainly fascinating, ghost stories. In July 1985, two men were walking along Pitville Circus Road. It was late and the neighbourhood was quiet. As they neared the old Despard home, they saw a tall woman dressed in black moving along the footpath of St Anne's Close (a modern cul-de-sac built on part of Denore's former garden) towards its junction with the main road. The face of the person was not concealed but as the figure was around seventy yards away they were unable to describe the features in any detail. The men continued along the main highway but being both struck by the strangeness of the woman's old-fashioned appearance, they walked back to St Anne's Close, but by this time the figure was nowhere to be seen…

Consult: B. Abdy Collins, *The Cheltenham Ghost* (Psychic Press Ltd, London, 1948); Andrew MacKenzie, *Hauntings and Apparitions* (Heinemann, London, 1982); Peter Underwood, *Hauntings: New Light on the Greatest True Ghost Stories of the World* (Dent, London, 1977).

The Dark Shades of Borley Rectory (1946-55)

This account of strange happenings connected with the famous Borley haunting is taken from the files of author and ghost hunter Peter Underwood, one of Britain's most experienced investigators, whose connections with the case spans over sixty years.

The haunting of Borley Rectory, famously known as the 'most haunted house in England', has been held in particular esteem by several generations of ghost hunters, and this controversial case, involving what is in effect the 'classic' haunted house, continues to fascinate and intrigue over eighty years after it first entered into the public consciousness through a series of sensational articles published in the columns of a national newspaper. Enduring stories of apparitions and ghostly figures, including the famous Borley nun, now one of the most famous ghosts in Britain, as well as violent poltergeist phenomena, strange lights and phantom footsteps, a ghostly coach and horses, buried bones as well as ghostly music and spectral animals, have not surprisingly created a 'Mount Everest of haunted houses' and many people, both believers and sceptics, as well as the public at large, have fallen under its intriguing spell.

Much has been written about the rambling thirty-room red-brick house, built in 1863 by the Revd Henry D.E. Bull to accommodate his large family, and the ghosts that are said to have walked there. The 'father of modern ghost hunting', the flamboyant Harry Price (1881-1948), an independent researcher who dominated the popular paranormal scene during the inter-war years, championed the Borley haunting in two full length books, *The Most Haunted House in England* (1940) and *The End of Borley Rectory* (1946). Only a few months after Price's death, the Society for Psychical Research (SPR) commissioned a trio of investigators that included noted and highly experienced researchers Eric J. Dingwall and Kathleen M. Goldney, to reassess Price's work at Borley in the light of posthumous accusations published by a London journalist that he faked phenomena inside the gloomy and deserted house in the summer of 1929. The 'Borley Report', published as *The Haunting of Borley Rectory* in 1956 and described as 'essentially a systematic attack on the honesty and integrity of Harry Price', has become almost as controversial as the material it attempts to de-bunk but at the same time remains essentially the talisman of sceptical commentators even today. Other critical works include Robert Wood's *The Widow of Borley* (1992), a sceptical examination of the Foyster years at Borley, the most controversial time period of the whole case and one we will look at briefly in a moment, as well as *We Faked the Ghosts of Borley Rectory*, an attempted exposure by the eccentric London-born Louis Mayerling (real name George Carter), a serial fantasist whose book was subsequently exposed as a hoax.

Writers who have been supportive of Borley as a true haunting, as well as opposing the view of Harry Price being a fraud, have included the former long-standing President of the Ghost Club, Peter Underwood – *The Ghosts of Borley* (1973) and *Borley Postscript* (2001) – as well as local Borley resident Edward Babbs – *Borley Rectory: The Final Analysis* (2003) – and paranormal enthusiast, the late Ivan Banks – *The Enigma of Borley Rectory* (1996). For *The Borley Rectory Companion*, a reassessment of the case in collaboration with Peter Underwood issued in 2009, the present authors came to the conclusion, after examining much original material pertaining to the case, that although Borley was undoubtedly plagued with exaggeration, misrepresentation and instances of fakery and hoaxing, several aspects of the reported haunting, particularly the sighting of phantom figures, the appearance of a mysterious light in the windows of the rectory bedrooms, as well as other reported phenomena including footsteps inside the house and sensations of coldness, cannot be as readily dismissed as the sceptics would wish, and as such Borley Rectory deserves to be regarded, for at least several periods of its existence (it was destroyed by fire in 1939 and demolished in 1944), perhaps not as the 'most haunted house' in England, but undoubtedly a genuinely haunted building.

In the closing years of the nineteenth century, the rectory and its environs gained a local reputation for strange and inexplicable happenings, although an unsubstantiated report credits a sighting of a nun-like apparition in the immediate area as taking place in the early 1840s, twenty years before the Revd Henry Bull took the decision to demolish an older building on the site and construct his new house. Ghostly figures were encountered inside the house, as well as seen walking in the garden, in the roadway outside and across the fields surrounding the rectory's large and expansive grounds. As well as the silent and lonely Borley nun, famously observed by four of the Bull sisters together in daylight on a summer July afternoon in 1900, both the Revd Henry Bull and his son Harry, who took over the living on the death of his father in 1892, claimed to have heard and seen a phantom coach and four horses rattling down the lane past Borley church, while the Bull's gardener and sometime groom, Edward Cooper and his wife, also reported seeing the ghostly coach sweep in towards the rectory from over the fields one night and cross the rectory lawn before disappearing from sight. The Coopers also claimed to have experienced poltergeist phenomena in the rectory cottage, a building which still stands today, as well as encountering the unnerving figure of a small black man which ran round their bedroom in circles during the night. When the surviving members of the Bull family left Borley in 1928 following the death of the Revd Harry, few could have conceived the idea that this strange and persistent local haunting would soon become one of the most famous cases of its kind in the country.

In early October 1928, the Revd Guy Eric Smith, originally from Calcutta, became rector of Borley and moved into the rectory with his wife Mabel together with their live-in maid, Londoner Mary Pearson. During the nine months that the Smiths lived in Henry Bull's old house they claimed to have had regular encounters with the unquiet ghosts of Borley: Mary Pearson told of seeing the nun standing in the garden and at least twice reported seeing the phantom coach crossing the lawn; the Revd Smith heard footsteps walking in the upstairs corridors, a voice crying out, and both he and on several occasions his wife showed villagers and visitors to the house an eerie light which appeared in the window of a first-floor bedroom which was closed up and empty; Mrs Smith claimed that the ghostly coach drew up outside the front door one evening and the servant bells rang by themselves at odd times of the day and night.

The Smiths were instrumental in bringing the Borley ghosts to a wider public. A letter to the editor of the *Daily Mirror* requesting details of a paranormal society who could investigate and explain away the mysterious happenings brought not only the required expert – Harry Price of the National Laboratory of Psychical Research and his secretary Lucy Kaye – but also a news-hungry reporter and subsequently hoards of sightseers and sensation-seekers who descended on the tiny hamlet at all times of the day and night, invading the grounds in order to try and see the eerie ghost nun for themselves. In July 1929, the Revd Smith and his wife abandoned the rectory and moved to nearby Long Melford, where they ran the parish for several months before finally quitting Borley for good in April of the following year. Six months later, in October 1930, fifty-two-year-old Lionel Algernon Foyster, a cousin of the Bulls, was inducted to the Borley living. His arrival at the rectory later the same month together with his young wife Marianne and their small adopted daughter Adelaide, was to usher in one of the most strange and controversial periods in the whole history of the Borley haunting.

The Foysters stayed in the lonely Essex hamlet for five years, during which time they gave the impression of being at the centre of a frightening and violent explosion of intense and unrelenting paranormal activity. For nearly a year and a half, the Revd Foyster kept a written record of the daily activities of the Borley ghosts (or 'goblins' as he called them) as they seemingly wreaked havoc inside the shadowy lamp-lit rooms and corridors of Borley Rectory. This diary, later re-worked by Foyster as a potential but ultimately unpublished novel entitled 'Fifteen Months in a Haunted House', is a catalogue of eerie and disturbing psychic violence: door slamming, bell-ringing, stone throwing, strange smells and disembodied footsteps and voices; wine bottles were thrown and smashed to pieces and stones and chunks of brickwork rolled down the staircases; several small fires broke out spontaneously inside the house and pathetic messages calling on the rector's wife for help were scrawled on the walls of the house. Household objects appeared and disappeared and Marianne Foyster claimed to see apparitions: the figure of the Revd Harry Bull and a sinister black bat-like monstrosity that struck her a violent blow with its outstretched wing.

In early 1932, a local Spiritualist group from nearby Marks Tey held a 'rescue circle' at the rectory, following which the violence and disturbances of the previous fifteen months began to subside. The Foysters eventually left Borley in 1935, the legacy of their stay proving to be a keystone upon which much of the later sensationalist aspect of the 'most haunted house in England' would be built. The truth of what went on inside Borley Rectory during that time will now never be known for sure. The Foysters' domestic arrangements throughout the 1930s, and particularly the period that Lionel Foyster was rector of Borley, were in themselves a bizarre and unnatural mixture of the absurd and the disturbing, and certainly contributed, in a non-supernatural way, to the apparent psychic bedlam that allegedly went on: Marianne, twenty years her husband's junior, took a lover, a London-born florist who went under the pseudonym of Francois d'Arles. D'Arles (real name Frank Pearless) was a mysterious figure who, according to contemporary accounts, appeared to dominate the Foyster household; Lionel Foyster, crippled with arthritis and often bed-ridden for long periods, seemingly knew and approved of his wife's affair and may even have been a voyeur to their sexual activities. The reported assaults by ghostly figures can reasonably be assigned to Marianne's affair with d'Arles, which was known to be violent at times, and it has been suggested that to alleviate the boredom of living in a lonely country backwater, the bored and frustrated Marianne Foyster took to and enjoyed playing ghostly games on her increasingly frail and impressionistic husband. The later revelation that Marianne entered into a bigamous marriage in the final year of their time at Borley, something which the Revd Foyster supported and incredibly assisted by pretending to be the bride's father, goes some way to supporting the view of Luton-born ghost hunter Tony Broughall, that the rectory building was in fact only haunted by 'a succession of very strange occupants that fate had brought together'.

Following the departure of the Foysters, gloomy Borley Rectory and its grounds remained empty and untended. The next incumbent, Alfred Henning, a London-born cleric originally from Forest Hill, aware of the building's unenviable haunted history, chose to live at nearby Liston with whose parish by that time Borley had now been amalgamated, and Henry Bull's once grand residence quickly began to fall into disrepair. In May 1937, Harry Price returned to Borley after an absence of several years. His bold experiment, to rent the rectory for a year and install a regular rota of observers to monitor the building and its grounds for signs of paranormal activity, was ground-breaking but only partially successful. A number of investigators, controversially drawn from the ranks of the general public via an advertisement in *The Times* rather than from specialist groups such as the Society for Psychical Research, reported unusual happenings – door slamming, footsteps, odd noises and the movement of objects – but the spectacular poltergeist phenomena of the Foyster years had seemingly left the rectory with them.

As Harry Price began working his numerous observers' reports and collected Borley papers into what would become the first of his two popular monographs on the case, the Church authorities started selling off slices of the old rectory grounds as building plots and, in October 1938, Borley Rectory itself, together with the Rectory Cottage and a small parcel of land was bought for £500 by William Gregson, a retired Captain of Engineers from the Rusland Valley in the Lake District. Gregson, an area organiser for Oswald Moseley's black-shirted British Union of Fascists, had bought the rectory with an eye to capitalising on its eerie reputation. He quickly began writing to Harry Price describing apparently unusual experiences as well as suggestions for paranormal-related marketing, including coach tours to the rectory and guided tours of the haunted rooms. However, as Price worked away compiling his 'Borley dossier', Gregson quickly became impatient with his investment and on the night of 27/28 February 1939, Borley Rectory was badly damaged by a fire which started in the hallway and quickly spread unchecked throughout the building. Captain Gregson blamed the Borley ghosts, who were seemingly fulfilling a séance prophesy obtained through a planchette eleven months previously by Price's ghost hunters, but his insurers begged to differ and, accusing the owner of firing the house himself in order to collect a substantial amount of money through his buildings policy, eventually settled for a much lesser amount out of court. Ironically, if Gregson had held back for just over a year, he would have been able to reap the collateral rewards from the publication of Price's *The Most Haunted House in England* which despite paper shortages and the wartime conditions, was enthralling readers during the grim winter of 1940.

The Borley haunting was to play a large part in the remaining years of Harry Price's life. In the summer of 1943, responding to suggestions made by Canon W.J. Phythian-Adams, he carried out excavation work in the rectory's ruinous cellars in the hope of finding evidence of human remains that would lend support to the theory, given by communicating 'entities' during séances held at Borley during the tenancy investigations, that the phantom nun had been a French novice, 'Marie Lairre', who was strangled to death and buried on the site by a member of the wealthy Waldegrave family in the fifteenth century. Despite Price's general distrust of séances and planchette information, on 17 August 1943, parts of a female skull were unearthed which, after being studied and photographed, were given a Christian burial in nearly Liston churchyard in 1945.

If the bones found by Price and his team in the rectory ruins were indeed that of 'Marie Lairre', then their respectful re-interment in consecrated ground was seemingly not enough to quieten her troubled spirit. A nun-like apparition has continued to be seen several times at Borley since those times, particularly during the 1950s and early 1960s, and may well have been photographed by Eddie Brazil during a visit to Borley church in 1972. The church itself has become a focal point for both paranormal happenings and subsequent investigation since the loss of the rectory to psychical research and today interest in the case seems undimmed – ghost hunters still gather in the locale on 28 July (the anniversary of the Bull sisters' encounter with the phantom nun on the rectory lawn) in the hope of seeing the ghosts walk, while beginning in 2010, local police have been obliged to cordon off the village on Halloween to prevent disturbances reminiscent of the 'rowdy scenes' that plagued the Revd Guy Smith and his wife when they unwittingly first brought the haunting to the attention of the general public eight decades before.

What, out of the multitude of reports and accounts of paranormal phenomena spanning over a century that are associated with the Borley case, deserves to be included in the present survey of Britain's most extreme hauntings? Of all the experiences connected with Borley Rectory, perhaps the most intriguing and disturbing are those of Montague Elelman, a London journalist who first visited the site of the 'most haunted house in England' in the mid-1940s. Following Harry Price's initial publicising of the haunting in his first Borley book, syndicated newspaper articles had spread reports of the case across the world, with the result that Elelman first heard of the rectory ghosts

The demolition of Borley Rectory in 1944, two years before the visit of journalist Montague Elelman. *(University of London Library)*

while a serving soldier in North Africa. Following demobilisation, he made the decision to investigate the case for himself in the hope of selling a story to one of the London dailies. By the time the newspaperman finally arrived at Borley, in March 1946, the rectory had been completely demolished and the former grounds were overgrown and deserted. Scattered bricks and rubble indicated only the outline of Henry Bull's once fine residence, but the cellars, now open to the sky, were still discernible despite being partially filled with debris and earth. After walking around the site for some time, during which he was able to interview two passing Borley villagers, Elelman eventually left for London, taking with him a length of charred timber, possibly part of the collapsed roof or a section of one of the floors, as a souvenir. For the next nine years, Elelman subsequently claimed that strange and unusual happenings, all with a direct connection to the famous Borley haunting, took place while the innocent but seemingly supernaturally-charged piece of wood was in his possession…

The first incident took place immediately upon his return to London. At the time, Elelman was staying at his sister's house and, arriving back there late in the evening, placed the length of burnt timber on the mantelpiece in his bedroom and went down to an improvised supper alone. The journalist had not informed anyone of his intention to visit Borley that day and the lateness of the hour meant that it would be breakfast time the following morning before it would be possible to discuss the trip with his sister. After a short time there was the sound of a sudden commotion from the upper part of the house and Elelman looked up to see his sister, in a state of distress, standing in the open doorway. She claimed that while crossing the first-floor landing she happened to glance through the open doorway of her brother's bedroom and had been shocked to see a tall black figure, unmistakably that of a nun, standing silently in the middle of the room. The couple went upstairs but the bedroom was empty and, deciding that for the moment it would be best to withhold details of his recent outing until the following morning, Montague persuaded his sister that she had been uncharacteristically jumping at shadows.

Over the next few nights, Elelman and other members of the household had a number of strange and inexplicable experiences. After waking unexpectedly from a dream the night following his sister's encounter with the nun, Elelman, in the process of lighting a cigarette in an attempt to quieten his nerves, suddenly heard a loud scream, unmistakably human and in the house somewhere. Thinking his sister and her husband were being attacked by a burglar, the journalist jumped out of bed and hurried across to their bedroom where, to his complete amazement, the couple were asleep in bed. The following day Michael Elelman, the newspaperman's brother, on a business trip to London from the Midlands, stayed over at the house and was given the spare bed in the same bedroom. After the household had retired and the two men lay in their beds quietly talking, the room light suddenly turned itself on. A few hours later, around half past two in the morning, both Michael and Montague were awakened by a ringing sound, as if a large clock were chiming the hour. Having lived in the house for several weeks, Montague knew that his sister and her husband did not own a clock with chimes, and the sound, which despite investigation they were unable to trace, was without doubt coming from somewhere close inside the building. All of these incidents took place in or near the bedroom where the apparently innocuous piece of Borley wood lay innocently on the mantlepiece over the fireplace. The next night, however, was quiet and in the days that followed there were no further disturbances.

Several weeks later, Elelman moved out of London, accompanied by his bizarre Borley trophy, and took up temporary lodgings some thirty miles away in a house at Westcliffe-on-Sea. During the first few days after his arrival, the front doorbell rang by itself on several separate occasions when there was clearly nobody at the door – during one incident, Elelman's landlord, convinced that local schoolchildren were playing an extended game of 'knock down Ginger', purposely left the front door open and, when the bell began ringing continuously, by looking through the inner glass vestibule door, was astonished to see that the porch lobby was empty – while a visitor to the house claimed to have seen a dark-clad figure cross the first-floor landing as she stood talking with the owner in the hallway below. A search of the upstairs proved that the visitor and the lady of the house were the only people present at the time.

Over time, Elelman began to notice a similar pattern in connection with the mysterious piece of rectory wood. Immediately after it was moved to a different location, strange things appeared to happen in its immediate vicinity which, after a few days, gradually ceased, almost as though whatever force had been disturbed was able to return to an eerie and unknowable state of suspended animation. Phenomena associated with the Borley wood during the time that it was either in Elelman's possession or in the keeping of friends and associates included shuffling footsteps, voices, sensations of coldness and drops in temperature, as well as unusual noises and glimpses of a dark figure or black shadowy shape, often seen standing motionless beside the relic or passing to and fro past the door of the room where it was temporarily kept on loan. Eventually, in 1955, some nine years after his initial visit to Borley, and at the insistence of his wife, Veronica, Montague Elelman gave the length of burnt wood away permanently and it was never seen by him again. Not surprisingly, its whereabouts today, if it in fact still survives, is unknown.

In 1963, Elelman gave a radio broadcast in which he described his experiences and in April 1974, he presented long-standing President of the Ghost Club, Peter Underwood, with a copy of the script. In an accompanying letter, the journalist stated that everything he had described in it connected with the haunted wood was completely true.

What are we to make of this story today? Is it another journalistic tall tale exploiting the dramatic side of what, by the early 1960s when Montague Elelman made his broadcast, was an exceedingly well known and much sensationalised haunting? Or is this account evidence of the ability of paranormal forces to become essentially attached in such a way to seemingly ordinary physical objects that they can project themselves and manifest in completely different locations, often miles away physically from the original centre of psychic or supernormal activity? A number of well-attested cases included in the present book describe just this sort of happening, so such a possibility should not be dismissed out of hand, and interestingly, as well as being of particular value eviden-tially, is the fact that on a number of occasions the persons who experienced apparent phenomena, including Elelman's landlord and his wife in Westcliffe-on-Sea, as well as a cleaner at his London office where the length of wood was stored on one occa-sion, were totally unaware both of its presence and its ghostly associations. Montague Elelman insisted that his story was true, but he qualified it by admitting that personally 'I think it includes coincidences – and perhaps it's possible for people themselves to create ghostly sights and happenings out of the stories – false or otherwise – that are in their heads, and for those things to be seen by other people too.' Such is the mystery and attraction of the paranormal, as well as the equally enigmatic legend of the 'most haunted house in England'.

Consult: Paul Adams, Eddie Brazil & Peter Underwood, *The Borley Rectory Companion: The Complete Guide to 'The Most Haunted House in England'* (The History Press, Stroud, 2009); Edward Babbs, *Borley Rectory: The Final Analysis* (Six Martletts Publishing, Sudbury, 2003); Ivan Banks, *The Enigma of Borley Rectory* (Foulsham, Cippenham, 2006); Eric J. Dingwall, Kathleen M. Goldney & Trevor H. Hall, *The Haunting of Borley Rectory* (Gerald Duckworth & Co. Ltd, London, 1956); Louis Mayerling, *We Faked the Ghosts of Borley Rectory* (Pen Press Publishers, London, 2000); Harry Price, *'The Most Haunted House in England': Ten Years' Investigation of Borley Rectory* (Longmans, Green & Co. Ltd, London, 1940); Harry Price, *The End of Borley Rectory* (George G. Harrap & Co. Ltd, London, 1946); Paul Tabori & Peter Underwood, *The Ghosts of Borley – Annals of the Haunted Rectory* (David & Charles, Newton Abbott, 1973); Peter Underwood, *Borley Postscript* (White House Publications, Haslemere, 2001); Robert Wood, *The Widow of Borley – A Psychical Investigation* (Gerald Duckworth & Co. Ltd, London, 1992).

The Haunting of Ardachie Lodge (1953)

The case of Ardachie Lodge is a forgotten classic. The crawling ghost of Mrs Bruen that haunted a now demolished hunting lodge in the Scottish Highlands remains one of Britain's most unnerving phantoms.

A curious aspect of a number of British hauntings is that the apparitions that cause the most alarm and fear to those who encounter them are of people who, when in life, are considered to be the weakest and most vulnerable in society, namely old and elderly women. Why this should be is worth considering. No doubt physical characteristics play their part: the ravages of time on flesh, skin, hair and bones, together with the shuffling gait and creaking stoop of advanced years, all add to the picture of unease and menace. For Walt Disney's *Sleeping Beauty* (1959), the beautiful, wicked queen becomes a much more unsettling figure, albeit a cartoon one, when she transforms herself into a hideous, hooked-nosed hag. Similarly, in Dickens' 1861 novel, *Great Expectations*, we pity the young Miss Haversham as she sheds tears after being jilted on her wedding day – she is a figure we feel for, not fear. Yet, move onward several decades to an older, withered Miss Haversham, a living ghost, insane and decayed, shuffling wraith-like in a shabby wedding dress through her crumbling house, and she becomes an object of dread and revulsion. Further fictional reference points are to be found in such characters as M.R. James' Mrs Mothersole, Robert Bloch's (and later Hitchcock's) psychopathic Mrs Bates, the hideous dwarf in Daphne du Maurier's 1971 short story *Don't Look Now*, and Susan Hill's highly regarded *The Woman in Black* (1983), whose real life counterpart we have already encountered.

In December 1952, Peter McEwan and his wife, Dorothy, moved into Ardachie Lodge, a stone building which stood close to the shores of Loch Ness and near to the town of Fort Augustus in the Scottish Highlands. The McEwans, who were both qualified psychologists, had been living in London since their marriage two years earlier, but because of a medical condition, Dorothy McEwan had been advised that a country environment would improve her health. The couple were accompanied by their two baby children and Peter McEwan's father, who roomed in a cottage in the grounds of the lodge. They planned to raise pedigree pigs and sheep and the old hunting lodge, with its numerous outhouses, seemed ideal for the purpose.

By the summer of 1953, the family was sufficiently established to be able to employ a housekeeper together with a farmhand to help with the livestock. Their advertisement, which was placed in a London newsagent, was answered by the MacDonalds, a couple in their forties who were tired of the metropolis and wanted to return to Scotland. Originally from Edinburgh, they were unfamiliar with the Highlands, yet such was their determination to make a new life north of the border, that they accepted the post without knowing the identity of the family they were to serve or even the location of the house. In fact, Mr MacDonald was in effect burning his bridges for in London he had been employed as a postman and, in giving up his job, had also lost his pension. However, both were keen to make as good an impression as they could during their first probationary month with the McEwans.

Mr and Mrs MacDonald arrived at Ardachie on 17 August 1953 after the long and tiring journey north. After meeting the McEwans they were given a brief tour of the house and the grounds and also instructed in their duties. However, it was obvious to their new employees that both were tired from their trip and Dorothy McEwan bade them an early goodnight and afterwards joined her husband and father-in-law for supper. Later that evening, around half past ten, as the McEwans were gathered in the sitting

Haunted Ardachie Lodge in the Scottish Highlands, where the apparition of a sinister crawling ghost was seen in the 1950s. *(Authors' collection)*

room, the MacDonalds burst in looking agitated and anxious. Immediately apologising for the intrusion, they asked if there was anything wrong with their room. The McEwans looked perplexed. Mrs MacDonald then asked if anyone had come up the stairs in the last half hour and entered the room opposite to theirs: both Peter and Dorothy McEwan were adamant that no one was in the house except themselves. When pressed, Mrs MacDonald declared that shortly after going to bed, she had heard footsteps ascend the staircase, move along the corridor and enter the room opposite. Her husband had slept through the noises. When she looked out into the corridor, she found it deserted. Soon after, the footsteps returned and Mrs MacDonald woke her husband. He also heard the slow, rhythmic tread, but he said he thought the sounds were coming from the walls of the bedroom. Both heard the footsteps come along the corridor and enter the room across the landing, but when they looked inside, it was empty.

The McEwans tried to reassure the couple, saying that the house was old and all manner of sounds might be expected from an aged building as it settled for the night. Despite the explanation, their reasoning was rejected by the MacDonalds and the frightened housekeeper insisted that the noises she had heard were human footfalls. The couple returned to their room, now convinced that there was something strange about the house. An hour later, the household was once again roused when the MacDonalds, now plainly terrified, complained of rapping sounds which they claimed were emanating from the walls of their bedroom. Three or four blows at a time were heard throughout the room. When Mr MacDonald switched on the light, the noises ceased.

Both couples decided to retire downstairs to the kitchen to discuss the situation. Peter McEwan suggested that the two men should return to the bedroom, where they sat in darkness for ten minutes, listening but hearing nothing. Despite this, Mrs MacDonald refused to sleep in the room and she and her husband were moved to the guest bedroom, which was some distance away separated by two flights of stairs and another corridor. As soon as she entered the new room, Mrs MacDonald crossed to the far wall and placed her head against the fireplace, as if listening for something. Then she said, 'There is an old woman in here.' As she turned from the wall she suddenly stiffened in shock. As if in a state of trance, she stared in horror at a corner of the room as the three spectators looked at her in astonishment. Dorothy McEwan told her to stop as she was frightening them, but Mrs MacDonald seemed not to hear and continued to stare ahead in fear across the room. Then she raised her arm and began beckoning something invisible to the others towards her.

After some moments, a highly distressed Mrs MacDonald appeared to awaken from a dream. She looked around the room and seemed puzzled, asking the others if they had seen the old woman with a cap on her head and a shawl around her shoulders. She had straggling grey hair and had been beckoning her to follow. As the woman motioned, Mrs MacDonald said she could hear the sound of flapping wings and felt the strength being washed out of her body.

It was now obvious that the woman would not sleep in the room in which she claimed she had seen the apparition, and the increasingly exasperated McEwans suggested that she and her husband use the empty bedroom opposite theirs which was away from the earlier scenes of alarm on the far side of the house. Both doors would be left open with the lights on, and Mrs MacDonald would have nothing to fear. However, within ten minutes of retiring in the new room, the MacDonalds once again heard faint tapping sounds coming from the walls. Peter and Dorothy McEwan were roused from their bed for a third time and all four gathered again, this time on the landing at the top of the main staircase. They had stood there for some minutes discussing the night's events when Mrs MacDonald suddenly froze with fear. Looking towards the end of the landing she said, 'There she is again. Can't you see her? She is crawling towards us on her hands and knees with a candle in her hand.' Once again none of the others could see the figure, yet Mrs MacDonald insisted she was there. Peter McEwan urged his new housekeeper to speak to the apparition. 'What is troubling you?' she managed to murmur, but was unable to continue. The apparition moved away around a corner of the landing and then returned, crawling with difficulty towards the hysterical housekeeper who became so frightened that the others had to quickly take her downstairs to the sanctuary of the kitchen. By now the whole household felt fearful and it was decided that they should abandon the lodge for the rest of the night and sleep in Peter McEwan's father's cottage, which stood nearby. The next morning, Peter McEwan visited his neighbour, Mrs Beckett of Cullachy House. She had been a friend of the previous owner of the lodge, Mrs Bruen, and he hoped she would be able to tell him something about the history of the house.

Ardachie was built in 1840 as a large shooting lodge for a local landowner, Charles Gillespie. It was constructed in the Georgian style, incorporating parts of some older farm buildings that originally stood on the site. Many local people still had vivid memories of the busy months of the year when the shooting parties were in residence. During the inter-war years, the house was owned by a Colonel Campbell, and after his death the lodge was purchased by the Bruens, who had previously owned property in Ireland. Old Mrs Bruen lived there with her sister, and both had been very popular with their neighbours. Peter McEwan asked Mrs Becket to describe the old lady. She had indeed worn a kind of shawl and a small cap and her hair was grey and straggling. Had she died in the house? McEwan asked. The answer was no, although she had lived at Ardachie until a few months before her death, she had eventually been admitted to a nursing home in Inverness. It seemed that Mrs Bruen had suffered from a crippling form of arthritis, and this, compounded by a stroke, made it very difficult for her to move around in the last months of her life. The old lady was in the habit of crawling around the house on her hands and knees at night holding a candle, keeping an eye on her servants, who she suspected were stealing from her. Peter McEwan was now even more puzzled. Was it possible that his housekeeper had seen the ghost of Mrs Bruen crawling through the house, and why was it that only Mrs MacDonald could see the phantom?

That night it was decided that the MacDonalds would sleep in their small kitchen downstairs, and they retired to bed early, at around half past nine. As Mr MacDonald slept, his wife awoke and remembered she had forgotten to bring in the milk, which the shepherd left outside the back door each evening. As she went towards the kitchen door the noises started, raps and knocks which seemed to sound throughout the room. Hesitantly, Mrs MacDonald went to the door and opened it. To her horror, at the foot of the stairs was the figure of the old woman on her hands and knees. She looked at the apparition for some moments, but could not discern any clear features. The wraith seemed barely human and soon it began to crawl very slowly towards her. Now extremely frightened, the housekeeper turned and rushed back into the kitchen, slamming the door shut.

This experience was too much for the McEwans, and together with their children and Mr and Mrs MacDonald, they once again abandoned the house for the night. By now, Peter McEwan decided he had to seek specialist advice in the hope that some light might be thrown on the strange happenings that his family and the MacDonalds were experiencing. For some years he had been a member of the Society for Psychical Research and he enquired if there were any members in his locality who might be able to help. Some days later, two SPR members, a Mr Ross and a Mr Matheson, arrived at Ardachie to investigate the curious incidents. Later that night, the household assembled in the MacDonald's small kitchen, which doubled as their bedroom, and settled down for a vigil. The room was in semi-darkness, illuminated only by the glow from the open kitchen range. Mr MacDonald and Mr Ross sat on one bed, Mr Matheson on the other, while Mrs MacDonald sat between them in an armchair. The MacEwans stood near the open door. For some minutes all was quiet, yet soon the observers heard rapping noises, like tapping on wood, coming from the window wall. The sounds came in a slow tempo, three raps at a time with a short interval between. Soon, deep sighs began to emanate from Mrs MacDonald which seemed to be synchronised in some way with the mysterious noises. As the others watched, the housekeeper appeared to become transfixed: her arms hung rigid by her side, and her attention was focused, vacantly, on the open door. Suddenly she let out a scream and shrank back. Hurriedly the main lights were switched on and Mrs MacDonald seemed to regain her composure. She told the others that she had clearly seen the figure of the old woman enter the room, although the observers saw nothing.

It was decided to give Mrs MacDonald time to recover and most of the party left the room. When they returned, she was in bed. Once again the lights were turned off and the vigil continued. Some moments later the rapping resumed and Mrs MacDonald's breathing became laboured. This lasted for some minutes before the housekeeper sat up and asked her husband if she had been dreaming. Then she said, 'The rose tree has been neglected, someone has removed the rose tree.' After this she became silent once more, but as she lay back on the bed the rapping noises began again. One of the SPR men, Mr Matheson, suspecting that the housekeeper might be making the noises herself, quickly shone his torch on Mrs MacDonald, but none of the watchers saw her hands move. However, at this juncture, Mrs MacDonald became distressed and it was decided to bring the vigil to an end. All returned to their rooms. The two researchers were allocated the room where the ghost had first made its appearance, yet they passed the night without any disturbance. Although the house seemed quiet throughout the small hours, the MacDonalds subsequently claimed that the rapping noises had continued until five o'clock in the morning.

The next day the investigators departed, clearly unimpressed by what they had witnessed, leaving the McEwans with more questions than answers. One thing which intrigued Peter McEwan was Mrs MacDonald's trance-state reference to the missing rose tree. When he and his wife had arrived at Ardachie, they had instructed the part-time gardener to clear out an old greenhouse in the garden so that it could be used for growing tomatoes. The greenhouse contained only a peach tree and a large old rose. The rose tree had been transplanted outdoors, but had subsequently died, something that Mrs MacDonald could not have known. He also recalled that on the day that the MacDonalds had arrived at Ardachie and were being shown around the grounds, Mrs MacDonald had become agitated and uneasy as she entered the rose garden. Peter McEwan's neighbour, Mrs Becket, had already informed him that the previous owner of Ardachie, Mrs Bruen, had a passion for the rose garden, being particularly fond of a rare early flowering rose tree. McEwan could not bring himself to tell Mrs Beckett that the rose tree had been destroyed when the gardener cleared out the greenhouse.

It soon began to dawn on Peter McEwan that the disturbances at Ardachie Lodge might well have something to do with the destruction of Mrs Bruen's favourite tree, yet even as he contemplated the idea, the thought seemed preposterous. But there were things that couldn't easily be explained: how could Mrs MacDonald know what Mrs Bruen looked like, and how could she have known about the rose tree? It seemed impossible that the MacDonalds would have been aware of Ardachie's former owner, her appearance and her love of roses and the garden from others who were employed at the lodge. Only two people working at the house had known Mrs Bruen when she was alive: the nanny, Jenny Maclean, and the gardener, David Coutts, and both were away from Ardachie on the day the MacDonalds took up their duties. Was it possible that Mrs MacDonald was faking the haunting and producing the rapping sounds herself? It was only she who had witnessed the apparition of the old woman, and, together with her husband, heard the first instances of knocks and raps. For McEwan, it seemed completely foolish that the couple, who had given up their lives in London and were determined to make a success of their new career, would alarm and alienate their new employers by declaring that their home was haunted in such a way.

On the night of 22 August, Peter and Dorothy McEwan sat yet again with the MacDonalds, and once more the familiar raps and knocks were heard. However, on this occasion, it was impossible to determine their origin and the session was inconclusive, but by this time it hardly seemed to matter. The strain on the McEwans was becoming unbearable, and for the safety and sanity of his family, Peter McEwan arranged for his wife and children to take a short holiday for a few days. It was also the end for the MacDonalds: they were asked to leave, and on 29 August 1953 were driven to the railway station to catch the connecting train to London. They had arrived at Ardachie twelve days earlier full of smiles and high hopes; now they boarded the train in tears.

With the MacDonalds gone, peace returned to Ardachie, but the events of the past two weeks had taken their toll, and Dorothy McEwan now felt she could no longer remain in the house. Her husband put the estate on the market and it was sold to a veterinary surgeon, who carried on the farming business successfully. Later the lodge was sold to a Major Vernon, the owner of the adjacent Glen Doe estate. He chose not to live at Ardachie and the lodge was closed up and left empty. Whether there were any further outbreaks of paranormal phenomena at the house after the McEwans had sold it on is unclear. Nevertheless, rumours concerning Ardachie Lodge began to circulate in the locality, and the building gained the reputation for being a haunted house with stories of an exorcism being performed in the building during the MacDonalds time there, in which candles were lit and a Mass being said in all the places that the ghost of the old woman had been seen. Despite the ruination of their Scottish idyll, the McEwans became convinced that they had been dealing with authentic paranormal phenomena at Ardachie. Undoubtedly, Mrs MacDonald was unknowingly psychic and acted as a catalyst for supernatural incidents to occur. The couple remain fleeting figures in the annals of psychical research and nothing is known of their subsequent history or whether the former housekeeper had further unnerving encounters with the supernormal.

On a grey winter's day in 1968, an Army team arrived at Ardachie Lodge. The house, now ringed by a screen of untended trees and a jungle of rhododendrons, had stood abandoned for many years. Rumours persisted that the place was still haunted and that the spectre of old Mrs Bruen continued to crawl her way through the empty rooms and corridors at night. But on this bleak, bitter day, Army explosives would put an end to the stories. They packed charges of dynamite around the walls of the house and operated the detonators. The empty windows of the lonely lodge looked out on to the unkempt garden for the last time. When the dust had settled, the debris was bulldozed and soon all traces of the haunted building were gone. By the end of the day, Ardachie Lodge was no more and the strange events which had taken place there for twelve disturbing days in 1953 soon faded from memory.

Consult: Colin Wilson, *Poltergeist!: A Study in Destructive Haunting* (New English Library, London, 1981).

Chapter Two

ROOMS OF FEAR

Haunted Houses, Churches and Other Buildings

The Ghosts of the Theatre Royal (1920s-Present)

For over 100 years, a persistent and convincing haunting has afflicted one of the country's oldest play-houses, involving a wealth of varied and intriguing phenomena that appear to be linked with the building's eventful past.

The Theatre Royal, Margate, built in 1787, is the oldest theatre in the county of Kent and the second oldest existing playhouse in Britain. Its origins are, to say the least, convoluted. In the late eighteenth century, Francis Cobb, an influential Margate businessman, was the landlord of the Fountain Inn, in King Street, as well as the head of his own Cobbs' Brewery. Situated at the rear of the inn was a stable that was also used as a makeshift theatre. This was rented to a retired sea captain named Charles Mate who already had control of a theatre in Dover. The cost of renting the stable was £20 per year, but Charles Mate decided to invest £200 and open a new theatre on the site. However, in 1785, Sarah Baker, England's first female theatre manager, brought her company to Dover and approached Francis Cobb, requesting his permission to open a new theatre in Margate. Cobb refused, but Baker was intent on having a theatre of her own and subsequently, in just over a month, had a wooden playhouse erected at a cost of £500. It opened for the summer season in July 1785, the same month that Charles Mate opened his season in King Street.

After three months, Mate found the competition too strong, and having by this time lost interest and money in his theatrical venture in Margate, he returned to his theatre in Dover. Not surprisingly, an acrimonious relationship developed between Francis Cobb and the Baker company, with the result that local townsfolk, under the influence of Cobb, sent a petition with over 900 signatures to Parliament, requesting a Royal

Charter. The 'Margate Playhouse Bill' was introduced and the Royal Charter awarded. The licensee would effectively have the power to send Sarah Baker back to Dover and prevent other rival companies from invading Margate. The licence holder would also be permitted to give dramatic performances from 1 May to 31 October each year, and was permitted to sell alcoholic drinks on the premises. The permit remained valid for 125 years, which no doubt pleased Francis Cobb and his brewery.

With Sarah Baker gone, Charles Mate decided that he would try again in Margate, and formed a partnership with Thomas Robson, a singer from Covent Garden in London. Charles Mate's former Margate theatre was re-opened and re-named the Theatre Royal. Both men had ambitious plans to succeed in Margate and towards the end of 1786, their co-owned Theatre Royal was closed and preparations were made for the building of a new theatre. The site of the proposed building was to be on the east side of Hawley Square at the junction with Prince's Street. The land belonged to an estate and was purchased for the princely sum of £80. The cost of the theatre was approximately £4,000, and on 27 June 1787, amid much ceremony, it opened its doors to the public for the first time. However, the partnership between Robson and Mate did not work effectively, with the result that Thomas Robson decided to sell his share of the Theatre Royal to a London actor by the name of Thomas King. Soon after this transfer of ownership, Mate also sold his share in the theatre to one of the owners of London's Drury Lane for £2,200.

In 1874, the structure was radically altered, marking the transition of the building from a Georgian boxed playhouse into a Victorian theatre. During its lifetime, the Theatre Royal has suffered a number of ups and downs and, in order to survive, its management has resorted at times to various alternative uses: a barracks, a chapel, warehousing, a cinema, a wrestling venue and a bingo hall. Despite these vicissitudes, it has survived and today remains an ever popular venue with local theatre-goers. Thespian activities apart, the theatre is also renowned for something which its appreciative audiences are probably not aware of as they sit enthralled in its centuries-old auditorium – ghosts.

In 1867, Sarah Thorne became theatre manager. Although she was an actress, albeit a mediocre one, Thorne's skill lay in her teaching of drama, and she set up one of the first acting schools in Britain in a house adjacent to the theatre. Under her guidance, the Royal experienced its most successful period, staging many productions which had previously drawn large crowds in London. Tragically, on 27 February 1899, she died from a severe attack of influenza aged sixty-two. In her later years, she had also acquired the lease of a theatre in Chatham, but her heart remained in Margate. When dying she was heard to declare, 'So long as the Theatre Royal is there, so shall I.' In the years following her death a number of strange incidents were reported at the theatre which led many to believe that the ghost of Sarah Thorne had indeed returned to haunt the building she had loved so much in life. Unaccountable noises and, from time to time, the appearance of a misty, filmy form on the stage and in the auditorium, were witnessed by theatre staff and actors, while Sarah Thorne's son also reported that he had encountered the apparition of his mother on several occasions inside the building. However, there are many who believe that the phantom, if it is Sarah Thorne, is not the only ghost which haunts the building.

In the nineteenth century, a demented actor who had been summarily dismissed from a production at the Royal, bought himself a box for the next night's performance. During the play he is said to have leapt from the box into the orchestra pit, breaking his neck. After the turn of the century, because the actor's ghost was, on many occasions, seen to appear sitting motionless in the very same box, the theatre management were forced to withdraw it from use and it was left curtained and empty. Yet, despite this, the apparition was repeatedly viewed drawing back the curtains of the box during performances. The phenomena only ceased when the box was finally bricked up as part of new fire precaution work carried out during the early 1920s.

In 1934, the lease of the Royal was taken over by Caspar Middleton. He knew nothing of the theatre's haunted reputation, and was strongly sceptical of the whole idea of ghosts and the supernatural. However, within weeks of his appointment he had witnessed an apparition on three separate occasions. One night after the performance had ended, he was coming out of the circle buffet when he saw a figure walk through a doorway from the stairs leading to the gallery, and go slowly around the circle before disappearing through a wall on the opposite side. At one time there had been an opening with a flight of stairs which had led down to where Sarah Thorne had once had an office, although he couldn't be sure if the apparition was that of Thorne herself. On another night, when the theatre had closed and all was quiet, he saw the figure again. He reported that the ghost passed so close that he could have almost reached out and touched it. He saw the phantom for a third time as it stood motionless by a door in the stalls which had once led to the box where the ghost of the crazed actor had been seen. Middleton described the apparition as a woman dressed in flowing, bluish-grey draperies, a description which several have suggested is the attire of the sleepwalking Lady Macbeth, a role often performed on the Theatre Royal stage by Sarah Thorne during the late 1800s. Middleton did not report what he had seen but made enquiries into the history of the theatre. Even when informed that the Royal had a haunted reputation, he remained silent. What finally made the whole affair public were the extraordinary and frightening experiences of two unsuspecting actresses that took place soon afterwards.

On the night of 22 August 1934, members of the theatre repertory company were rehearsing at midnight for their opening performance of a new play. As the stage was laid out for another company appearing that week, the rehearsal was being held in the circle buffet. One of the players, Margaret Carrington, had left the buffet and was standing under a small gaslight at the side of the circle, reading her part. The rest of the theatre was hushed and in darkness with the fireproof curtain down on the silent stage. Suddenly Miss Carrington was startled when she heard a gentle moan or cry break the stillness. She glanced up and was astonished to see a figure leaning out of

Interior of the Theatre Royal, Margate, haunted by numerous ghosts, including that of a crazed actor. *(Authors' collection)*

a box on the other side of the auditorium, seemingly gesturing and waving its arms about. Miss Carrington was terrified, for she knew whatever it was was not natural and she could not help from screaming. Her cries brought one of her female colleagues out of the buffet to see what was happening. She too saw the waving figure and immediately fainted. By now the commotion had drawn the attention of the manager, Caspar Middleton, and he came hurriedly into the auditorium. Looking across the theatre he also saw the waving, swaying figure leaning over the edge of the box. Despite what he had previously experienced, Middleton thought it was someone playing a practical joke, yet he couldn't understand how anyone could have entered the theatre to carry it out as both the doors to the stage and the box itself were locked. He quickly made his way across the circle and through the door where he had previously seen the apparition standing, and up into the box itself. No one was there, and nothing had been disturbed. While Middleton was making his way hurriedly across the theatre, Miss Carrington's eyes were still held, transfixed, upon the waving apparition: a bluish-grey transparent female figure. Then, to her utter amazement, the figure gradually rose up into the air over the front of the box and then disappeared into the theatre roof.

Following this extraordinary incident (it is most unusual and impressive for a ghost to be witnessed by a group of people collectively), the haunting became public and other evidence to support it came forward. Soon after, psychic investigators took up the case and organised several vigils inside the building which at the time proved inconclusive. What wasn't in doubt, however, was that the Royal was the scene of paranormal activity, and had at least two ghosts, one of whom was supposed to be that of the late Sarah Thorne. However, when a niece of Thorne heard of the ghostly activity, she visited Margate and told Caspar Middleton that it in fact might not be the ghost of her aunt which was haunting the theatre. Many people had believed in the ghost as far back as the 1880s, and Sarah herself had often described how she encountered a supernatural figure in the form of a monk in a vault within the basement. The vault was believed to be a section of passageway from a medieval building which had once stood on the site of the Royal. One day, as Sarah used the passage, she came face to face with a ghostly figure wearing a grey habit and promptly fainted. She remained lying helpless for some three hours before she was eventually discovered.

The following years saw the haunting continue and there were reports of inexplicable happenings at the theatre which included strange noises and half-glimpsed ghostly shapes. During the Second World War, bomb damage forced the Royal to close but it reopened in 1948 and once again manifestations were soon experienced. Late one July night, no less than thirteen people, including the then manager Robert Butler, testified to hearing the prolonged screams of a woman as well as disembodied footsteps hurrying across the empty stage. Another reported phenomenon was a mysterious orange ball of light which, hardly bigger than a marble, travelled over the footlights and across the stage, growing to the size of a football before disappearing into the passageway leading to the stage door.

The strange incidents continued on into the next decade. In 1954, two workmen who had stayed on late one night, were frightened into a rapid departure from the theatre when they heard, in the circle overhead, the sound of agitated pacing footsteps. Both investigated the sounds but could find no explanation for them. Throughout this period, all those who had contact with the theatre agreed that there was an overwhelming sense of unease throughout the building. Heavy doors which had been secured and bolted last thing at night were found to be standing open the next morning. Lights which had been put out after locking up were discovered blazing the next day. The caretaker at the time reported that he found the place extremely eerie, particularly when he was alone there late at night. At times he often heard sibilant whisperings and muffled noises sounding throughout the auditorium, and regularly had the feeling that he was being watched.

During the early years of the 1960s, it appeared that instances of paranormal phenomena in the Margate theatre were lessening. Throughout the day, at least, staff, actors and members of the public, heard or saw nothing out of the ordinary. However, we may wonder, after the last performance had ended, and the lights were extinguished and the doors locked for the night, what strange occurrences took place within the silent theatre. Is a building any less haunted if disembodied footsteps sound in the dark corridors or empty rooms and there is no one there to hear them? One person who did get to experience a night alone in the theatre was decorator Alfred Tanner. In January

1966, he was contracted to paint the auditorium for the then manager, Harry Jacobs, and to minimise inconvenience in the daily running of the Royal, it was agreed that the painting would be carried out during the night. Tanner would commence work at 10 p.m. and continue on until 6.30 a.m. the following morning. Not being a local man, he was unaware of the theatre's haunted reputation. Perhaps if he had, he might have thought twice about taking the job.

Several times during his first night in the theatre, Tanner reported hearing soft voices and whisperings throughout the auditorium. At one point he heard what sounded like someone coughing. Puzzled, the decorator explored the building but could find nothing to account for the noises. It was during his second night there that the incidents became somewhat more alarming. Once again there were the sounds of whispering and coughing. At 1.30 a.m., he heard the booking office door slam shut and when he went to look he found it standing wide open. Soon after, the backstage door slammed heavily. Tanner went to investigate and found the door closed and bolted. He resumed work but was once again disturbed, this time by the sound of footsteps as though an invisible person was walking across the stage towards him. Suspecting a practical joke, Tanner was about to issue a challenge when to his utter astonishment he saw what seemed to be a disembodied head float into view. It came round the curtains on the left of the stage and drifted across to the right. The decorator later stated that it was the head and shoulders of a woman with frizzy hair, two slits for eyes and a thin receding chin. He watched it for a few seconds, whereupon it reached the other side of the stage and disappeared from sight. His eyes were then quickly drawn to another door in the auditorium where a heavy set of curtains had been lifted clear of the wall and folded on a large semi-circular wooded pelmet. As he watched, the curtains were lifted up and then slowly dropped back down, as if someone was moving them down from the pelmet. Bravely, Tanner made his way over to the curtains and examined them. As he did so he had the uncomfortable sensation that someone was standing behind him. He nervously looked to his rear but there was no one there. Yet the feeling that there was something or someone behind him persisted. The atmosphere in the theatre had become unsettling, as if something dreadful was about to happen. By now Mr Tanner had had enough. He locked up the theatre and made his way home, but was so shaken by what he had witnessed that he was unable to sleep and sat up for the rest of the night reading.

The next morning he returned to the theatre and informed Harry Jacobs of his curious experiences of the previous night. The manager didn't know what to make of Tanner's story. One might think that an old theatre at night could well be a place of unexpected noises and sounds which would feed an overactive mind with all manner of dark fancies. But the painter was adamant that what he saw and heard was not his imagination, and he refused to work again in the theatre alone. As the two were going up a staircase, Alfred Tanner stopped by an old photograph of Sarah Thorne in her Lady Macbeth sleepwalking costume and exclaimed, 'That's the face I saw last night!'

It is unclear if Jacobs was previously aware of the theatre's ghostly history although it seems likely that he was. However, ghosts or not, the painting job had to be completed and it was arranged that Tanner would be accompanied the next night by a friend, Lawrence Rodgers. Soon after they commenced work, both heard strange noises in the auditorium which culminated in a terrific crash, as if something had been thrown from the balcony into the stalls. When they went to investigate, the men could find nothing to account for the sound. At this Mr Tanner gave up and went home, but Rodgers went along to the police station to report the strange happenings, with the result that at two o'clock in the morning, eight policemen searched the theatre from top to bottom but failed to find anything unusual.

By now the haunting had come to the attention of the local Margate newspapers. An interested reader of the *Thanet Gazette*, James Chell, a teacher who for some years had studied psychical research, read the report of the most recent hauntings and obtained permission to hold a night vigil within the theatre. He duly arrived at the Royal with his dog to be told that another man also wished to carry out an investigation the same night. The two men agreed to join forces. Chell and Thomas Redshaw, who had not met before, began preparing for their vigil. As soon as the theatre had closed for the night both men searched the building thoroughly to make sure that they were alone. Then, after ensuring that all the external doors were secure and not capable of being opened from the outside, they turned off the electric lights at the main switchboard situated on a high platform behind the stage backcloth. The theatre was left in darkness, save for two small gas lamps, one each side of the auditorium. At half past midnight, the two men settled down to see what the night would bring.

After half an hour of waiting, the theatre suddenly seemed to become very cold: both men became aware of noises and scratching sounds behind the stage backcloth, and also the sound of furniture being moved. Mr Chell's dog, which had been previously silent, now sat up and began to howl, her hackles raised. Chell and Redshaw investigated the noises but could find nothing to account for them. The stage was empty of any furniture or props. Almost as mysteriously as they had begun, the sounds ceased and the temperature in the theatre returned to normal, yet an hour later the same intense cold returned, and suddenly there was a loud explosion and all the lights in the auditorium came on. The two men went immediately to the platform behind the backcloth, climbed the ladder and saw that the heavy, ironclad light switches, which they had earlier switched off, were now back into the 'on' position, a physical impossibility as all three switches could not have been worked simultaneously by one person.

The two men once again searched the building. As they did so, both noticed the smell of dead leaves at the side of the stage where once three boxes had looked down on to the performers. After a few minutes, the smell changed to one of roses, accompanied by another sudden drop in temperature. Both Chell and Redshaw found this particularly unpleasant, but as before, the coldness passed and the atmosphere returned to normal. All was quiet for the next forty-five minutes, when, without warning, the entire auditorium lighting went out. When the men climbed the platform and inspected the switches by torchlight, they found that the three heavy metal levers had been returned to the 'off' position. Once again it would have been impossible for any lone person to do this.

James Chell returned to his seat in the auditorium and began to write up his notes. As he sat there he became suddenly aware of the ticking of what sounded like a substantially large clock, which lasted for exactly four minutes. There was no such timepiece in the theatre and it was later revealed that none had existed in the building within living memory. Once again there was a period of calm during which both men sat in the auditorium listening to the dark, silent theatre. At around 3.15 a.m. they became aware of a large patch on one wall which now replaced the box from which years before the demented actor had committed suicide. The patch, dirty brown in colour, moved slightly and then disappeared. Some moments later it reappeared, remaining for about thirty seconds before, once again, vanishing. Soon after, the whole theatre seemed to come alive with sinister noises – rustlings and scratching sounds – that filled the entire auditorium but were impossible to locate with accuracy and gradually died away. Just before 4 a.m., the two men thought they could feel a presence in the vicinity of the upstairs gallery and both realised that the theatre had again become intensely cold. Shining a torch up into the gallery revealed the strange brown shape they had seen previously. As they watched, it seemed to glide from one pillar to the next and then return to its original place, whereupon it vanished. The investigators quickly made their way over to the spot but could see nothing, although both were aware of a feeling of malevolence, as if something evil was with them in this part of the building.

By this time Chell and Redshaw had had enough and decided to bring their vigil to a close. They locked up and walked away from the theatre up to the main road. After a few minutes they were caught up by a policeman on a motorcycle who asked them their business. They explained their night-time visit to the Royal and that they had only left the building fifteen minutes before. The constable informed them that a quarter of an hour before, the police station in Margate had received a report of a loud explosion coming from within the theatre. The two men had heard nothing so the disturbance must have taken place after they had left the building. The strange sound seemed similar to the noises that had accompanied the switching off of the lights inside the auditorium, but on a much larger scale. The incident remains unexplained.

In September 1972, ghost hunter Andrew Green (who we will encounter in greater detail in a later part of this book), visited the Theatre Royal and spoke with manager Harry Jacobs. Although Jacobs claimed he had not experienced anything unusual himself, he felt unable to dismiss a number of experiences that had been reported by various staff members, and confirmed that a fortnight before a similar incident to that involving Alfred Tanner, also concerning a decorator working in the theatre, had taken place. On this occasion, the painter had fled from the building 'shaking with fear', upsetting a tin of paint over himself in his desperation to get away. Thirty years later, the theatre was still being visited by paranormal researchers: a team from the *Ghost Detectives* television series spent a night in the building during which séances were held on the empty stage. Today, strange incidents are still reported occasionally from the Royal, and if the ghost of Sarah Thorne still treads the boards in her beloved theatre it would appear she is scarcely alone.

Consult: Andrew Green, *Our Haunted Kingdom* (Wolfe Publishing, London, 1973).

Legacy of Doom: The Strange Case of Langenhoe (1937-62)

An important candidate for one of Britain's most haunted buildings, the story of the now demolished Essex church of St Mary's in the remote village of Langenhoe contains many and varied accounts of strange and inexplicable happenings. It remains one of the great hauntings of the twentieth century.

Essex is said to be one of England's most haunted shires, home to a host of ghostly tales as well as stories of witchcraft and Black Magic; the birthplace of the notorious seventeenth-century Witchfinder General, Matthew Hopkins, it is often referred to as the 'Witch County'. Its haunted capital, as we have seen, is undeniably the tiny village of Borley, but twenty miles south, near the town of Colchester, lies another haunted site which many believe equals, and even surpasses, the incidents which are alleged to have occurred at Henry Bull's famous rectory. Curiously, both locations are connected, not only historically but also in the nature of the paranormal phenomena reported, and although this haunting did not achieve the fame or notoriety of the 'most haunted house in England', it is a tale of ghosts, poltergeists, phantom women, and an evil which has plagued this Essex village perhaps for centuries. For this is a forgotten ghost story – the strange case of Langenhoe.

Langenhoe (Anglo-Saxon for 'long hill') is situated on rising ground above bleak marshland near Mersey Island. The village centre lies along the B1025, and today a turning off the main road down a long lane brings the curious traveller to the remains of a desolate graveyard hidden by tall trees. A few solitary headstones lean in the tall grass, and despite the proximity of several modern farm buildings, there is a loneliness to this remote spot. This is the site of Langenhoe church, built in the fourteenth century, damaged by an earthquake in 1884, demolished in 1962, and believed by many to have once been the most haunted church in England.

Early in 1937, the Revd Ernest Merryweather was inducted as rector. Born in the North of England, he had never before encountered the paranormal nor had any interest in the subject. Yet soon after his arrival he began to experience strange incidents at

Langenhoe, Essex: The haunted church on the marshes. *(Peter Underwood Collection)*

his new church, occurrences that were to gain in frequency and intensity over the next twenty-year period. Initially these were seemingly insignificant episodes, such as the rector's valise (a small case for carrying his vestments and books) unaccountably locking itself when left in the vestry. Within the environs of the church and the churchyard, every effort to open the valise met with defeat, yet Merryweather found the case would open normally when he was in the lane away from the building. On 20 September 1937, a still autumn day with not a breath of wind, the rector was alone in the church. Without warning the west door, which was standing open, slammed shut with an incredible crash that seemed to shake the entire building. These early odd incidents were recorded by the Revd Merryweather in his diary, a practise he would continue up until his departure in 1959. Many of the entries describe typical poltergeist activity, such as the movement of objects within the church and the sound of thudding noises which were heard coming from the vestry, as if clods of earth were being thrown at the door. The rector was not the only experient, as inexplicable incidents were witnessed on several occasions by members of the Langenhoe congregation.

The phenomenon of ghostly music has been reported on many occasions in numerous locations over the years by psychical researchers (see Melvyn Willin's *Music, Witchcraft and the Paranormal*, Melrose Books, 2005) and Langenhoe is a case in point. On 28 September 1950, while in the vestry, the rector heard the voice of a young woman singing. The sound, which resembled plainsong, seemed to emanate from the west end of the building. When the sound died away, Merryweather heard what he took to be heavy footsteps walking slowly up the aisle of the church. The rector quietly went through the vestry door, whereupon the footsteps ceased abruptly and he found the nave empty. The same ghostly singing was heard again a week later when the rector arrived at the church to find two workmen crouched by the west door, attempting to look in through the keyhole. The men beckoned to him to come forward and as Merryweather approached, the sound of singing could clearly be heard coming from the empty church. All three men then explored the building, even climbing the spiral staircase to the tower, but could find nothing; the church was deserted.

Another aural feature of the Langenhoe haunting involved sinister whisperings and voices inside the church. Following an outbreak of hooliganism in the local area, where people had been assaulted by a number of youths, Ernest Merryweather took, rather dramatically, to carrying a dagger for his own protection. While alone at the church one day, he had placed the dagger firmly in a belt around his waist under his cassock. As he stood in front of the altar for a moment, he felt the knife being pulled from his belt and, as it clattered to the floor, he heard a female voice say, very clearly, 'You are a cruel man'. On another occasion, the rector arrived at the church and as he walked into the vestry, heard voices coming from the direction of the chancel. Two or three people seemed to be having a whispered conversation, with a male voice dominating, although no actual words could be distinguished. The talking ceased after a few minutes, to be followed by a deep, sorrowful sigh. The rector immediately went into the church but, as with the incident experienced previously with the two workmen, the building was empty. The Revd Merryweather's diary contains other similar entries, of hearing other sounds and voices in the church as well as unexplained footsteps in the churchyard outside.

As with the haunting of Borley Rectory, apparitions and phantom figures also feature in the Langenhoe story. On Christmas Eve, 1950, as Ernest Merryweather was walking up the nave towards the chancel, a curious vague form seemed to suddenly appear from nowhere, glide across the nave in front of him, and disappear into the pulpit. Merryweather described the figure as possibly that of a man dressed in a tweed suit. On separate occasions during Sunday services, as the rector stood by the altar officiating, he saw the figure of a woman in what appeared to be late medieval or Tudor dress cross the west end of the church and vanish into the stone wall. On another occasion, whilst practising at the organ in the empty church, the rector felt as though he was

The Revd Ernest Merryweather, who chronicled the Langenhoe ghosts for twenty years. *(Peter Underwood Collection)*

being watched from behind. Turning from his seat, he saw a woman wearing a modern cream dress looking intently at him; the experience was fleeting and almost instantly Merryweather realised that the person had gone.

Perhaps the most extraordinary incident of the entire Langenhoe haunting occurred not in the church, but in the nearby Langenhoe Hall. One day in the autumn of 1947, the Revd Merryweather was being shown around the house by its then owner, Mrs Cummings. On reaching a particular room, the rector commented on the pleasant view it commanded over the surrounding marshland. His host, however, did not care for the room, saying that she felt there was an unusual atmosphere which at times she found unpleasant. After Mrs Cummings had left the room, Merryweather lingered for one last look from the window before turning to follow her. As he did so, he had the impression of walking straight into the *unmistakable and frantic embrace of a naked invisible woman*. The rector reported that the phenomena lasted only seconds but was emphatic that it was not his imagination.

Such was the rector's concern for what was taking place at Langenhoe, he ultimately sought the advice of his superior, the Bishop of Colchester. Rather than being dismissive, the Bishop lent a sympathetic ear to the rector's plight as he himself had experienced apparent poltergeist phenomena several years previously during the Foyster incumbency of Borley Rectory. Whilst visiting the house during the height of the disturbances, a stone had been thrown at him which narrowly missed his head before smashing into a fireplace.

Although Merryweather had not up to that time undertaken any research into the history of Langenhoe, he was later to learn that villagers had for many years considered the immediate area around the church as being haunted. Local legends tell of a 'Lady in Black' who walks around the churchyard at night, and there is an account of two sisters who, in 1908, reported seeing the figure of a woman dressed in old-fashioned nun-like clothing which moved slowly along the pathway between the gravestones before disappearing into the north wall of the church. Merryweather was also to discover that Langenhoe and Borley were historically connected. In 1583, Nicholas Waldegrave, Lord of the Manor of Borley and son of Sir Edward Waldegrave, acquired the manor of Langenhoe on his marriage to Catherine Brown, who, with her sister Jane, had inherited the Langenhoe estate in the same year. The Waldegraves, as patrons of the living, would have been responsible for the appointment of the rectors of Langenhoe as well as those of Borley. During the seventeenth century, their chosen clergymen officiated at both churches, an arrangement which seems to have continued into the early 1700s, with the livings of Borley and Langenhoe being combined in 1661, 1680 and again in 1758.

Not only are there historical connections between the two villages, but also a curious mirror-like symmetry of supernatural happenings: at Langenhoe, the majority of paranormal activity took place in the old church, while the rectory (apart from

Merryweather's astonishing ghostly embrace) played little part in the haunting; at Borley, although the church has its own haunted history, much of which dates from the end of the Second World War, the rectory was the main focus during the 'most haunted house' heyday of the Bull family and later the Smiths and the Foysters.

Beginning in the late 1940s, veteran British ghost hunter Peter Underwood took an interest in the case, and the first account of the story appeared in his 1974 book, *A Host of Hauntings*. In September 1949, together with the Revd John Dening, he carried out an all-night vigil in Langenhoe church, during which a violent thunderstorm obliterated any aural phenomena that might have occurred inside the much haunted building. A further investigation, held the following year, again yielded negative results. In 1958, several séances were held at Langenhoe church in an attempt to establish a cause for the haunting. The communicating 'entities' allegedly contacted included the tyrannical Sir Robert Attford, the Lord of the Manor during the reign of King James I, who had supposedly murdered his serving girl lover, Mary Felicity, in the church in the early 1600s. A similar tale tells of a past rector who had also done away with his illicit sweetheart within the precinct of St Mary's, and there are other allegations of murderous violence: one of the Lords of the Manor in the fourteenth century was Lionel de Bradenham, a lawless man who was in the pay of the Borley Waldegraves, and who allegedly committed several murders. Underwood, however, was disinclined to accept the séance evidence as providing a truthful explanation of the haunting, and from scant records of the life of de Bradenham, there is certainly no historical evidence that anyone was actually murdered inside Langenhoe church. Also, it should be noted that in many hauntings, local legends and traditions are often moulded to fit and substantiate particular aspects of the reported phenomena.

Is there possibly a more sinister reason for the strange phenomena which has been experienced at Langenhoe over the years? Tragedy and death seem to haunt this lonely village as much as the restless spirits who once walked the environs of its lost church; and is there an ancient curse or hex, the origins of which are now lost in the mists of time, that gives evil a free reign? Four-hundred-year-old Langenhoe Hall in particular has seen its fair share of disaster: three people have committed suicide within its walls, one of whom is believed to have been a member of the Waldegrave family. In the nineteenth century, nine children of the then owner of the Hall all died in infancy, their mother passing away shortly after the last child. Albert Lowenstein, the Belgium financier who owned the estate during the First World War, committed suicide by jumping out of a plane over the English Channel. The estate was then bought by a man who failed to make a success of his investment and drowned himself in a sluice pipe by Adder Marsh. Soon after the First World War, a driven herd of horses awaiting transportation to the Continent were panicked when a terrific snowstorm struck Langenhoe. The resulting chaos caused the deaths of many of the drovers. Since then, many suicides have been reported at the spot where the herdsmen died. Langenhoe Rectory has also had its share of misfortune.

Over the years it has witnessed a number of serious and strange accidents, and also the suicide of a previous owner. Further tragic episodes continued into the 1940s when a young man accidentally shot and killed his fiancée in a cottage in the village; and two years before the church was demolished, seventy-two-year-old Edward May died while cutting down undergrowth in the churchyard.

Clearly a legacy of doom has hung over this lonely village for many years, yet whether this series of unfortunate events has any bearing on the reasons for the haunting we can only speculate. Whatever the origins of the strange phenomena at Langenhoe, there are many people, including the present authors, who accept that a number of the paranormal incidents reported there were indeed genuine. It is possible to attribute at least some of the auditory phenomena – knocks, bangs, creaks and taps – in the church to the fragile condition of the building's fabric. Following the Essex earthquake of 1884, the church was never structurally sound and even after restoration the walls and floors remained out of true alignment. However, not all of the reported activity can be explained in this way and the incidents of footsteps, voices, spectral singing, as well as the sighting of apparitions, must be given special consideration.

Although many people experienced the curious happenings at Langenhoe, the principle witness to the phenomena was the Revd Merryweather. His diary entries chronicling the events span a period of twenty-two years, and record almost every aspect of reported paranormal episodes. It is his testimony, in much the same way as with Rosina Despard at Cheltenham, which carries much of the argument for supernormal phenomena in this remote and lonely spot. Peter Underwood described him as a shrewd man who would not be easily fooled or carried away by his imagination, and was as puzzled, critical and sceptical of the events he experienced during his incumbency as anyone else; in short, a good witness. Although, as has been said above, the rector claimed not to have experienced similar happenings prior to his arrival in Essex, it seems most probable that he was unknowingly psychic, perhaps confusing or masking this fact as part of his innate spiritual nature and vocation within the Church of England, and that his arrival at Langenhoe acted as a catalyst for phenomena to occur. If there is any truth to the 'stone tape' theory, that physical surroundings can absorb an impression of violent and tragic events and later, under a combination of circumstances or conditions and with the right person present, can play back these 'recordings' in the form of paranormal noises and apparitions, one would certainly expect it to apply to Langenhoe. Perhaps the church itself, which had stood through all of the troubled times of the surrounding area, acted as a focal point, absorbing and later allowing impressions of these happenings to return again in some unknown way.

In 1959, Ernest Merryweather retired from the ministry when Langenhoe was combined with the neighbouring parish of Abberton. St Mary's became redundant and, after the furnishings and fittings were removed, the doors were locked and the church was abandoned to rats, mice, and perhaps its host of lost and indigenous phantoms.

In 1962 it was demolished, its disused graveyard, now consumed by weeds and net-tles, being the only reminder of former times. The Revd Merryweather died in 1965, by which time the strange events which had taken place at this lonely village on the marshes over the previous two decades had all but faded from living memory.

During research for this book Eddie Brazil, accompanied by his wife, paid a visit to Langenhoe and was fortunate to meet Steven Wormell, the current owner of Langenhoe Hall. Mr Wormell has lived in the Hall all his life and in particular as a child can remember the demolition of St Mary's in the early 1960s. Although he had not experienced anything out of the ordinary, he confirmed that the upstairs room in the Hall in which the Revd Merryweather had his strange encounter with the naked apparition, even though it faces south, is always cold, and like a previous owner of the Hall, Mrs Cummings, he did not care for the room or its atmosphere. During a tour of the grounds, Mr Wormell pointed out the room and said he would have liked to show the visitors inside but his son was at that moment in bed asleep. Looking up at the drawn curtains, Mr and Mrs Brazil both reflected that within that room seemingly occurred one of the most bizarre incidents in the entire history of paranormal phenomena.

A short time later, Brazil and his wife made their way over to the now abandoned and empty churchyard. Among the leaning and eroded gravestones, both were con-scious of experiencing a strange physical sensation, as if some force was sapping their energy. Mrs Brazil felt this unpleasant sensation more than her husband and, quickly becoming nauseous, had to return to the car. Before joining her, Brazil took a series of photographs, acutely aware that he was standing on the site of one of the allegedly

Scattered gravestones – all that remain to mark the presence of one of England's most haunted churches. *(Eddie Brazil)*

most haunted buildings in the country, the exact location where inexplicable footfalls, apparitions and unknowable singing had been experienced, and where, in June 1951, while working alone in this very churchyard, the Revd Merryweather had the feeling of being watched by a legion of unseen figures. As the researcher and his wife drove away down the main road it began to rain and the strange story of Langenhoe seemed suddenly far away, although both sensed that within its abandoned graveyard, something else and far more unsettling still remains.

Consult: Paul Adams, Eddie Brazil & Peter Underwood, *Shadows in the Nave: A Guide to the Haunted Churches of England* (The History Press, Stroud, 2011); John C. Dening, *The Restless Spirits of Langenhoe* (John C. Dening, Brandon, 2000); Peter Underwood, *A Host of Hauntings* (Leslie Frewin, London, 1973).

The Northfleet Horror (1962)

This little-known haunting of a 1930s council house involved three separate families for a brief period during the early 1960s. The case contains some of the most chilling apparitional phenomena included in the present survey.

An inexplicable and terrifying case of haunting took place in 1962 in the town of Northfleet, which lies near Gravesend, twenty miles south-east of London. Twenty-eight-year-old Sidney Maxted and his wife, together with their children, Kevin, aged six, Linda, aged four and baby Clair, moved into No.16 Waterdales, a small semi-detached house a short walk from Northfleet Cemetery. Waterdales, then as now, is an extremely long thoroughfare with most of the housing dating from the 1930s. Prior to the family taking up residence, the house had no history of paranormal activity, and during the previous years many tenants had lived there in relative peace.

After a short time in the house, Mrs Maxted gradually became concerned about the noises she often heard during the daytime coming from the first-floor front bedroom, which was situated over the family living room. These sounds seemed very like footsteps, as though an unseen person was pacing to and fro across the floor. Sidney Maxted also heard the footsteps and like his wife found them difficult to explain. However, the noises in the bedroom became a real source of unease to Mrs Maxted, and in an attempt to set her mind at rest, her husband offered the explanation that the footfalls must be those of their next-door neighbour in the adjacent house, No.14, that they were able to hear through the party wall of the building, the acoustic effect being increased by the fact that one of the bedrooms of the adjoining house was sited over the entrance hall to the Maxted home. It was a simple fault of bad design and 'jerry building', and although Mrs Maxted's fears were temporarily calmed, her anxiety remained nonetheless.

The house in Waterdales, Northfleet, where three successive families encountered frightening paranormal activity in the early 1960s. *(Eddie Brazil)*

Sometime later, events took on a particularly sinister nature. The Maxted children began complaining of scratching noises which came persistently from underneath their beds, and of their bedcovers being yanked away onto the floor; the children themselves claimed they were being mysteriously pulled or struck at by invisible hands. As the disturbing phenomena increased, the children became more distressed and began sleeping in their parents' bedroom, unwilling to stay in their own room during the night.

In February 1965, matters came to a head. One night around 2 a.m., Mrs Maxted got up to attend to baby Clair. As she made to get back into bed after changing and settling the infant, she looked across to the doorway and was surprised to see the figure of a young child coming into the bedroom from across the landing. Thinking it was her four-year-old daughter, she responded automatically and called out, 'Linda'. The figure immediately moved across the room and advanced towards her. As it approached it suddenly began to grow in height, until it had become a tall figure which bent menacingly over the bed. Mrs Maxted's terrified screams awoke her husband, at which point the apparition thankfully vanished. This harrowing experience proved too much for the family and the next day they gave notice and left the house.

The need and desire for affordable council housing was no less important in the mid-1960s than it is today and, soon after the Maxteds vacated No.16 Waterdales, Northfleet Council allocated the property to twenty-five-year-old Eric Essex, who moved in with his wife Margaret and their infant baby. Mr Essex had been made aware of the strange occurrences which had taken place within the house. However, his need to provide a comfortable and secure home for his family was paramount, despite the rumours of ghostly happenings. However, it wasn't long before strange things began to take place. One afternoon, Mrs Essex was sitting with her mother in the living room when they both heard footsteps together with what sounded like furniture being moved, coming from the bedroom above. They called to Eric, who at the time was in the garden, and all three rushed upstairs but found no sign of an intruder. All agreed that it would have been impossible for anyone making the noises to have escaped from the house undetected. As well as footsteps, the following months saw the family plagued with strange smells which came and went mysteriously throughout the entire house. They resembled musty or mouldy stenches rather than the smell of chemicals or odours that might conceivably have been caused by household cleaning products. There was also occasionally a low-pitched hum, again throughout the house, which had the effect of causing a ringing sensation in the ears. Mr and Mrs Essex tolerated these oddities until one night in August 1966, which saw events reach a climax curiously similar to the finale of the Maxted tenancy.

About 2 a.m., Eric Essex was awakened by the sound of footsteps moving about in the hallway and on the staircase. Getting out of bed he inspected the landing and the rooms below but found them empty. On returning to bed he quickly became aware of a whistling sound in his ears. It was then that he realised that the bed was vibrating or shaking, and that one end was being lifted up. Wondering what was happening he sat up and looked to his side. To his horror there stood a figure: the form of a woman whose long dress trailed down to the floor. The apparition was glowing with a pinkish-orange luminance, but what made Eric Essex recoil with terror was that from the shoulders upwards it was *completely headless*. As with the Maxteds, the Essex family hurriedly vacated the house the next morning vowing never to return. Eric Essex was later to say that the encounter was absolutely terrifying, and one that he never again wanted to experience.

The house now remained empty until another tenant could be allocated the property. However, despite its vacant state, strange sounds were still heard coming from within. Mrs Margaret Harrison, who had been resident at No.14 Waterdales for about three months, regularly heard the sound of heavy footsteps ascending the stairs at all hours of the day and night. One night when she was alone in the house whilst her husband was away on business, Mrs Harrison had the unnerving experience of hearing a heavy, booming sound, as if some massive object was thudding or bouncing down the stairs. It seemed whatever was making the noise reached the bottom of the landing and then bounced violently up to the hall ceiling which was directly above Mrs Harrison's bedroom. There was a powerful thud under her bed, which then transformed itself into a scraping or scratching sound. The noise seemed to be emanating from across the whole floor and grew in volume, as if something below was trying to claw its way up into the bedroom (see also the experiences of Gail Brown and Shirley Bruce, pp. 80-82). The experience proved too frightening for Mrs Harrison, and like the previous neighbours, she and her husband quit the house.

The haunting of No.16 Waterdales is a puzzling case. As mentioned previously, the property prior to the Maxted family taking up residence had no history of paranormal activity. Yet for four years, three families experienced disturbing phenomena which ultimately forced them to leave their respective homes. The case conforms in many respects to a typical poltergeist haunting in as much that a house is undisturbed until a person, usually a repressed adolescent, becomes the focus or living agent for paranormal incidents after moving in. After a period of time the phenomena ceases and the house once again becomes normal, as is clearly demonstrated in several of the cases included in the later part of this book. There is a possibility that poltergeist agents were present in both the Maxted and Essex families. Coincidence might stretch also to Mrs Harrison, who was physically so near to No.16 that she too became a focus of poltergeist activity. An alternative explanation is that for a four-year period the house on Waterdales was haunted by an evil spirit or 'entity' intent on frightening and harming all those families who had the misfortune to be present at the time.

Consult: George Owen & Victor Sims, *Science and the Spook: Eight Strange Cases of Haunting* (Dennis Dobson, London, 1971).

A Memory of the Future (1960s)

An unusual case of the crisis apparition of a living person appearing nine years before the actual events portrayed in the supernatural vision took place.

In 1936, shortly before his death, the eminent English writer and scholar, Montague Rhodes (M.R.) James, who 'had written better ghost stories than any man living', was asked by his friend, the Irish diplomat Sir Shane Leslie, what were his thoughts on the reality of the paranormal. James replied: 'Think on it, some of these things are so, but we do not know the rules.' James was right – the first reported instance of poltergeist phenomena occurred in what is now modern Germany, 800 years before the birth of Christ, and in AD 100, the Roman scholar, Pliny the Younger, set down what is regarded as the first account of an organised ghost hunt, which took place in a haunted house in Athens. Yet 2,000 years on, modern psychical researchers have failed to fully understand why and how paranormal incidents occur. If we are to comprehend what M.R. James calls 'the rules', it would seem that we must look beyond the traditional realm of the supernatural with its panoply of ghosts, hauntings and supposedly earthbound spirits, and ask if the paranormal has just as much to do with the living as it does with the dead? Can a ghost or a supernormal incident be an example of a vision of a future event, or indeed the apparition of a living person? The following account demonstrates this particular phenomenon. It is disturbing in its content as it features the malevolent manifestation of a family matriarch, a figure more normally associated with love and compassion, and not with evil menace.

Within the archives of the Society for Psychical Research there exist countless accounts of what are known as 'phantasms of the living'. Sometimes referred to as 'crisis ghosts', they are encounters with apparitions which occur seemingly at the moment of death or during a period of great upheaval or emotional struggle in the life of a person who forms the subject of the ghostly experience. An example that involves the apparition of a healthy living person rather than someone on the brink of death is given by writer Colin Wilson in his book, *Beyond the Occult* (1988). Wilson's secretary at the time was required to attend a meeting at an office in the Cornish town of St Austell. A delayed start had put her behind schedule and when she encountered heavy morning traffic she realised she would be late. As the traffic jam moved slowly along she became more and more frustrated. As the time ticked away she became increasingly stressed, and knowing she wouldn't be able to make the meeting on time thought about turning around and heading back home. She eventually arrived at her destination, flustered and tense, some forty minutes later. As she entered the building she met two colleagues who asked where she had gone to. The secretary misunderstood the question and replied that she had been stuck in traffic. 'No,' one of the men explained, 'Fifteen minutes ago we saw you enter the building and then turn around and hurry back outside again.' She informed them that this was impossible as at the time she had still been in her car some distance from the building, yet the men were insistent that they had both seen her in the way they described. It seems that the young woman, anxious and worried about missing the meeting, had in some way managed to telepathically transmit an image of herself into the office, and her thoughts on abandoning her trip and returning home had manifested in the way she was observed entering the building and then hurrying back out. It would seem that this experience as described by Wilson is related, in a non-fatal way, to the psychic mechanics that create apparitions of the seriously ill or injured who are moments away or have passed the moment of death. But if sorrow, love, despair or frustration can generate such telepathic visions, can anger and hatred do likewise?

Beatrice Laity was born in 1927 in the town of Redruth in Cornwall. From the beginning, she and her two elder brothers had an unhappy childhood. Both parents seemed incapable of giving love or affection to their children and Beatrice lived her early years in sadness and bewilderment at her mother's vicious way of life both in thought and action. Her father, an ex-naval man, was of a hard, unforgiving nature, and if the chastisement he meted out to his children was responded to with tears and weakness, he punished them even more severely. Throughout these difficult years, Beatrice's only safe haven of compassion was that of her elder brother, Lionel, who likewise endured the path of family misery and tried as best he could to soften his sister's mental anguish. One gesture in particular became a symbol of the deep love and understanding between them. When Mr Laity bullied Beatrice to the point of tears, Lionel would sense when his sister was at breaking point and, manoeuvring so that his father could not see, he would gently touch her on the crown of her head and let his hand slide down to the nape of her neck. Instantly, Beatrice knew that she was not alone in taking her father's anger, but was in some way sharing it.

At the outbreak of the Second World War in 1939, the family moved to Plymouth and the two elder boys immediately joined the Royal Navy, leaving Beatrice alone to endure the coldness of her parents. She was just fourteen when the whole of her frail world collapsed: the brother she worshipped was killed when his ship was attacked by a lone

German bomber when anchored in Falmouth harbour. Beatrice was devastated and her parents' unwillingness to show any sympathy or understanding of the loss only added to her grief. Soon her heartache was driven to almost suicidal despair when her second brother was killed when his ship was again attacked by enemy planes. Unbelievably, again there was no compassion or emotional support from her parents following the tragedy, and Beatrice's grief and anguish built up dangerously in her isolation and loneliness. She rejected her deep belief in religion and it seemed the only road to peace was destruction by her own hand. One night when she felt it was time to leave the misery of the world behind, she suddenly felt the pressure of a light hand smoothing her head from crown to nape, and she knew that from somewhere her brother Lionel had come to comfort her. This time it wasn't her tears he was stopping, but her death. From that fleeting, soft touch, her hatred and despair vanished as she could now face her sadness and sorrow knowing in time a light would once again shine in her life.

That light came five years after the war ended when, in 1949, she married, at last finding peace and happiness in her husband and children of her own. Her unhappy past was something to be forgotten for now the future seemed full of promise and family joy. However, in 1961, Beatrice was to have an experience that would bring the nightmares of the past back in to her secure and settled world. One night she was suddenly awoken, her senses instantly clear and aware of something ominous within the room. There, standing at the foot of the bed, was the figure of an elderly woman with distinctive bushy hair but with her face veiled in shadow. The form remained silent, yet Beatrice knew that the woman was filled with an unbelievable hatred towards her, a detestation which increased as the figure began to move menacingly towards the head of the bed. Beatrice called out but the figure continued to move silently and threateningly forward. Desperately invoking her deep religious beliefs to dispel the apparition she began to pray. Whether it was this, or whether it was the physical act of her clinging to her sleeping husband for salvation that worked is unclear, but at that moment the form of the woman slowly began to fade and then was gone.

In 1969, Mr Laity died, and although family relations had in no way improved over the years, out of duty rather than love Beatrice decided to provide a home for her lonely and now elderly mother. However, time had not mellowed the old woman and her daughter's secure family existence, together with her three children, seemed to only add fresh fuel to her former animosity and bitterness. One night in 1970, Beatrice awoke to hear a faint shuffling sound outside her bedroom and a moment later, the dark shape of a figure moved past the frosted glass of the bedroom door. She at once got out of bed, opened the door and looked out into the darkened corridor. The landing was silent and empty, yet a growing sense of unease began to descend over her, and in the back of her mind, the memory of that fearful apparition from nine years before started to take shape. At the end of the corridor her daughter's bedroom door stood open and Beatrice hurried apprehensively towards it, fearing that something was wrong. In the faint glow coming through the landing window, she saw with horror the same grey shape standing silent and menacing at the foot of the bed. The outline, the bushy hair, the slight stooping posture of advanced years, was identical with the ghostly figure she had seen nearly a decade before. Beatrice walked forward into the room and instinctively stretched out a hand to ward it off and was horrified to make contact with the cold, bony flesh of a solid human body. In panic she switched on the dim bedroom light and was astonished to see her mother standing over the sleeping child's bed. The old woman gazed down on her granddaughter, her eyes blazing with hatred, and then turned towards her own daughter with an expression of evil malice. Mrs Laity stared at her for what seemed an eternity before she silently shuffled back to her own room. Beatrice was so distressed and physically afraid of what might happen that the next morning she went to see her doctor. On his advice her mother was sent to stay with a relative some distance away, where she died six months later.

The case is a strange one. Is it possible that on the night in 1961, Beatrice witnessed an apparition of her demented mother's malice at a future date, an event that had not even happened, and in so doing saved her daughter from harm and herself from plunging back into a nightmare of heartache and tragedy which she had taken years to escape from. We will never know…

Consult: Colin Wilson, *Beyond the Occult: Twenty Years' Research into the Paranormal* (Bantam, London, 1988).

The Child on the Stairs (1966)

This account of the haunting of an eighteenth-century South London house involves a disturbing mixture of both physical and mental phenomena. The origins of the disturbances remain unexplained.

In 1966, forty-two-year-old Mrs Joan Benson was living with her children in an eighteenth-century house in the Stockwell district of South London. She had recently separated from her husband and now had the stressful task of maintaining a home for her family of four girls and two boys, all under the age of seventeen. Built in 1723, the Benson house was a rabbit warren of rooms spread over five floors. It had remarkably survived inner-city development and now provided a suitable residence for the large family. Mrs Benson's nights were spent mainly alone in front of the television while her children were elsewhere in the house or out socialising with friends.

As is the norm (if there is such a thing as normality in a haunting of this nature) the phenomena commenced unremarkably with the odd unexplainable noise or movement of objects in an upstairs room, most of which were quickly forgotten. However, there were also the sound of footsteps ascending the stairs and the sudden slamming of doors that Mrs Benson heard during the day whilst alone in the house, and which were not dismissed so lightly, and eventually things soon took a dramatic turn. One Saturday night as she watched television alone, she became aware that the living room had gradually become intensely cold. Without warning, Mrs Benson was astonished and shocked to view the figure of a young child dressed in a nightgown, which appeared to glide across the room and vanish through an opposite wall. At first Mrs Benson was unsure if she hadn't seen a real child enter and leave the room, such was her amazement. Shaking her head, and not a little unnerved, she went into the kitchen, lit a cigarette and wondered if the stress of the estrangement from her husband was beginning to tell. Eventually, convincing herself that the vision of the child had been an hallucination brought on by tiredness and worry, she made a concerted effort to put the eerie vision out of her mind.

However, during the following weeks, instances of inexplicable phenomena gradually increased and the sound of footsteps in the rooms and on the staircase became more frequent. Mrs Benson also began to hear soft whisperings and indecipherable mutterings throughout the house, in a similar way that, back in the 1920s, the Revd Guy Smith and his wife claimed to have heard strange 'sibilant' whisperings in the rooms and corridors of lonely Borley Rectory. The London housewife described the sounds as particularly disturbing, almost as if two people were engaged in a secret and malicious conversation with herself as the unsuspecting subject. Unsurprisingly, she became increasingly anxious as the catalogue of unusual incidents continued but at the same time refrained with some effort from sharing this distress with her children. Things took a more frightening turn when Mrs Benson was awoken on several nights by having her hair pulled, and on occasion her arms pinched, seemingly by an invisible assailant. Sitting up in bed she always found the darkened room empty. Curiously, as the phenomena continued, her children appeared to be completely unaffected. We may view this as odd as in most hauntings of this type, the focus is invariably a child or teenager, who either unconsciously causes the phenomena or is affected by it.

One day, as Mrs Benson stood at the top of a flight of stairs, she had the clear impression that hands were being laid on her shoulders, and that there was a force behind them, as if someone wanted to push her violently off the landing. Although the unseen person gave the impression of being the same height as her, the hands which touched her were soft and small like those of a child.

The penetration of paranormal 'entities' into the world of dreams and the unconscious minds of sleepers in haunted buildings is an intriguing and little-explored aspect of psychical study, but in almost cinematic style, the Stockwell haunting culminated in just such a way with a regular series of bizarre and disturbing nightmares. In one, Mrs Benson dreamt that she had suddenly come awake and, sitting up in bed, could hear soft whisperings on the landing outside the room. As she looked across to the bedroom door, it ever so gently swung open. Moments later a child's head peeped around into the room and looked at her with a most evil expression. Perhaps even

Stockwell, South London: The haunted house (between the two refuse bins in the foreground) where Mrs Joan Benson encountered the frightening child on the stairs. *(Frederick Brazil)*

more disturbing was when, soon after, Joan Benson dreamt she was standing on the top-floor landing of the house at night. As she stood in the darkness she could hear soft footsteps gradually ascending the stairs and out of the shadows appeared a young child dressed in a nightgown coming up the flights towards her. As the figure started on the final steps up to the topmost landing, Mrs Benson said that it began to change into the grown figure of a woman, but still retained its cherubic, smiling baby face...

Finally, Joan Benson sought the help of her local GP, who smiled, listened attentively and proscribed tranquilisers. However, salvation from the sinister child ghost came ultimately from unlikely quarters, namely the property maintenance department of Lambeth Council. The council's need to renovate and repair the eighteenth-century house required the Benson family to temporarily relocate to alternative accommodation while building work was carried out, with the offer that when completed they could either return to their former home or continue to reside in what was a recently built modern house; Mrs Benson, unsurprisingly, chose to stay in her new home and leave her strange experiences in the Stockwell mansion to the past.

As in both the Pontefract and Northfleet cases, no convincing explanation for the cause of the phenomena in the Benson house has been found. As her children were unaware of what was happening, and also because Mrs Benson suffered from nightmares and was under a great deal of emotional strain at the time, some observers have suggested that the haunting was entirely psychological and literally all in her mind. Prior to the family taking up residence, the house had no reported incidents of paranormal activity, as was the case when new tenants moved in after the Bensons had left. Nevertheless, Joan Benson, who died in 1999, maintained her belief that for most of the summer and autumn of 1966, she was the personal victim of an evil ghost child.

Disturbing and certainly fascinating as this account of malevolent paranormal phenomena is, we have to admit that we are still at a loss to understand why such things occur. The simplest answer would be to put the incidents down to the actions of 'evil spirits' who are intent on harming those they choose, seemingly at random. Yet, as we have already noted, such an idea is nonsense to established science and who can blame the scientists for adhering to their view? Science can only operate within the realms of concrete evidence, repeatable experiments and absolute truths. However, in saying that, perhaps we should remember the famous maxim of psychoanalyst Carl Jung, whose continuing interest in the paranormal eventually drove a wedge between himself and his mentor Sigmund Freud: 'I will not commit the fashionable stupidity of regarding everything I cannot explain as a fraud.' What we are left with in cases such as the Stockwell haunting are the testimonies of those who have experienced the phenomena. Either they are lying, were mistaken, or were hallucinating. Yet, if what they experienced is in fact a reality, then both psychical research and established science have still to come to terms with the existence of paranormal activity which is far sinister and darker than anything we might imagine could go 'bump in the night'.

[N.B. This account was given to one of the present authors – Eddie Brazil – by the experient.]

A Clawing Terror (1975)

The first of three unnerving hauntings in our survey collected during the 1970s by writer and researcher Peter Moss involves a brief but chilling encounter with a night-time apparition and frightening aural phenomena – the case remains obscure and unexplained.

In the autumn of 1974, Shirley Brown arrived in the Scottish city of Dundee to begin her training as a student nurse. Coming from the beautiful but remote island of Orkney, the lights and bustle of a mainland city was still an exciting prospect, and she looked forward to not only completing her studies, but also forging new friendships. In early 1975, she and a fellow student, Gail Bruce, moved into a small one-bedroom flat in an old tenement building in the city centre. The flat was cramped but liveable: as well as the single bedroom there was a small bathroom and a kitchenette accessed off a medium-sized living room. Both students got on well together, enjoyed their studies, and were free to run their own lives. Strangely, given what the two women would eventually be confronted with, their first ten months at the tenement flat progressed in a relatively normal and humdrum fashion, with nothing out of the ordinary or any signs of impending alarm. Yet, in January 1976 all of this quickly changed.

One morning Shirley, who was not on duty until the afternoon, did not wake until Gail was about to leave for her morning shift. Before Gail went off to work she found Shirley staring at her with a very strange expression. When she asked if there was anything wrong, Shirley turned over in bed and said nothing. Her friend said they needed to have a chat at lunchtime. Over their midday meal, Gail explained that the previous night she had been unable to get to sleep and had laid awake into the small hours. At about 3.30 a.m., the hall light came on. Immediately afterward, she heard the sound of someone moving about in the bathroom with slow padding steps. Not unnaturally she was terrified and assumed someone had got into the flat, yet this was not possible for she knew that the front door was locked. The footfalls soon stopped and the light went out, plunging the hall into darkness. Unbeknown to Gail, Shirley too was finding it hard to sleep and had lain in bed wondering what had caused the sounds, and why the hall light had been switched on and off. Puzzled by the noises, Gail had looked across the room and was astonished to see an elderly woman with short grey hair and dressed in a pale blue nightgown standing beside Shirley's bed. What mystified Gail even more was that Shirley and the old woman seemed to be deep in an intense and whispered conversation. Moreover, there seemed to be an overwhelming impression of evil in their strange and secretive mutterings. Momentarily she had closed her eyes, and then reopened them, to find the figure had gone. Curiously, next morning, Shirley seemed to have had no recollection at all of talking with the old lady. Nonetheless, the two women were very frightened by the incident and agreed that they would never spend time in the flat alone again.

One week later, Shirley was lying in bed just before midnight reading as she waited for Gail to finish in the bathroom, when she heard the soft footsteps of someone moving about in the tiny kitchen adjacent to the bedroom. With rising fear she knocked on the wall which divided the two rooms, hoping that it might be Gail preparing a late-night snack. However, instead of a gentle tapped reply from her flatmate, there came the terrifying sound of what she could only describe as 'giant talons' that clawed at the wall with super-human strength and violence. Shirley screamed out, and when Gail came rushing in from the bathroom, the terrible sounds suddenly ceased. The two young women were utterly panic stricken and sat on the edge of the bed holding onto each other in terror. Soon after, the ferocious sound of the talons tearing at the wall came again, this time with increased ferocity, as if whatever was in the kitchen was determined to claw its way through the brickwork and into the bedroom. Incredibly, for nearly fifteen minutes the frenzied tearing and scraping continued. Eventually the two nurses could take no more and, pulling on a few clothes, prepared to flee from the flat, but to their horror, they quickly realised that their keys were in the living room, which was now seemingly occupied by something terrible. Mustering as much courage as they could find, the two petrified women realised they would have to enter the living room and confront whatever lay within. Summoning up courage, they burst open the door and switched on the light. Instantaneously there was a blinding blue flash and the living room bulb fused. At the same time, the savage sound of the claws scraping at the wall abruptly ceased. Gail and Shirley rushed across the darkened room, grabbed the keys from the table and fled from the tenement.

The students quickly made their way through Dundee's deserted streets to the sanctuary of a friend's apartment. Had it not been for the genuine state of shock the girls were in, their story would almost certainly have been dismissed as nothing more than a bad Halloween joke. Over coffee Gail and Shirley related their harrowing experience. Neither of them dared spend another night in their own flat, though they did go back the following morning to collect their belongings. Everything was quiet with nothing out of place, and the wall of the living room-kitchen, in spite of the savage clawing they had heard, had not the slightest mark upon it.

Gail Bruce and Shirley Brown eventually found alternative accommodation in another part of the city. Although shaken by what they had experienced, both felt they should at least try to look into the history of the tenement to see if they could throw any light on the strange happenings. However, thinking it over, they declined, lest they uncover something more shocking, inviting the harrowing encounter to become a permanent nightmare.

The experience of the two student nurses is indeed curious. As mentioned above, for ten months the two women lived in peace in the tenement with no hint of anything remotely paranormal occurring. We must ask, what triggered the onset of the phenomena? Who was the old woman whom Gail had seen talking to Shirley on the night the disturbances started, and why did the haunting take the unnerving aural form that ultimately made them abandon their home? Could it be at one time the flat was occupied by an elderly woman who had passed away whilst in residence, and whose ghost now wanted the intruders out of what she still considered her property? Perhaps the sibilant whisperings with Shirley, and the savage clawing at the wall were her way of saying, 'Get out, this is my flat!' Of course, we will never know. The sceptic would argue that the girls imagined the whole event, but Peter Moss, who interviewed both women, was convinced that they were telling the truth. As far as we can ascertain, there have been no more disturbances at the tenement, and the two women never again experienced the terror of that night.

Consult: Peter Moss, *Ghosts Over Britain* (Sphere Books Ltd, London, 1979).

The Weeping Woman of Flitwick Manor (1994)

The haunting of Flitwick Manor dates from the mid-1990s and was seemingly precipitated by the discovery during building refurbishment of a hidden attic room. The unnerving figure of a grief-stricken woman in black was seen several times over a period of several weeks by both staff and visitors.

In 1976, English screenwriter Nigel Kneale, most often remembered today for his ground-breaking *Quatermass* science-fiction dramas of the 1950s, scripted six television plays which were made into a single series by ATV under the collective title *Beasts*. Broadcast in the autumn and early winter of the same year, each story presented an eerie and macabre interplay between humans and animals, arguably the most unsettling of which was the disturbing episode entitled 'Baby'. In an atmosphere of growing unease, a young country vet and his pregnant wife (played by Simon MacCorkindale and Jane Wymark) are haunted by the ghost of a witch's familiar, whose mummified body is accidentally discovered bricked-up in a wall by building contractors refurbishing a six-teenth-century cottage. The idea of ghosts and horrors being released in such a way is a popular fictional plot line, and one that Kneale himself had used before to great effect eighteen years before in his *Quatermass and the Pit*, where latent psychic forces are set free by London Underground workmen who come across a buried alien spaceship while car-rying out extension work to the eerily titled Hobbs Lane railway station.

Other writers have been drawn to a similar plot device over the years. The narrator of H.P. Lovecraft's 1922 short story *The Hound* comes to a grisly end after plundering a jade amulet from a wizard's grave, while several of English ghost story master Montague Rhodes (M.R.) James' seminal tales, such as *Oh, Whistle and I'll Come to You, My Lad* (1904) and *A Warning to the Curious* (1925) feature hidden and seemingly innocent items (in these instances a whistle and a buried crown) which, when disturbed, release vengeful spectres who exact their revenge on the unwary protagonists. How far-fetched and remote from reality the concept of supernatural or paranormal forces being connected with ordinary, inanimate objects really is should be judged against several of the cases included in the present survey. As we will see, the evidence for such haunted relics as the Hexham Heads, the Seton sacrum bone, and even the Wookey Hole arrowheads, is such that this type of phenomena cannot be dismissed completely out of hand.

The discovery of hidden rooms which both contain and release supernatural forces has also been exploited by novelists and screenwriters. For the highly regarded 1945 Ealing Studios film *Dead of Night*, a macabre collection of sinister vignettes that starred amongst others Michael Redgrave, Googie Withers and Mervyn Johns, writer John Baines explored the concept of a household object giving access to a supernatural room from another world in the memorable episode entitled 'The Mirror'. The look-ing glass of the title harbours an evil presence that gradually insinuates itself into the mind of a newlywed husband and, twenty years later, the same theme was combined with material by another ghost story aficionado, R. Chetwynd-Hayes, to form a similar episode in director Kevin Connor's *From Beyond the Grave* (1974), another portmanteau-style presentation, this time by Hammer Films' rival Amicus Productions. Here actor Jack Watson plays sinister aristocrat Sir Michael Sinclair, a Jacobean occultist who man-ages to survive death by living in a ghostly room out of time created through a mixture of human sacrifice and Black Magic, and made chillingly accessible to an unwary couple from the real world via 'The Door', one of several items with eerie powers sold during the course of the film by antique dealer Peter Cushing.

For the practical ghost hunter, the geography of British hauntings is littered with haunted rooms and chambers that have been chronicled over many years in the literature of psychical research. Many notable houses, castles and stately homes have their own individual 'haunted room' where incidents of paranormal activity appear to be concentrated. A few names from what would be an extremely long list include Glamis Castle (where a secret chamber is said to have once housed a disfigured monster), Borley Rectory (the notorious Blue Room), Willington Mill, Craigievar Castle, Chingle Hall and Sandford Orcas Manor House. The house at the centre of America's famous 'Amityville Horror', 112 Ocean Avenue on Long Island, New York, where dysfunctional twenty-three-year-old Ronald DeFeo Jnr shot his entire family of six people to death in November 1974, and where subsequently a wealth of paranormal phenomena including demonic possession, poltergeist activity and haunting was alleged to have taken place, was found to contain a secret basement room – the 'Red Room' – where strange presences were allegedly felt and which a family dog refused to enter. The Amityville case, famously presented to the public in a sensational book by author Jay Anson and a subsequently enduring film franchise, remains highly controversial and over the years researchers have cast much doubt on the claims, by construction surveyor George Lutz and his wife Kathy, for genuine paranormal activity in and around the property.

In England, one case of haunting in which paranormal activity, including the sighting of apparitions, took place following the discovery of a secret hidden room, and for which convincing evidence exists for genuine phenomena, is that of Flitwick Manor, at one time a private house now converted into a luxury hotel. Although an account of the haunting reads like something from the plot line for a film or novel, eyewitness testimony collected and presented as part of the well-respected *Strange But True?* television programme in the 1990s shows that where the world of psychical research is concerned, fact is stranger than fiction.

The village of Flitwick, located nine miles north-west of Luton in Bedfordshire, has a recorded history stretching back to Domesday times. The manor of Flitwick was originally held by the Earls of Albermale. Later, King Charles I sold it to the City of London and in the early 1630s it was conveyed by the City trustees to Edward Blofield, who set about building a new house for himself and his family. The original manor house was a two-storey building which has been drastically altered and extended through the years. In 1735, the house and estate was owned by the Dell family who carried out a programme of alteration work, and in 1783 the house passed into the ownership of the Brooks family through the marriage of George Brooks to Anne Fisher, who had inherited the house as part of the settlement of a previous marriage. George Brooks and later his son John Thomas Brooks, who was born at Flitwick in 1794, also extended the manor house and developed the grounds and gardens. John Brooks was a keen horticulturalist and an early member of the Royal Horticultural

Flitwick Manor, Bedfordshire, where building work in the mid-1990s seemed to release the unquiet spirit of a weeping woman in black. *(William King/Luton Paranormal Society)*

Society. He developed a botanical garden at Flitwick and today the herbarium created by his maiden daughter, Mary Ann Brooks, still survives. She died in 1848 at the young age of twenty-six after a long illness and was survived by her father for another ten years. The Brooks stayed at Flitwick Manor for an unbroken period of nearly 150 years until the early 1930s when it again passed into private ownership, and the eerie haunting which later plagued the building some fifty years later would appear to have its roots during the time that the manor and its estate were in their hands.

In 1990, the Grade II listed manor house was sold to a hotel chain and in the autumn of 1994, refurbishment work began to update the building for its new use. The house had last undergone building work in 1936 when noted local architect Sir Albert Richardson had designed and overseen some updating for the then new owners, the Lyall family, as well as in 1984 when the premises were converted into a restaurant; now extensive work involved remodelling and redecoration, including stripping and recovering the roof. Once scaffolding had been erected and sections of the original tiling were removed, builder Jim Sparkes made an unusual and intriguing discovery. Inside one of the attic areas was a concealed room accessed by a small doorway which had lain hidden behind brickwork for what seemed to have been many years, and it became clear on further investigation that at one time the mysterious chamber had been accessible from inside the manor house itself: Sparkes was able to trace the outline of a second blocked-up doorway that was concealed behind panelling in the upper part of the building. The discovery of this secret room, which by its location appeared to have at one time been part of the old servants' quarters from the Brooks era, coincided with the beginning of a period of strange and disturbing incidents at Flitwick Manor, as though something that had lain isolated and undisturbed there for many years had now been released…

During the time that the refurbishment was taking place, the hotel was still receiving guests and although the staff didn't know it at the time, only three days were in fact to elapse between the discovery of the secret room in the roof by Jim Sparkes and his fellow builders and the start of a wave of paranormal activity in the newly refurbished Flitwick Manor. John Hinds, a company purchasing director on a brief overnight stay following a business conference, was the first to encounter what appeared to be the newly revived ghost of Flitwick. Hinds retired to bed around one in the morning and lay relaxing in his bed with the lights off. After only a few minutes he was suddenly aware of a heavy thump on the counterpane, as though something had dropped onto the bottom half of the bed from above. Switching on the bedside lamp, Hinds looked about but could see nothing either on the bed covers or lying on the floor, while the bedroom appeared to be undisturbed as it had been a short time before.

Turning off the light he again tried to get to sleep but, after what seemed like only a few minutes, there came a disturbing shuffling sound as though someone or something was moving across the floor towards the bed. Struggling up, Hinds rapidly switched on the bedside lamp again and this time was horrified to see the clear outline of a female figure sitting only a few feet away from him at the bottom of the bed. Petrified, Hinds called out but the woman remained immobile and was seemingly unaware of his presence. Despite his fear, he saw that she was looking away across the room in the direction of the window, and as he watched the figure gradually faded away and was gone. Terrified that the woman might return, Hinds spent the rest of the night awake and with the room lights on, and the next morning checked out of Flitwick Manor vowing never to return. 'I consider myself to be a very sceptical person and I really can't believe that it was a ghost I saw,' Hinds later recalled, 'but I have no other explanation for it…'

John Hinds was not the only person to encounter the eerie phantom woman. The following night, the hotel receptionist Lydia Dawson finished a late shift and went upstairs to one of the guest rooms on the second floor that was used as sleep-over accommodation by staff staying on the premises. Completely unaware of what had taken place only twenty-four hours before, she found herself suddenly awake in what appeared to be the early hours of the morning: the time was in fact just after one o'clock and, standing close to the side of the bed looking down at her, was an old woman with white hair, dressed in what appeared to be dark-coloured and distinctly old-fashioned-looking clothes. Despite her own terror, Lydia saw that the woman seemed to be intensely upset and the figure, which appeared completely solid and lifelike, radiated an atmosphere of intense grief. Initially paralysed with fear, the receptionist was finally able to struggle out of bed and with her heart pounding madly, ran across the room and out into the corridor where at night the lighting was permanently switched on. After several minutes, she found the courage to open the bedroom door and, looking inside, was shocked to find that all the lights in the room were now switched on. Of the weeping woman, there was no sign…

Sonia Banks, at that time the acting manager at Flitwick Manor, like Lydia Dawson, was one of several of the hotel staff to have a strange and unnerving experience. Alone on the premises one evening, Mrs Banks made her usual rounds of the house, which involved locking up the outside doors and various ground-floor rooms, following which she went upstairs. As she made herself ready for bed, she was startled to hear the sound of footsteps which appeared to pass directly overhead, as though someone were walking through the roof space above. This was followed almost immediately by the sound of a door being slammed violently shut towards the front part of the hotel, which was the same wing of the hotel where Jim Sparkes had found the hidden room only a week or so before.

Soon after, Duncan Poyser, the hotel's head chef, also experienced unusual happenings while alone in the building at night. Like John Hinds and Lydia Dawson only days before, Poyser retired just after one o'clock, again in one of the second-floor bedrooms, and was lying on his back trying to get to sleep when he suddenly became aware of a heavy weight pressing down on the lower part of his legs, as though an invisible person was sitting across the bottom of the bed. As he struggled to sit up, Poyser could see that the room was quite empty but, despite this, the unseen force continued to hold him down against the mattress. Finally, with an immense effort, the chef managed to wrench himself sideways and, as the sinister pressure suddenly lifted, the young man found himself sprawled on the floor by the side of the bed. Shaken by what had happened, Poyser switched on the lights and checked the bedroom thoroughly but there was nothing to account for what had happened.

Was the appearance of the eerie weeping woman brought about by the discovery of the hidden attic room, and if so, who was she? Although her true identity still remains a mystery, one suggestion is that the old lady who materialised in such an aura of unhappiness to the terrified Lydia Dawson was Mary Brooks, the unhappy wife of John Thomas Brooks, son of the builder of Flitwick Manor. John Brooks died in 1858 and his wife went on to outlive her husband by twenty years. During that time she apparently never recovered from the death of their daughter, Mary Anne, and grieved constantly for the loss of her child. Perhaps this palpable sadness has somehow imprinted itself into the bricks and timbers of the old house she knew so well and where she spent so many unhappy days after the death of her husband, and this psychic residue was somehow disturbed over 100 years later by Jim Sparkes and his builders? A second theory ascribes the ghost as being that of a former housekeeper of the later Lyall family who was dismissed from her service on suspicion of poisoning one of the Lyall children, and whose room in the roof spaces of the manor house was the very same one that was opened up, years after it had been sealed following her departure from the estate. During the time that the Lyalls lived at Flitwick, the house had a local reputation for being haunted, particularly by the sound of an unseen person knocking on the bedroom doors.

Whatever the true origins of the weeping woman of Flitwick Manor, the appearance of her unhappy and frightening apparition was short-lived. After an initial burst of activity, the phenomena quickly died away, although visiting ghost hunters still consider the building to be haunted. The house continues to be used as an hotel and the mysterious attic room is now a guest bedroom – Room 12 – and odd things are still reported here from time to time. The apparition of an old woman has been seen at least once downstairs when a live band was playing at a function, and lights inside the house are reported to turn on and off unexpectedly. In his *Paranormal Bedfordshire* (2008), local researcher Damien O'Dell has presented evidence of two further female apparitions having been seen at Flitwick in recent times – the figure of a small child and a 'servant girl'. Their origins, like that of the unhappy weeping woman, remain a mystery.

Consult: Damien O'Dell, *Paranormal Bedfordshire* (Amberley Publishing, Stroud, 2008); Peter A. Hough & Jenny Randles, *Strange But True?* (Piatkus, London, 1994).

Chapter Three

SPECTRES OF VIOLENCE

Suicide Ghosts and Other Troubled Spirits

Three Lingering Deaths (1927 & 1970s)

The following accounts, two of which are previously unpublished, feature the seemingly paranormal echoes of three suicide-related deaths. These incidents took place in London in vastly different settings: a residential house, a cinema, and a public house.

In 1922, Mrs L. Probert and her nineteen-year-old daughter, Phais, moved into No.6 Lonsdale Road in Barnes, West London. The property, once an Edwardian house, had been converted into three small furnished flats with a separate basement. The Proberts occupied the ground floor and for five years lived peacefully with no hint of anything strange occurring. One evening in October 1927, they had gone to bed at their usual time and were soon both asleep. During the night, Phais was awakened by a creaking sound and, sitting up in bed, she looked across the room to the window and saw a heavy wickerwork rocking chair moving steadily back and forth as if someone had just got up out of it. Knowing this was impossible, she looked to the open window thinking a breeze was causing the chair to move. However, it was a still and windless night, and the rocking chair was too heavy to be moved by anything less than a gale.

Phais reluctantly got out of bed to investigate further and was conscious of faint waves of air pulsing across the darkened room. At the same time she became aware of a nauseating, foetid stench which was now permeating the room. Now more than a little anxious, she went towards the chair, whose motion was gradually diminishing. As she neared the window, the pulsing of the air increased as if something was flapping back and forth, and the dreadful smell grew almost intolerable. In the half-darkness she looked to see if the smell might have been caused by something organic an animal could have brought in through the window during the day, but could find nothing.

Puzzled she went back to bed and tried to sleep. The movement of the chair had ceased and gradually the disgusting smell, together with the strange sensation of the pulsing air, faded away. In the morning all appeared normal and Phais said nothing to her mother. Soon the strange events of the previous night were dismissed and the Proberts continued to live in the flat quietly and undisturbed.

Two years later, almost to the same date, Phais once again experienced the strange phenomena. Awaking in the night, she heard the creaking sound of the rocking chair which once again was moving to and fro, and the nauseating stench again filled the room. Now more than a little alarmed she got out of bed and looked around, certain that a stray animal must have brought its dead prey into the flat and had somehow managed to set the rocking chair in motion. As before there was nothing to be found and the rocking of the chair together with the foetid smell faded away.

Some days later, Phais visited the local butcher's shop which was only a few doors down from the flat. During a conversation with the owner, she half-jokingly suggested that the butcher should keep his old carcasses away from the local cats as they were in the habit of dragging the old bones into the nearby houses and causing a most dreadful smell. After hearing an account of the strange happenings, the butcher paused, looked at Phais and said seriously, 'That house is supposed to be haunted.' Phais returned a puzzled smile. 'Haunted by whom?' she asked. 'If we had been told that before we might not have taken it.' But there was no light-heartedness in the butcher's voice as he replied, 'Just over a year before you moved in, a middle-aged man living alone in your flat committed suicide by hanging himself from a hook near the window of one of the bedrooms. His body hung there for a fortnight before it was discovered. They say the stench when the police broke in was terrible.' For the remainder of their tenancy, the Proberts never again experienced the odd phenomena, and they eventually moved on. Before they left, however, they were informed that a couple who had previously rented the flat suddenly left one night without giving a reason. As far as we can ascertain the phenomena of the rocking chair and the vile smell was never reported by any subsequent tenants. Eventually the house was demolished, and the sad episode of one man's suicide together with its lingering aftermath drifted from living memory.

Fifty years on from the strange events in West London, a similar suicide-related paranormal incident, one with a more resonant supernatural echo, took place in a vastly different location than suburban Lonsdale Road. The Odeon cinema in Camberwell, South London, was built in 1939 on the site of the former Metropole Playhouse. With seating for nearly 2,500 people, it was one of the largest picture palaces in the capital, and regularly saw queues streaking back along Coldharbour Lane eager to see the latest Hollywood blockbusters. However, by the early 1970s, cinema attendances had dwindled, with the result that the lower stalls were taken out of use and audiences were confined to the upper circle.

The haunted Odeon cinema, Camberwell, South London, now demolished. The ghost of a suicide victim was encountered here in the early 1970s. *(Eddie Brazil)*

In the summer of 1973, Jane Smith arrived in London to stay with her elder sister, Helen, and her brother-in-law at their home in Camberwell. Coming from the relative peace and calm of a Wiltshire village, she was eager to take in the capital's sights, and was also excited at the prospect of replacing her dated wardrobe with all the new fashions the London boutiques could provide. One night early in her stay, she and her sister decided to go and see a film at the Odeon. Jane was unaware that the cinema had seen better days and, as a consequence, used only the upper balcony for seating. Half-way through the film she needed to visit the ladies' convenience and in the flickering half-light, her sister, in a hushed tone, told her it was downstairs next to the foyer. Jane made her way to the back of the auditorium and proceeded downstairs but, being unfamiliar with the layout of the building, she quickly became lost.

Making her way through a door into what she thought was the foyer, she found another flight of stairs which descended to a dimly-lit corridor. At the bottom the corridor turned a sharp left and led along to a further doorway. Suspecting that she must have come down too far, she nevertheless continued to the end to see if it led to the toilet. At the far end of another passageway, positioned on the wall, was an illuminated 'Ladies' sign. However, this was the toilet for the now disused stalls and the lavatory itself was in a dilapidated state, illuminated by a single, flickering florescent strip-light; discarded film posters and a stepladder were stacked against one tiled wall. Choosing the least disgusting of the cubicles, she made herself as comfortable as possible. Almost immediately she became aware of the sound of descending footsteps which seemed unnaturally loud and curiously out of place, particularly as the stairwell was isolated from the toilet room by three sets of doors. At no time did Jane assume that the sounds were in any way paranormal. The footsteps came into the lavatory and continued across the floor to the far end of the dimly-lit room and entered the last cubicle. This was followed by a sound that made Jane freeze with fear: the unmistakeable impression of a man sobbing and weeping as though in great distress. Panicking, she quickly buttoned her clothes and, pulling back the bolt on the cubicle door, opened it and stepped outside. Immediately the eerie weeping sounds fell silent. At this Jane hastily left the washroom and made her way back along the gloomy corridor and up to the main part of the cinema.

As she pushed open the door she was relieved to see an anxious Helen together with one of the cinema staff. 'Where have you been?' asked her sister. 'I followed you to the ladies' toilet upstairs but you weren't there.' Jane explained how she had got lost and found herself in the downstairs washroom, adding that there was now a man crying in one of the cubicles. The cinema attendant looked at her quizzically and said that those particular toilets had not been in use for several years. When Jane persisted with her story, the man called another male colleague and the two men descended to the washroom. They soon returned and informed the two women that the room was empty. Jane was incredulous but the attendants assured her that there was absolutely no one there. Somewhat unnervingly, they confirmed that the stairs were the only way out from that part of the building: the door from the lower corridor into the auditorium had been sealed up several years before.

Disturbed by the incident, the two women left the cinema. When they returned home that night, they related the strange incident at the Odeon to Helen's husband, who listened with a curious expression but said little about the episode. Soon Jane Smith's fortnight in London came to an end and she returned to the family home in Wiltshire. Some days after her departure, Helen and her husband were discussing the strange event in the cinema toilet. 'You do know that the Odeon is supposed to be haunted?' he told Helen. He had heard a story from an old friend who had been a projectionist at the cinema back in the 1960s. A precise date could not be given, but it seems that either in the late 1940s or '50s, a middle-aged man is said to have hanged himself from the overhead pipes in one of the cubicles. Soon after the tragic incident, the cinema began to acquire a haunted reputation. The story and rumours of ghostly happenings was common knowledge between the cinema staff when the projectionist arrived, and even though he had not experienced anything out of the ordinary during his years at the Odeon, fellow workers had often reported seeing the apparition of a distraught man in the auditorium and also hearing the sound of footsteps in the corridors and on the stairs. Some staff members were fearful of walking alone in certain areas of the building, and the toilet in which Jane had heard the sound of the distressed man, the scene of the alleged suicide, was considered the most haunted part of the building. Did Jane Smith encounter the unhappy spirit of a suicide victim on that night in 1973? We will never know. The Odeon closed in 1975 and thereafter stood empty and abandoned. After being used as a clothing warehouse it was demolished in 1993 and today the site is occupied by a block of flats.

The final account of what we may call the phenomena of 'lingering death' occurred within a stone's throw of the Odeon cinema. Once again it concerns a number of suicide-related paranormal incidents, and as with the previous case would appear to be phenomena which has not been previously or subsequently reported. In June 1975, twenty-two-year-old Kay Bradshaw (pseudonym) arrived in London from her home in Buckinghamshire to begin work as a barmaid at the Fox on the Hill on Denmark Hill, Camberwell. The hostelry is a large public house split into two buildings which contains six bars and a restaurant. The oldest and smaller part of the complex, which possibly dates from the eighteenth century, consists of a public and a saloon bar, as well as accommodation for ten staff. Part of the pub's garden was said to be the site of a burial pit for the victims of the Black Death which had periodically ravaged England over the centuries. In the Middle Ages, Camberwell, then a tiny hamlet, would have been considered sufficiently distant from the city to dispose of London's plague-ridden dead.

Bar work at the time was much sought after by those hoping to establish themselves in the capital as it not only provided a steady job but also free meals and cheap

The Fox on the Hill pub, Denmark Hill, London. During the summer of 1976, sinister phenomena connected with the ghost of a suicide victim was experienced here. *(Eddie Brazil)*

accommodation. On arrival, Kay, being a new girl, was allocated an attic bedroom and lived peacefully at the Fox on the Hill for almost a year without experiencing anything out of the ordinary. The summer of 1976 was a memorably hot one with the mercury consistently topping eighty-six degrees, and for the staff at the Fox, the hours were long and the work tiring, but Kay was enjoying her first experiences of London and made several new friends.

As seems to be the pattern in many reported paranormal cases, the phenomena was to commence in a puzzling yet low-key manner. One night in June 1976 after a long shift in the pub's restaurant, Kay decided to take a bath. The bathroom was situated on the landing a short distance from her bedroom and was shared by all staff members. As she relaxed in the hot tub, letting the aches and tiredness of the day seep away, she was jolted out of her reverie by the bathroom being suddenly plunged into darkness. Leaping out of the bath, she groped about in the blackness and found the pull cord but no light came on. Her first thought was that there had been a power cut but a thin slither of light under the door to the landing showed that the power was still on in the rest of the building. Donning her bathrobe, Kay opened the door and it was then that she noticed the light bulb lying on the floor. Picking it up she found it was still warm. Although this was to be expected, it seemed impossible for the bulb to have fallen soundlessly from its socket and also not to have broken on impact. Moreover the bulb was of the bayonet type, which needed an upward action to remove it from the socket. More mystifying was that there had been no sound of the bulb hitting the lino. One moment the light was on, the next the room was in darkness with the bulb lying motionless next to the bath. Although puzzled by the incident, Kay concluded that there had to be a rational explanation – perhaps the socket was loose and the bulb itself ill-fitting?

The next few weeks followed without incident. However, following another hot and tiring day, Kay went to the bathroom to run the bath water. As she opened the door and stepped inside she automatically put her hand to the light cord and was alarmed when it suddenly seemed to swish up and wrapped itself around her neck in a whiplash movement. The light came on and she could see that the lower half of the cord had twisted itself tightly around her throat. Grabbing the cord she immediately untangled it and stepped back out onto the landing in shocked surprise. It seemed to her that the cord had intentionally made a movement towards her throat, yet the idea had to be preposterous. How could it have twisted itself into a noose in such a chilling way? The light switch cord was still gently swinging back and forth as she gingerly looked back in the bathroom. She tried the switch two or three times to see if it was working properly, and then examined the cord, wondering what could have made it jerk in such a sudden and unpleasant way, eventually taking the flex and carefully wrapping it around a nearby towel rail.

The incidents in the bathroom left Kay not only anxious but also baffled and she confided to her colleagues about the strange episodes. They listened with interest, but were soon treating her story, much for Kay's reassurance, with bluff good humour, adding that she was either working too hard, drinking too much, or, as an Australian workmate waggishly suggested, hadn't paid her electric bill. There were no more odd incidents experienced in the bathroom, and soon the on-going work in a large public house together with the distractions of a busy social life, let the strange occurrences retreat to the back of her mind. However, what she was soon to encounter at the Fox was to prove not only equally as inexplicable, but also far more terrifying.

One night after another busy session in the bar, Kay retired early to bed for some well-needed rest. It was a warm night and the bedroom window was left open with the curtains drawn back. She read for some minutes before turning off the bedside lamp. Around half-past two in the morning, she was awoken by a rustling sound coming from somewhere nearby. The bedroom was bathed in the soft, dim, neon street lighting from outside and, sitting up, she looked sleepily around to see what was causing the sound. On the back of the bedroom door hung a jacket which had recently been dry-cleaned. It was still wrapped in its polythene covering and Kay could see that the surface of the transparent material seemed to be gently rippling, as if a breeze was playing against it, although the night was still with not a breath of wind. The rustling of the polythene continued for about a minute and then abruptly stopped. Thinking that it must have been an internal draught coming from the landing, she laid her head back down on to the pillow, but as she turned over she was suddenly shaken out of her slumber by the sight of a dark figure standing immediately next to the bed.

Kay looked up in open-mouthed fear at the form which now began to bend menacingly over her. In the half-darkness she could make out that the person was a man and that his face seemed somehow disfigured: the eyes were no more than black slits and, as he came closer, she could see large teeth in an ugly open mouth which was stretched wide in a mad, malevolent grin. Kay screamed in terror and leapt from the bed. She ran to the door and fled out onto the landing and down to a female colleague's room. The commotion brought several people from the nearby bedrooms and seeing Kay in her distressed state, they tried to calm her. She was insistent that there was a man in her room and that he had tried to attack her. Two men went quickly up to the attic room to investigate but found it deserted. 'There has to be someone there,' insisted Kay, 'he was right by the bed!' but she was assured that the room was empty. Eventually the police were called and a thorough search of the staff accommodation was carried out, but the officers could find nothing out of the ordinary, and despite their reassurances, Kay spent the rest of the night on a sofa in a friend's room.

By now Kay had begun to wonder if the incidents in the bathroom and the man in the bedroom were in some way connected. Despite her colleagues' continued assurance that there was nothing to worry about, she asked if she could switch rooms and exchanged with her Australian workmate who, with typical bravado, said that if he met the sinister 'man in black' he would offer him a beer. Eventually, knowledge of the strange incidents began to filter down through the rest of the staff, and the experiences were soon being discussed in hushed tones by a number of customers. One quiet afternoon as Kay worked in the downstairs bar, she was engaged in conversation by an elderly gentleman who had been a regular at the Fox for many years. Learning of Miss Bradshaw's encounters, he asked if she knew anything about the Chinese man who had committed suicide in the pub. He went on to say that back in the 1950s, the Fox had employed a Chinaman who, like Kay and her colleagues, lived for a time with his wife in the accommodation block. He was a hardened gambler and would often stay out all hours losing his money at cards or at the bookmakers. The couple had terrible rows and one day she had had enough and walked out. His pleadings for her to return came to nothing, the continued gambling and drinking got out of hand, and he inevitably descended into despair. One day he didn't show up for work and was found hanged by his belt next to the door in his bedroom.

Kay listened intently, her face withholding any expression of shock or surprise at the story of the suicide, and her own experiences in the bathroom and bedroom began to merge into an uncomfortable realisation of what she had already begun to suspect. She vacantly replied, 'How terrible,' and added what seemed a pointedly obvious question, 'In which room did it happen?' 'A room at the top, in the attic, I think,' was the reply. Kay remained at the Fox on the Hill until May 1977, after which she left to take up a position at another pub in the West End of London. There were no more strange incidents reported, either from the bathroom or from staff who subsequently occupied the attic bedroom. However, there is a curious footnote to this story which may or may not be connected to previous events.

The room into which she moved after she saw the figure in the attic had once been occupied by a couple from New Zealand. The Fox had a regular turnover of overseas staff with a large contingent from Commonwealth countries and they often furnished the rooms with items they had picked up on their travels around the world. One such memento stood in Kay's room, an ornate metal birdcage which had been purchased in a Hong Kong market. Standing some 3ft high, it was fashioned somewhat like a Chinese pagoda with a large carrying handle, and having been bought for its design rather than to house birds, it had eventually been discarded by the New Zealand couple when they returned home, and now belonged to no one in particular.

One night, a few weeks before she was due to leave the pub, Kay awoke in the small hours to find the room bathed in a soft, blue light. At first she thought it was an emergency light from a passing ambulance or police car out in the street, but this was not so. She looked from the bed and saw that the blue light was in fact emanating from the top of the pagoda birdcage, pulsing out with a kind of rhythmic glow. She watched transfixed as the light seeped across the room, coldly illuminating the walls and ceiling. The effect continued for over a minute, eventually reaching a crescendo of brightness before it began to gradually die down and finally faded away. Kay leapt from the bed and immediately switched on the room light. She examined the birdcage but could find no explanation for the strange glow. Even though the night was mild and the bedroom comfortably warm from the central heating, she found that the metalwork of the cage was inexplicably cold to the touch. Mindful of her previous experiences, she at once took an item of clothing which she wrapped around her hand and, picking up the cage, moved it out onto the landing, hoping in hope that a fellow colleague would claim it and give it a new home. The next morning, much to her pleasure, Kay found that the birdcage had gone, presumably taken by

Former barmaid Kay Bradshaw, who encountered the malevolent ghost of the Fox on the Hill. *(Eddie Brazil)*

a workmate. However, enquiries amongst her colleagues were met with stony silence or puzzled expressions. It seemed that no one had removed it. Kay was insistent that she had left it on the landing and that someone *must* have claimed it. Despite her best efforts to locate the cage it was never seen again, and, soon after, Kay Bradshaw left the Fox on the Hill and has never returned.

If the incidents described above demonstrate anything, they show that we still have not deciphered the paranormal code that shows just how and why these events take place. Suicide is a terrible and desperate act, and one which we might reasonably accept could, in a way we have yet to comprehend, leave some trace behind, but how echoes of such events can make a rocking chair move back and forth, doors open and close, a light switch cord tie itself around a person's neck, or manifest the figure of a man in a darkened room, are unexplainable. For Phais Probert, Jane Smith and Kay Bradshaw, their experiences were not only disturbing, but frighteningly real. No doubt they were the right people in the right place and time, and as such were given a glimpse into a world which we may never fully understand. The basement flat in Lonsdale Road and Stockwell's Odeon cinema have long gone, yet the attic room at the Fox on the Hill public house still remains. As far as we know, no further paranormal incidents have occurred there, although it is possible that the spirit of an unhappy man still lingers within, waiting to reveal his presence to the next suitable person.

Consult: Peter Moss, *Ghosts Over Britain* (Sphere Books, Ltd, London, 1979). [N.B. Details of the Stockwell hauntings were given to one of the present authors – Eddie Brazil – by the experients.]

The Face at the Window (1944-70)

This account of the haunting of a house in West London with a dreadful history of suicide and murder comes from the files of the late Andrew Green, a well-known writer and researcher of the paranormal. Green had several personal connections with the case and as a youth claimed that he had actually managed to photograph one of the haunting apparitions.

One bright autumn day in September 1944, Arthur Green, then an acting senior air-raid warden and rehousing officer, had cause to visit a large detached house in Ealing, West London, accompanied by his teenage son, Andrew. No.16 Montpelier Road was a substantial Victorian villa and, as a local man, Arthur Green knew it, as well as its reputation for being a haunted house, well. The building seemed to keep a terrible secret which over the previous sixty years had been gradually revealed in sudden flashes of violence and unhappiness, and for the seventeen-year-old Andrew Green, who had already kindled an interest in the subject of ghosts and the super-natural, it was to be a day he would remember for the rest of his life, as his personal experiences on that wartime visit would form a foundation for his later career as a ghost hunter and successful author of several books on the paranormal. His connection with the house in Montpelier Road was to span twenty-five years, during which time he was able to document a number of strange and inexplicable incidents in a building that was undoubtedly inextricably linked with the dark and unpleasant side of human nature.

Andrew Green was born in Ealing on 28 July 1927 and by the time of his death in May 2004, ghosts had formed a large part of his adult life. Initially educated at Borderstone Grammar School, he later studied science and philosophy at the London School of Economics, graduating with a Bachelor of Science degree in 1971 and an MSc four years later. During the 1970s, Green began working as a full-time author, but in the preceding years he had enjoyed a varied career with spells in the Civil Service, publishing (including his own modest publishing house, Malcolm Publications), clerical work and pharmacy. All of Green's published works reflected his lifelong interest in psychical research and the supernormal, and he joined a roster of successful contemporary authors including Jack Hallam, Peter Underwood, Antony Hippisley Coxe, Andrew MacKenzie and Marc Alexander, who were writing popular guides and gazetteers on British ghosts and hauntings for an eager modern audience primed to explore the twilight world of the unseen by the occult revolution of the 1960s.

During his ghost-hunting career, Andrew Green was a member of the discipline's two leading paranormal societies, the Ghost Club and the Society for Psychical Research, although the politics of each organisation, as well as Green's own views, soured his relationship with both on occasion. Like many people working in the field, he felt the need to be independent, and at various times founded his own psychical groups, beginning in 1949 with the Ealing Society for Psychical Research, essentially a small group of friends who came together for trips to allegedly haunted places; and later the equally short-lived Lewisham Psychical Research Society, as well as the National Federation of Psychical Research Societies. Green travelled around the country and in over forty years of active investigation visited dozens of locations, at times being rewarded with unusual experiences: in 1952, at Prittlewell Priory near Southend-on-Sea, then being used as offices for the local council, he obtained the strong mental impression of a monk-like figure in the vicinity of the 'Minstrels' Gallery' where two weeks earlier a member of staff had reported seeing a phantom figure, while four years later he investigated a poltergeist case in

Ghost hunter Andrew Green (1927-2004), whose examination of the Montpelier Road haunting spanned over twenty-five years. *(Bowen Pearse)*

Wycliffe Road, Battersea, and received a letter purportedly penned by 'Donald', the ghost itself, supposedly the earthbound spirit of Louis Capet, the illegitimate son of Charles II of France, although in fact written by the fifteen-year-old daughter of the house while in a dissociative state.

As well as the obligatory castles and stately homes, Green investigated many ordinary and unassuming locations where residents and local people claimed to have had strange experiences: they included sightings of a faceless motorcyclist on a housing estate in Croydon, the ghostly figure of a former employee seen walking near the storage tanks at an oil refinery at Coryton, Essex, the apparition of a grey lady seen by staff and pupils at Kilworthy House School at Tavistock, Devon, the eerie footsteps that haunted an antique shop in Ewell, Surrey, and apparitions and other phenomena experienced by the staff of a ladies' fashion boutique in Chatham High Street. Probably his most high-profile investigation was an all-night vigil, accompanied by a hoard of newspapermen, at the Royal Albert Hall in London immediately prior to the 1996 BBC Proms, where workmen behind the scenes had claimed to see ghostly figures in the basement area. Green toured the vast building but was unable to substantiate reports of a haunting.

Green, through a combination of his own scientific training and personal experience, eschewed a spiritualist explanation for paranormal phenomena, believing that ghosts

and hauntings, rather than being due to the activities of discarnate spirits and entities, had their origins in natural and quantifiable forces within the universe, something
he had in common with another contemporary ghost hunter, the eccentric scientist
Benson Herbert, who ran the Paraphysical Laboratory (or 'Paralab') from a cottage
on the edge of the New Forest, and whose organisation Green was for some time a
member. Both Green and Herbert, along with fellow investigators Peter Underwood,
John Cutten and Geoffrey Croom-Hollingsworth, took part in the well-respected 1975
BBC television programme *The Ghost Hunters*, which featured footage of Herbert in
action carrying out a planchette experiment at a haunted pub, while Green himself
was filmed demonstrating ghost-hunting equipment at his own house, an eighteenth-
century former tied farm cottage at Robertsbridge in East Sussex.

Green published a number of books covering his involvement with and study of
the paranormal: they include *Ghost Hunting: A Practical Guide* (1973), *Phantom Ladies* and
Haunted Houses, both from 1975, together with *Ghosts of the South East* (1977) and *Ghosts
of Today* (1980). However, it was in his first published work, *Our Haunted Kingdom*, published by Wolfe Publishing in 1973, that Green set down the details of his experiences
at No.16 Montpelier Road in 1944 and first acquainted the general public with one of
London's most sinister and disturbing hauntings.

Ellerslie Tower was an impressive three-storey red brick building, named after the
70ft-high crenelated structure incorporated into its south-east corner. By the time of
Andrew Green's wartime visit, the house had been renamed Hillcrest Tower and part
of its substantial garden had been sold off for redevelopment. Montpelier Road had
been laid out in the early 1880s in an area of high ground designated as a catchment
area for affluent families (the German-born British historian Sir Nikolaus Pevsner
famously described Ealing as the 'Queen of the Suburbs') and construction of what
became No.16 had followed soon after, although, despite the opulence of its design
and pleasant surroundings, No.16 was soon to become a building much afflicted with
unhappiness. In 1887, a twelve-year-old girl named Anne Hinchfield took her own
life by jumping from the top of the high tower, and according to Andrew Green's
researches, she was the first of twenty suicides to take place from the same spot in the
house over a period of nearly fifty years, a chilling total that undoubtedly would have
given the great villa a notorious local reputation for dark and mysterious happenings,
one that may also have possibly prompted its later change of name.

In its early years, Ellerslie Tower was the home of the Wallace-Dunlop family, a
name now closely associated with the Suffragette movement. Scottish-born Marion
Wallace-Dunlop (1865-1942) went down in history as the first woman to go on hunger
strike after being charged with wilful damage – she was sentenced to a period of impris-
onment in 1909 for defacing the stonework of the House of Commons with a rubber
stamp. For a period beforehand, the house was let to the Vincent family from Western
Australia; theirs was a large household with a retinue of servants (Alice Vincent had

three stepchildren and a daughter of her own) and the family stayed at Montpelier Road for some years. After their departure in 1907, Marion Wallace-Dunlop returned to the family home. She eventually left Ealing in 1912 and the house passed to a succession of new occupants whose time in the rambling hilltop building became continuously linked with despair and the tragedy of human self-destruction.

In 1934, forty-seven years after the death of Anne Hinchfield, this sinister connection finally played itself out in an explosion of murderous violence when a nursemaid threw a young child in her care from the top of the brick tower and immediately afterwards jumped to her own death, a terrible event with which Andrew Green had an intimate connection: his mother, then working as a nurse, had been on duty at the time and had been called to the very scene of the tragedy. Years later, Green would describe how, as his mother had waited on the overgrown lawn at the rear of the house while a doctor made an examination of the bodies, she saw a line of footprints appear in the wet grass as though an invisible person was walking past. The footprints continued towards a garden seat which then appeared to move as though whatever was passing through the garden had paused momentarily to rest…

The events of 1934 brought to a close a long and troubled chapter in the eventful history of the house in Montpelier Road. Not long after the murder and suicide, Hillcrest Tower was sold, although it remained empty throughout the rest of the decade and it was to be nearly twenty years before the building would be lived in again. During the summer of 1944, the house, by now a grim dilapidated hulk lying neglected and alone amidst increasingly wild and overgrown grounds, was requisitioned by Ealing Town Council for use as a depot for furniture and other items salvaged from bombed-out buildings in the surrounding area. Although the once grand rooms and numerous corridors provided adequate storage space, a raft of repairs were needed to make the building suitable for the purpose, and the attention of the council rehousing officer assigned to oversee the conversion was drawn to a particular area on the first floor, where an extremely unpleasant smell, over and above what would normally be expected in an empty and closed-up building, made working in that part of the house particularly difficult.

During the course of the repair work, Hillcrest Tower quickly gained a reputation amongst the council employees for being haunted. The sound of footsteps and doors closing in parts of the building known to be empty at the time, as well as the frequent disappearance of tools and other items (a phenomenon common in poltergeist cases) and the continued presence of the disturbing smell, made a number of workmen refuse to go back inside and, ultimately, a replacement crew from the neighbouring suburb of Greenford was employed to finish the job. However, visitors to the house transporting items for storage regularly complained about the unpleasant atmosphere inside the building as well as the mysterious smell which, despite re-plastering and new floorboards, was regularly encountered, according to Andrew Green, on a twenty-eight-day cycle.

An enlargement of a photograph taken by ghost hunter Andrew Green at a haunted house in Ealing, West London, in 1944. It has been suggested that the apparition of a suicide victim can be seen in the top left-hand window. *(Paul Cawthorne)*

Through his duties as an air-raid warden, Arthur Green had access to the building and, aware of his son's growing interest in the supernormal, agreed to open up the house so that they could look around and Andrew was able to take photographs. While his father went to check that the various doors and windows on the ground floor were secure, Andrew wandered around on his own through the numerous high-ceilinged apartments, including the first-floor room, where the peculiar and recurring smell continued to be reported (and which Green found had been used by the last occupiers as a chemical laboratory). Not surprisingly, given the house's unenviable history, the young man was keen to explore the tall tower which had been the focus of so much tragedy in the past, and made his way to the upper storey where, strangely, he seemed not to be alone…

Recalling the visit nearly thirty years later, Green was able to describe his experience: 'Scrambling up the ladder on the third floor to the tower roof I had an impression that I was being physically helped, feeling a pair of hands on my waist, but the only other occupant of the building was on the ground floor.' The tower commanded an impressive view out across North London, but as the teenager scanned the distant houses over the treetops of the wild and overgrown garden, he became aware of a sudden and increasingly powerful compulsion, as though willed by an insistent inner voice, which encouraged him to step forward and walk over the waist-high parapet, as though the wide expanse of lawn below the tower was only a few inches away. Unbeknown to the young ghost hunter, Green's father had followed him up into the tower and suddenly arrived to pull him back from the edge. 'At that moment I was convinced I would not be hurt. Later, I realised that the suicides may well have suffered from the same impelling command and were not victims of a real death wish.'

Green and his father climbed down from the tower and made their way to the ground floor. It was mid-afternoon and as they walked around the outside of the empty building, Green decided to take a photograph from a vantage point on the far side of the wild and untended lawn. No one was in the house at the time, and Arthur Green was waiting on the other side of the house, yet in one of the first-floor windows, what appears to be the figure of a young girl can be seen looking wistfully out at the photographer – the unhappy ghost of Anne Hinchfield, whose footsteps may be those heard by several council men working on their own inside the house, or a simulacrum created by a combination of light and shade on the window glass? The image has been championed by some and dismissed by others – all 'ghost' photographs are subjective and several famous images from the past including the Minsden Chapel monk, the Wem Town Hall girl, as well as Indre Shira's classic Brown Lady of Raynham Hall, have been debunked in recent years – but there can be no denying that Hillcrest Tower was a building where a residue of its troubled past continued to live on.

By the early 1950s, the house had been given a new lease of life by being divided up into separate flats and in 1952 Andrew Green had cause to visit the property again. One tenant, Kenneth Yandell, a producer at the BBC, was also the director of a local amateur dramatic group of which the young ghost hunter was a member, and rehearsals for a forthcoming play (appropriately enough Frank Harvey's *The Poltergeist* which had been filmed by Southall Studios in 1947 as *Things Happen at Night*) were held in Yandell's flat. Ultimately the drama was never staged but a series of unusual happenings took place during the pre-production meetings at Montpelier Road. Although Green made no mention of details concerning the first of the many violent deaths that had taken place in the old house, one female member of the cast appeared to fall into a trance-like state during the first rehearsal in which she seemingly took on the personality of the tragic Anne Hinchfield. A week later, several of the dramatic group present in the flat heard the tread of footsteps walking through the apartment as well as the sound of a closing door, which they were adamant did not come from any of the adjacent flats.

Kenneth Yandell and several other tenants also reported unusual experiences of their own. A couple who occupied part of the building near to the tower often heard limping footsteps, as though from a person walking with a stick, passing along what had been the original corridor leading into the top-floor room below the roof area, while other residents claimed to have seen the bell push of their front door moving by itself. During the time that Kenneth lived at Montpelier Road, he experienced the mysterious smell which had plagued the building during the time the council workmen had been in the house during the war – Green realised from his previous visit in 1944 that Yandell's bathroom was the site of the former chemical laboratory – and his dog also exhibited great signs of distress during the same periods. During the 1960s, Green met television scriptwriter Jack Edwards who, at that time, was living in the same flat at Hillcrest Tower that had been vacated by Kenneth Yandell and his wife. Like the original occupants, Edwards also complained of regularly experiencing a sulphurous gas-like smell, even though a domestic gas supply had not been laid into the apartment.

The origins of the strange happenings in the Montpelier case remain a mystery. In 1970, the building was demolished and today a block of flats, Elgin Court, occupies the site. Many years after his wartime experience, Andrew Green met a former employee who, as a young woman, worked as a maid at the house; a local woman, she claimed that during her time there, Black Magic ceremonies were carried out regularly in one of the tower rooms, and Green himself reported seeing 'magical symbols' cut into the walls while exploring the building in 1944. Whether the melancholy atmosphere inside the house was in some way a left-over of these times is debateable and perhaps an explanation for the strange forces present on occasion at Montpelier Road is nearer to the theories of Cambridge academic Tom Lethbridge (1901-1971), the 'Einstein of the Paranormal', who felt that the appearance of apparitions at haunted sites such as the hilltop location of Ellerslie Tower are due to the effects of natural forces and energy within the earth itself rather than the actions of entities and discarnate spirits. Whatever the real explanations, the mystery remains and No.16 Montpelier Road, Ealing, deserves recognition as one of London's most enigmatic and haunted buildings.

Consult: Andrew Green, *Our Haunted Kingdom* (Wolfe Publishing, London, 1973); Andrew Green, *Haunted Houses* (Shire Publications Ltd, Princes Risborough, 1975).

Of Ghosts and Murder: The Killing of Charles Walton (1945)

The wartime murder of a simple countryman in the Warwickshire village of Lower Quinton remains one of England's most enigmatic and officially unsolved crimes. The strange tale of Charles Walton involves ghosts, ritual murder and witchcraft in equal measure.

One of the most persistent and widespread of our native British ghosts is the appearance, often at remote and rural locations such as old cemeteries, footpaths, as well as lonely lanes and byways, of large black phantom hounds, most commonly known to both ghost hunters and folklorists alike by the collective title of 'Black Shuck'. There are many derivatives and variants of these ghost dog hauntings, some of which are associated with the former sites of gibbets and gallows, and they go by a number of striking and colourful local names. The North of England is known as the hunting ground of 'Padfoot', an animal the size of a donkey whose feet are turned backwards; in Lancashire a similar beast is called by a number of names including 'Trash', 'Striker' and the 'Boggart' which, when seen, utters a terrible screeching sound before sinking down into the ground and disappearing; in Northumberland and parts of Yorkshire the 'Barguest' is described as being a large black dog with blazing eyes, while 'Shuck' or 'Shag' haunts the cemeteries and graveyards of East Anglia on dark stormy nights, terrifying wayward travellers unlucky enough to cross its path with its single flaming eye.

Over in Bedfordshire, lonely Galley Hill on the north-eastern outskirts of Luton, the scene of a Roman massacre and later an execution site for seventeenth-century witches, is known for the 'Hell Hound', which is said to have appeared during a thunderstorm one dark night in the early 1700s, when it danced in the flames of a lightning-struck gibbet. The legend of the 'Black Dog' phantom hound is most strong in the West Country where it is known from a number of locations including Uplyme in Devon and the Blackmoor Gate crossroads on Exmoor. One phantom hound that breaks the tradition, however, is the Scottish 'Lamper' that haunts the wilds of the Hebrides Islands and whose appearance is considered to be an omen of approaching death. This ghostly dog is said to be white rather than the traditional black and to have no visible tail.

One particular 'Black Shuck' haunting which is specifically regarded as a portent of doom is that associated with Meon Hill, an expanse of hillside above the Warwickshire village of Lower Quinton, a rural hamlet on the edge of the Cotswolds four miles south of Stratford-upon-Avon. The area has a brooding atmosphere of strange secrets and mystery that stretches back over countless years. Ten miles to the south-east are a collection of ancient megaliths known as the Rollright Stones: a stone circle called The King's Men, together with a solitary upright, The King Stone, and the four remaining uprights and possible cover-stone of a chambered long barrow called The Whispering Knights. All these names derive from local folklore which claims they are the petrified remains of a Danish king and a company of his faithful knights who were turned to stone by a witch to prevent the monarch becoming the new king of England; and it is witchcraft that is a sinister thread which runs down through the years around Lower Quinton, a place now inextricably linked with tales of ghosts and murder.

In 1875, in the village of Long Compton, a mile north of the Rollright Stones, a seventy-five-year-old villager, Ann Turner (or Tenant), was brutally killed by a local man, John Haywood. Haywood, a simpleton, claimed that the old woman was a witch who, through the working of magic charms, had blighted the village and brought him personal bad luck. On the evening of 15 September, as she returned home from a visit to the village bakery, Ann was attacked by Haywood, who in an explosion of superstitious rage, stabbed her several times in the head and legs with a pitchfork. She died a few hours later and the farmworker was quickly arrested and sent for trial. Found guilty but insane, he was committed to the Broadmoor Asylum for the Criminally Insane where he died fifteen years later at the age of fifty-nine. The 'witchcraft' murder of Ann Turner was a notorious local event that was to cast long shadows down through the imaginations of future generations over half a century later.

At Lower Quinton, as in many rural districts, the ominous appearance of ghostly black dogs was a well-known country superstition, and the lonely slopes of Meon Hill were regarded as a haunted place where it was wise to avoid lingering after dark. How this tradition came about is unclear, but the presence in the village of a local man named Charles Walton appears to have a certain amount of significance. Walton, a countryman and farmworker and one of six children, was born on 12 May 1870 and lived in and around Lower Quinton all his life. He is known to history as an enigmatic figure about whom today it is difficult to separate fact from fiction. A widower, Walton earned a living working on local farms, clearing ditches and cutting hedges, and in his youth appears to have demonstrated a talent as a horse trainer. Following the death of his wife, he lived with Edith Walton, an adopted niece in her early thirties; a neighbour, Mrs Beasley, helped with shopping, and if it had not been for the chilling events of St Valentine's Day, 1945, Walton would have faded into obscurity, a slightly eccentric but nonetheless benign and harmless local character.

Charles Walton plied his simple trades on the farms on and around Meon Hill and it was here according to some accounts – contemporary local gossip as well as modern commentaries – that as a young man he had a strange and frightening encounter with the supernatural. Versions of the experience differ but the consensus is that Walton, a novice ploughboy in his mid-teens, saw on a number of occasions the apparition of a phantom black dog which proved to be a personal harbinger of ill-luck. Whether the hedge cutter actually spoke about this personally or discussed the incident with his immediate family in unclear and at this distance of time the truth of the matter is impossible to ascertain. What is clear is that in 1930, the Revd James Harvey Bloom,

rector of Whitchurch and the father of actress and novelist Ursula Bloom, published a volume of local history entitled *Folklore, Old Customs and Superstitions in Shakespeare Land* which has become inextricably linked with the wartime events in Lower Quinton. In his book, Bloom describes how, in 1885, a fifteen-year-old boy from the village of Alveston on the outskirts of Stratford, five miles north-east of Lower Quinton, while walking home from work on nine successive evenings, met a strange black dog at the same spot on the edge of the village. The youth told a number of people, including a shepherd and a carter with whom he worked, about the creature but no one was inclined to take him seriously. On the ninth and final evening, as the lad made his way home in the twilight, the dog appeared again

Enigmatic countryman Charles Walton, whose wartime 'witchcraft' murder remains unsolved. *(Authors' collection)*

and as he approached, he saw that on this occasion it was accompanied by a human figure. Drawing nearer, the ploughboy was horrified to see that the person was actually a headless woman who rushed past him in the gathering darkness, her silk dress rustling as she moved. The ghosts proved to be the prophets of ill omen: that evening word came to the family that the ploughboy's sister had taken ill and died. According to the Revd Bloom, the young lad's name was Charles Walton…

Versions of this eerie story have transposed the happenings to the slopes of Meon Hill, where the number of appearances of the spectral hound and its unsettling companion are generally reduced to three. As with the account given by James Bloom, the ghost dog was accompanied on the third and final evening by a headless woman; one version has the dog itself changing into the apparition. All versions allege that the fifteen-year-old ploughboy was the Charles Walton who lived quietly in the small thatched cottage known as 15 Lower Quinton and is the incident that connects the countryman with the twilight world of the unseen and assigns Meon Hill as being a haunted place. Whether Walton actually acknowledged to the people of Lower Quinton that he was the person involved in the Revd Bloom's ghost story is unclear. There is a possibility that he was, but the closing part of the tale, that the phantoms either brought about or gave warning of the death of a family member, appears not to be supported by physical evidence held by the Office of National Statistics at Somerset House: there are no records of this Charles Walton having a sister who died in 1885, which would lend support to the belief that the event took place on Meon Hill; or at least no records have come to light at present.

What is clear is that Walton was known locally as an odd character, a man steeped in the old ways of the country. It was said he demonstrated some form of clairvoyant ability and was able to charm the birds from the trees and could imitate the calls of every bird in the neighbourhood. Some went further and alleged an involvement in local witchcraft, that Walton knew the identities of villagers and people from the surrounding area who practised magic; and also that the old man was a coven member himself who possessed the 'evil eye'. It was well known that he bred 'natterjack' toads and that the garden behind his tiny cottage was alive with the creatures. In several parts of the country, toads have had a long association with witchcraft: East-Anglian witches were said to concoct a magic lotion from toad spittle and the sap of the sow-thistle, while in Cambridgeshire, 'toadmen' were said to have special power over horses, something that is of interest when we remember Walton's apparent affinity with horse training in his youth. Crime writer Donald McCormick, who investigated the Walton case in the 1960s, claimed to have found evidence that these pet toads were on occasion harnessed to a toy plough and sent running out across the ploughed fields around Lower Quinton, a sinister pastime that the red-headed seventeenth-century Scottish witch Isabel Gowdie also confessed to carrying out in order to stunt the growth of local crops. Gowdie was burnt at the stake in 1662 and, unbeknown to the inhabitants of Lower Quinton, an equally horrific fate was to befall the gentle Warwickshire countryman in the closing months of the Second World War, nearly 300 years later...

In 1945, Charles Walton was seventy-four years old. Afflicted with rheumatism, he walked with a stick but continued to take on casual labouring work on the local farms whenever he could obtain it. He was a familiar sight in the lanes and fields around Lower Quinton with his grizzled grey hair and drooping moustache, dressed in his customary heavy boots, collarless shirt and three-piece suit with a tin watch on a chain across his waistcoat. Since the previous summer he had been working regularly for Alfred Potter, a local landowner whose farm, known as The Firs, stretched up onto the slopes of Meon Hill.

Around six o'clock on the evening of 14 February, Edith Walton became concerned as to the whereabouts of her uncle, who had not returned from a day's hedge-cutting around one of the more remote fields on the Potter farm. Darkness had now fallen and it was out of character for Walton not to be back home by this time. Together with Mr Beasley from the neighbouring cottage, she walked the short distance to Alfred Potter's farmhouse and he agreed to accompany them out onto Meon Hill to look for the elderly man. Potter claimed to have seen Charles Walton earlier in the day cutting the hedgerow around a field known locally as the Hillground, and it was to this spot that the three made their way. Arriving at the field they began looking about in the gloom and soon made a terrible discovery: Walton was lying dead under one of the hedges that he had been slashing earlier in the day; he had been beaten to death and his body savagely mutilated.

Harry Beasley and a hysterical Edith Walton, together with another passing villager, went back down the hill to raise the alarm while Alfred Potter remained in the field near Walton's body. Soon local police officers together with detectives from the Stratford-upon-Avon CID were at the scene and shortly before midnight, Dr James Webster of the West Midland Regional Laboratory arrived to examine the body. Webster was an experienced pathologist who, eight years before, in June 1937, had carried out a post-mortem on the body of Mona Tinsley, the ten-year-old victim of child-killer Frederick Nodder, who had gone missing from her home in Newark five months before. Mona's heavily decomposed body had been recovered from the River Idle and for the paranormalist the case is an interesting one as the highly regarded Spiritualist medium Estelle Roberts (1899-1970), with the permission of Chief Constable Barnes of the Newark Borough Constabulary, had been involved in the search for the missing child. Through her spirit control 'Red Cloud', Roberts had provided convincing information about the child's murder by seemingly contacting the spirit of Mona Tinsley herself (see *Ghosts & Gallows*, The History Press, 2012). On this occasion, Webster's forensic report detailed a series of horrific injuries that has made the Lower Quinton murder one of the most notorious and sinister of the twentieth century.

Charles Walton had been overpowered and beaten to the ground, initially with his own walking-stick which was found discarded several feet from the body, the handle smeared with dried blood and hair. He had fought back but his killer had been stronger and had attacked the old man with his own slash hook, a double-edged hand implement used to cut back undergrowth and trim hedgerows: the windpipe had been severed and the throat had been disfigured with a cross-shape wound; there were also deep wounds to the chest (including several broken ribs) and the metal hook was found at the scene with its sharpened end buried in Walton's neck. In a final act of savagery, the country-man's own pitchfork had been driven with immense force into the ground, a prong either side of his neck, pinning him to the earth; according to at least one account of the murder, it took the combined efforts of two policemen to pull it free. Webster concluded that the attack had taken place in the early afternoon, around four to five hours before the body was discovered by Edith Walton and the men from the village.

The following day, the Warwickshire Police made the decision to request assistance from Scotland Yard and on 16 February three officers from London arrived at Lower Quinton. They were Chief Inspector Robert Fabian, who later became familiar to television audiences in the 1950s as *Fabian of the Yard*, together with his assistant, Detective Sergeant Albert Webb, and a Special Branch officer, Detective Sergeant Saunders. Fabian would later spend his retirement writing a series of popular bestsellers chronicling his adventures, some of which were subsequently dramatised by the BBC, but of all the cases he worked on in his professional career, that of Charles Walton was to prove the most intriguing.

The London policemen were given local help by Detective Superintendent Alex Spooner from the Warwickshire CID: Spooner thought it likely that the murder had been committed by Italian prisoners-of-war at an internment camp at nearby Long Marston, and DS Saunders, who spoke fluent Italian, carried out numerous interviews there but ultimately drew a blank. Fabian and Webb, together with local officers, took statements from the entire population of Lower Quinton – nearly 500 people – and in an effort to locate Walton's fob watch, which was found to be missing from the body, the Royal Engineers carried out sweeps of the countryside with mine detectors while aerial photographs were taken by spotter planes from the RAF. During the course of the investigation, Fabian heard rumours of Charles Walton's supposed involvement in local witchcraft and that his death was in fact an 'evil-eye killing': the previous year's harvest had failed and some residents of Lower Quinton apparently considered that the old hedge-cutter and his pet toads were at the root of the problem. At the time, the policeman was disinclined to give much credence to such tales, but this was to change in later years. After several weeks on the case and with no progress, Robert Fabian and his men were forced to return to London. An inquest on 20 March 1945 recorded Walton's death as an unlawful killing and today, over sixty-five years later, the case remains officially unsolved.

The alleged supernatural elements of the Lower Quinton case are the aspects of the crime which continue to fascinate both crime historians and paranormalists. In 1950, Miss Margaret Mead, an American expert on primitive religion, visited the area and expressed her confidence that Walton's death was an organised witchcraft killing. Alex Spooner retained a keen interest in the Walton case but ultimately was unable to progress the investigation further. Robert Fabian returned to Lower Quinton in his 1970 book, *The Anatomy of Murder*. Twenty-five years after the event, Fabian was more inclined to give credence to the suggested occult angle of the murder and that his investigation in 1945 had been hampered by a 'wall of silence' on the part of the inhabitants of Lower Quinton, who had been reluctant to provide information. He also claimed to have had an encounter with a black dog on a footpath across the side of Meon Hill during the time he was working on the case, which had disappeared mysteriously when he went back a few minutes later to look for it. Although in his public memoirs Fabian asserted with some confidence that the death of Charles Walton was 'clearly the ghastly climax of a pagan rite', in private the former policeman was more circumspect. Shortly before his death in 1974, Robert Fabian confided to author and criminal historian Richard Whittington-Egan that he was confident that the old man's sometime employer Alfred Potter was the murderer. The suggestion was that Walton had lent Potter money and in the early weeks of 1945 had been pressing the farmer for repayment, a scenario which, however, is not supported by contemporary statements from the murdered man's bank account. As such, this enduring mystery is well suited to take its place amongst the extreme hauntings of Britain…

Consult: J. Harvey Bloom, Folklore, *Old Customs and Superstitions in Shakespeare Land* (Mitchell, Hughes & Clarke, London, 1930); Robert Fabian, *The Anatomy of Crime* (Pelham, London, 1970); Brian Lane, *The Encyclopedia of Occult and Supernatural Murder* (Headline Book Publishing, London, 1995); Donald McCormick, *Murder by Witchcraft* (John Long, London, 1968).

Steeped in Violence: The Haunting of Killakee (1968-70)

One of Ireland's most haunted buildings, Killakee House near Dublin, has a history of paranormal happenings that includes the appearance of apparitions, the movement of objects and the sighting of a sinister phantom cat. The centre of a series of strange happenings beginning in the late 1960s, some researchers have suggested that the haunting may have its roots in the sinister history of the area that dates back to the beginning of the eighteenth century.

In 1968, Mrs Margaret O'Brien together with her husband Nicholas, a retired Garda Superintendent, bought and moved into an old semi-derelict house in a remote area of Rathfarnham, seven miles south of Dublin city centre. Known as Killakee House, the building and its estate had lain empty since before the Second World War and, unsurprisingly, this abandonment together with its rural location and what is in fact a singularly colourful and dramatic history, had given local people cause to regard it as being something of a haunted place. Nestling in the foothills of the Wicklow Mountains, whose heavily wooded slopes reached down to easily surround what was a picturesque rubble building complete with an open courtyard, stable block and small stone bell tower, the O'Briens had been inspired by the natural landscape to convert Killakee (from Coill á Chaeich or Blind Man's Wood) into a dedicated art centre where Irish artists and sculptors could come to both work on and exhibit their art, and the couple initially brushed ghost stories aside as they set about organising what was an extensive programme of refurbishment.

Originally termed the Stewards House, what is today Killakee House had been built in the mid-1760s by the Connolly family of Castletown, County Kildare, although some parts of the structure may pre-date this time. The surrounding area is steeped in the deeds and stories, both real and imaginary, from which tales of the supernatural are easily drawn. It was used initially by the Connollys as a hunting lodge and, much later, as a dower house by the local landowning Massey family, who were bequeathed the estate in the 1880s from the last surviving member of the White family, who purchased the estate from the Connollys in the early 1800s. Luke White, born in 1752, a bookseller and later Member of Parliament, was one of the wealthiest businessmen in Ireland with an estimated fortune (in 1799) of over £50,000. Around the same time that he bought a vast estate at Luttrellstown, including Luttrellstown Castle, from the 2nd Earl of Carhampton, White also became the owner of Killakee and set about building a vast country residence a short distance away across the road from the old Stewards House. This building (Killakee House proper) was a fine Victorian mansion of some thirty-six rooms, built in a Mediterranean style.

Luke White died in 1824 and his family lived on at Killakee for another sixty years. Nearly 100 years after Luke White's death, when Hugh Hamon Charles, the 8th Baron Massey, inherited the estate, his family was already in dire financial straits. Soon declared bankrupt, he was evicted from the once splendid house and for a time moved into the Stewards House before finally settling in the gatekeeper's lodge. Known as the 'Penniless Peer', he lived in virtual poverty until his death in 1958, by which time the original Killakee House was long gone. In 1924, when the bank repossessed Killakee, a caretaker, Edmund Burke, was appointed to look after the house and for a period it was rented to the Countess Constance Markievicz, known as the 'Red Countess', an Irish revolutionary nationalist politician who became the first woman ever to be elected to the House of Commons (although she never took up her seat). A member of the Irish Citizen Army, the Countess took part in the 1916 Easter Rising, and during her tenancy five IRA soldiers were shot dead on the Killakee estate. On 23 April 1931, Rupert Young, a Trinity student, was shot and killed by IRA men guarding a huge explosives dump hidden in a secret concrete bunker near the house, and for a time the mansion

Killakee House and tower, Rathfarnham near Dublin, whose violent history includes tales of devil-worship, murder and haunting. *(South Dublin County Libraries)*

was used by detectives from the Dublin Metropolitan Division of the Garda Siochána as a base for hunting down his killers and to combat 'irregular military activities' in the area. In 1941, the Killakee mansion was sold to a builder, who stripped the house for salvage, after which it was demolished. Whether this Killakee House was ever haunted has not been recorded, and it is with the old Stewards House of the Connolly family that we are concerned with here.

Killakee lies in the shadow of Montpelier Hill, a steep rise on which, around the same time, William Conolly, the Speaker of the Irish House of Commons, also built a second stone hunting lodge, one which, unlike the Stewards House, commanded views out in all directions over the surrounding countryside. This building occupied the site of a prehistoric cairn from which stones were taken and used as part of the new structure. Conolly died in 1729, after which the lodge became associated with the activities of Richard Parsons, the 1st Earl of Rosse. A Freemason and noted libertine, he was born in 1702 and became the 1st Earl on his sixteenth birthday. At one time the Grandmaster of the Grand Lodge of Ireland, Parsons followed the example of his close English contemporary, the likeminded Sir Francis Dashwood, 2nd Baronet and later fifteenth Baron le Despenser, and established the first incarnation of the Dublin Hell-Fire Club, with the lodge on the summit of Montpelier Hill as its principle meeting place. In West Wycombe, Buckinghamshire, for a period of four years beginning in 1748, Dashwood had employed local labourers and farmhands made idle through a series of poor harvests to dig out a network of interconnecting tunnels and chambers that sank deep into the chalk under West Wycombe Hill, and it was here that he held court over orgiastic ceremonies and pseudo-Satanic ceremonies dedicated to unrestrained excess and the parody of conventional religious worship and practice.

At Wycombe, Dashwood located the deepest of these artificial caves directly under the fourteenth-century church of St Lawrence to create a veritable 'church in Hell', and although the lodge at Killakee was not so grand in its design or bold in its construction, the Earl of Rosse likewise drew around him a company of young bucks and libertinous intellectuals whose activities, like the English 'Monks of Medmenham', involved a wild explosion of drinking, gambling, prostitution and possibly even murder. Those involved included Henry Barry, known as Lord Santry, a violent and drunken rake who killed a man in an unprovoked attack following a drinking binge in a tavern in Palmerstown in 1738, Colonel Jack St Leger, who co-founded the Club with Parsons, and Richard 'Burnchapel' Whaley, a notorious descendant of Oliver Cromwell. The Hell-Fire Club normally met at the Eagle Tavern on Cork Hill in Dublin, but the Conolly family also gave Parsons and his fellow revellers the use of Montpellier Hill, with the result that the lodge has become inextricably linked with stories of dark and sinister deeds involving gambling, pistol duelling, Satanism, black masses and even cannibalism.

Some form of devil worship was almost certainly practised by Richard Parsons and his cronies at Killakee. It was said that one chair was always left empty during the Hell-Fire Club meetings in case Satan himself decided to grace the club with a personal appearance, and on one occasion the Earl of Rosse placed a black cat in the seat of honour to make up for the master's absence. He also tortured and abused animals and, following a black mass in the hilltop lodge, soaked a black cat in spirits and set it on fire. These animal sacrifices appear to have been carried out with some regularity but, more sinisterly, one story that survives from this time concerns a human killing, when a local dwarf-like half-wit with a misshapen and enlarged head was beaten and suffocated to death during a ritual and secretly buried somewhere on the estate. Parsons' rakes also fought duels in the grounds around the Stewards House and at least three noblemen were shot to death there over the years.

Eddie Brazil was born in Dublin and as a child used to travel to Rathfarnham by bus. On a number of occasions, Eddie's grandfather would recount stories of the grim deeds of the Hell-Fire Club members of old which were well known in the area, and the Dublin mountains themselves were popularly touted as being the home of the Devil. A popular tale concerned a particular night when the Earl of Rosse and a group of revellers were seated playing cards with a mysterious silent stranger dressed in black. As he played his cards, the stranger glanced slyly around at the other men but continued to say nothing. At one point, one of the clubbers dropped his cards by accident on the floor and as he bent down to retrieve them had a chance to look across at the feet of the stranger opposite. Instead of riding boots, he saw that the man's legs ended in hairy cloven hoofs…

Richard Parsons died in Dublin on 21 June 1741, following which his grim Hell-Fire Club was disbanded. For some time up until his death, the Earl and his companions had held their nefarious meetings in the old Conolly Steward House, as the Montpelier lodge had become unusable due to a fire which had badly damaged the building. This had started in mysterious circumstances and numerous stories have become extant as to the origins of the blaze. Perhaps the least sensational and most likely of these is that Parsons and his fellow libertines fired the building as an act of revenge after the Conolly family, disgusted at the activities that took place, refused to renew their lease on the lodge. Another version has it that during the course of drunken revelries following a black mass ceremony, one of the Earl's footmen accidentally spilt wine on Richard Whaley's coat-tails, which enraged the wearer so much that he doused the servant in brandy and burnt him alive. In the confusion, which was ably assisted by the heavily inebriated state of many of Hell-Fire revellers, flames from the burning servant's body set fire to nearby draperies, starting a conflagration which destroyed a large portion of the building and in which several club members were killed. Whatever the true facts, the summit of Montpelier Hill experienced a cessation of dark deeds that lasted until the early 1770s, when a revival of the original Hell-Fire Club took place under the leadership of 'Burnchapel' Whaley's son, Thomas 'Jerusalem' Whaley, who presided over a further onslaught of debauchery that lasted nearly thirty years until his death in 1800. Whaley and his friends called themselves 'The Holy Fathers' and the pedigree of their depravities seems to have been as high as that of the Earl of Rosse's incarnation: they are said to have kidnapped a local farmer's daughter and, after torturing her to death, cooked and ate her flesh. No small wonder then that journalist Frank Smyth, who studied the Killakee case in the early 1980s, described it and the surrounding area as being 'imbued with more violence and savagery than most haunted places', and perhaps this has a bearing on the intensity of the strange phenomena that Margaret O'Brien and her husband began to experience soon after moving into their new home.

Much of the haunting of Killakee House concerns the appearance of a large phantom black cat, incidents of which, so local people informed Margaret O'Brien, had taken place with some regularity, both in the old Stewards building as well as the immediate environs of the estate, for the previous fifty years prior to the arrival of the new owners. Seemingly some form of supernatural residue from the shocking past days at Killakee, the ghostly creature was said to be the size of an Airedale terrier, and despite her initial scepticism, Margaret was shocked when, alone in the garden near the house, she began catching sight of a large black animal on several occasions vanishing away into the undergrowth, and as the days passed she was not the only person to see the creature in the grounds of Killakee House. Val McGann was a former Irish pole-vault champion from Ballinashoe, County Galway. In the late 1960s, he was beginning what would become a successful new career as an artist and landscape painter, and at the time was living in a trailer on the estate. He claimed to have encountered a huge black

The phantom cat of Killakee, as painted by artist Tom McAssey. *(Authors' collection)*

cat several times while out alone in the woods and went so far as to stalk it armed with a shotgun, but was never able to run it to ground. McGann described the animal as being 'about the size of a biggish dog, with terrible eyes'.

As the O'Briens continued working on the old Stewards House, incidents of paranormal activity in and around the building began to increase. In March 1968, artist Tom McAssey from County Carlow, together with two other men from Kilbeggan, were staying at Killakee decorating the interior of the house. One evening, as the three men were working in one of the main rooms off the front hallway, they all had a terrifying experience. A short time before, McAssey had closed and secured the main door of the house which opened onto the front courtyard. Soon one of the workmen noticed that the front door, which was held closed by a heavy bolt fixed into the frame, was again standing open, while at the same time the atmosphere in the room, which was being warmed by a portable Calor gas heater, suddenly became icy cold. The lights were out in the hall area but as the three men looked out through the archway leading into the old ballroom where they were standing, they all clearly saw the door open wide and felt a cold breeze coming into the house. Tom McAssey went forward and was alarmed to see what he took to be a tall figure dressed in black material standing just beyond the threshold. Its dark drapery was quite distinct although the artist was unable to see any kind of face or features. Convinced that one of the locals was playing a trick, McAssey advanced into the hallway and challenged the figure by saying, 'Come in. I see you,' to which a deep voice replied, 'You can't see me. Leave this door open.' At this point, McAssey was standing within an arm's length of the front door. The sound of the sinister stentorian voice made the other men lose their nerve and they both fled back into the ballroom. A split second later, the sinister figure uttered a long drawn-out snoring sound which panicked McAssey himself: he slammed the front door shut and, like the other workmen, ran back into the interior of the house, pausing only to look back into the hallway once he'd reached the relative safety of the old ballroom. The artist later described what he saw to a Dublin radio reporter: 'The door was again open and a monstrous black cat crouched in the hall, its red-flecked amber eyes fixed on me.'

As the weeks passed, other workmen employed at Killakee, as well as artists staying with the O'Briens, reported seeing and hearing strange things. On one occasion, two men walking into the ballroom from the stone-flagged hallway saw what they assumed to be the figure of a nun standing in the middle of the room with her back toward them. As they came forward, the nun suddenly vanished and a subsequent search of the premises quickly revealed no one matching the figure's description had been in the house at the time. This incident took place around midday although several workmen were scared by happenings at night and on several occasions became badly frightened. Other locked doors seemingly opened by themselves and in a separate incident, Tom McAssey again claimed to see another shadowy figure, this time standing in the main hallway. The demonic cat was also reported as appearing inside the house when all the doors and windows were closed and locked.

The disturbances continued with some regularity until, by the end of the summer, Mrs O'Brien decided that perhaps some form of religious ceremony would help alleviate the sinister atmosphere of Killakee and, following a request to the Church authorities, a local priest obliged and carried out an exorcism of both the house and the grounds. This appeared to have the desired effect and for over a year Killakee House was quiet: there were no appearances of either the phantom cat or the nun-like apparition and the O'Briens were able to operate the now completed art centre in peace. The centre ran courses in painting and drawing for beginners and professional artists, woodcarvers and sculptors were able to display their work in the newly refurbished gallery amidst the old Steward building's attractive rural surroundings. However, in October 1969, an impromptu and somewhat light-hearted 'séance' held at the centre by a group of visiting Irish entertainers seemed to again disturb the psychic fabric of the old building.

During the course of a small party, several guests that included journalist and songwriter Shay Healey, Danny Doyle – then a chart-topping Irish balladeer – and comedian Noel Ginnity, laid out a Ouija board-style circle of letters on one of the tables and attempted to communicate with the Killakee ghosts by means of a glass tumbler. Despite the levity of the occasion, the glass, which gradually became animated under the resting fingers of the party members, soon spelt out the name *Paul Foster* and followed this with what seemed to amount to a warning: *Go home, there is danger.* When asked what the danger was, the glass traced out the word *lights* and almost immediately the ceiling lights in the room began to dim, while at the same time those in the courtyard outside went out completely. A check on the main fuse board showed that none of the building's circuits had failed and there appeared not to be any kind of fault that would have caused the sudden drop in power.

Following the showbusiness séance, and perhaps even because of it, the haunting of Killakee House entered a new phase. For several months, the building seemed to be at the centre of an unprecedented outbreak of poltergeist-type activity that became increasingly violent and destructive: lights in the house began to switch themselves on and off, the sound of servant bells ringing in the front and rear hallways – on one occasion constantly throughout an entire night – despite the fact that these bells had been physically removed and were no longer present; crockery and bottles were found broken, and several pieces of furniture were destroyed, seemingly by invisible hands – these included two oak chairs, one of which was pulled apart at the joints while the other was simply smashed to pieces. Artwork on display in the O'Brien gallery was also a target for paranormal attack: several oil paintings were found torn into strips while a display of pottery was discovered in pieces on the floor as though it had been thrown across the studio.

A phenomenon well known to psychical researchers, particularly those investigating Spiritualist séances involving physical mediums, is that of 'apports', a term given to solid items such as flowers, jewellery, coins and even small ornaments, which materialise or appear within a controlled environment by paranormal means. Apported objects are a feature of a number of well-known cases including Borley Rectory and the Enfield Poltergeist, and although their presence at Killakee is perhaps to be expected given the intensity of the haunting, the nature of the apports recorded here seems to be almost unique in the annals of paranormal study, involving as it does the appearance and disappearance of knitted children's hats. These items, some clean and new, others dirty and worn, were found by the O'Briens lying inside the house during periods when other incidents of paranormal activity in the building were at their highest. A number of times, Margaret O'Brien found coins inside the hats and they appeared and disappeared during the night hours when the house was locked and secure and the owners were asleep in their bed.

The house also seemed on occasion to be filled with strange sounds and noises for which there was no physical cause or reason, a phenomenon often found in haunted house cases. During one incident, Mrs O'Brien was alone at Killakee while her husband was away on a trip to Cork. During the night, as she lay in bed with the house locked up and secured, Margaret heard the sound of a violent commotion coming from somewhere on the ground floor, as though pieces of furniture were being violently broken and thrown about. Going downstairs, she discovered that nothing had in fact been disturbed or was out of place, and there was nothing in the now silent rooms that could have caused the bizarre and unsettling noises. As well as the phantom cat, Margaret O'Brien also claimed to have seen human apparitions on occasion inside Killakee House, particularly in the art centre gallery which appeared to be a particular focus for the haunting. One day, during the time the centre was open to the public, Mrs O'Brien noticed a tall Eurasian man walking through the gallery who she was sure had not been with any of the visitors who were currently inside the house. As she went to talk with him she found that the person had disappeared and similarly, when she approached two nuns walking through the same room on a separate occasion, they too suddenly seemed to vanish into thin air. Sheila St Clair, a medium from Antrim, who visited Killakee at the beginning of 1970 accompanied by a television crew from Radio Telefis Eireann, claimed that the two nuns seen by Margaret were the unquiet spirits of two women – 'Holy Mary' and 'Blessed Margaret' – who acted as servants at the black masses held in the house by the Earl of Rosse 200 years before, and that much of the haunting was due to the atmosphere of evil created during those times by the blasphemous activities of the various incarnations of the Dublin Hell-Fire Club.

By July 1970, the O'Briens felt that the haunting had again got to the point where the intervention of a priest was necessary and at their request, a second exorcism took place at Killakee. Again, following the ritual the phenomena died down and in fact the most intense period of the haunting had passed and for the next seven years, until the house was sold to a new owner, Joseph Frei, the couple reported only experiencing occasional odd sounds and noises. As well as the rite of exorcism, perhaps the cessation of ghostly happenings at Killakee House was due to another equally dramatic and unexpected event. Early in 1971, during refurbishment work to the kitchen, a plumber lifting flagstones over a section of the original floor discovered the small brass statue of a horned and tailed devil, its hands raised in a mocking and provocative gesture. The presence of the figure seemed to reinforce in some way the seemingly demonic aspect of the Killakee haunting and this was followed by another sinister discovery that seemed to provide a physical connection with the area's notorious past. As the plumber dug down further into the earth under the stone flags, he revealed a shallow grave that chillingly contained a small but clearly human skeleton with a strangely enlarged skull. Was this the remains of the hapless dwarf said to have been killed by Lord Santry and his violent rakes back in the eighteenth century, clear proof of the truth behind the so-called legends and stories associated with the Montpelier Hill Hell-Fire Club? The truth will perhaps never be known. The skeleton was given a religious re-interment, following which the strange disturbances at Killakee practically ceased.

For some years a reminder of the strange days at Killakee House was a vivid painting by Tom McAssey of the demonic cat he saw in 1968 in the hallway, which was painted soon after the incident and hung in the very same hallway. The old Stewards House was operated as a restaurant for several years until the early 2000s and is now a private residence. In his *Irish Ghosts* (2012), Peter Underwood lists a further apparitional sighting of a man wearing a blood-stained shirt, possibly one of Richard Parson's rakes killed in a pistol duel when the Hell-Fire Club cast its shadow from the hillside over 250 years ago...

Consult: *Encyclopedia of Witchcraft & Demonology* (Octopus Books Ltd, London, 1974); Peter Underwood, *Irish Ghosts* (Amberley Publishing, Stroud, 2012).

The Strangling Hands (1976)

This unusual and disturbing account of a physical attack by a haunting apparition was collected by writer Peter Moss in the mid-1970s. Moss was able to interview the couple involved in the case personally and recorded what appears to be a strange and unsettling encounter with the supernatural.

In 1975, following a marriage break-up, Diane Glaze and her three children returned from Malta to live with her sister in the Scottish city of Aberdeen. After some months of reflection and wondering where life would now take her, she felt ready to once again enjoy herself and socialise. She soon met Isa Samat, a Malaysian student studying at Aberdeen University. Their friendship turned to courtship and then to love, and in 1976, as soon as Diane's divorce was made absolute, the couple married and set about making a new home together.

One night in July 1976, Diane was awoken during the small hours. The night was soundlessly hot, yet she experienced a sensation of chilling coldness which seemed to be of the spirit rather than of the physical body. Almost immediately this was followed, out of the darkness, by an inexplicable feeling of panic. Looking across the room, she was amazed to see the figure of a tall, gaunt-faced old woman standing by the bedroom door. Even though the rest of the room was in total blackness, the figure seemed to exude its own sickly glow which almost appeared to seep from its unnatural presence. From this strange illumination, Diane could make out the woman's grey hair, drawn back into an unkempt bunch but straggling lose at the sides, the yellow and grey dress in a diamond check pattern with the sleeves rolled up to the elbows, and the pale brown colour of the apparition's face and arms.

Terrified, Diane closed her eyes, hoping that when she opened them the frightening vision would be gone, but when she looked again across the room, the figure remained standing by the closed door. Time seemed to stand still, but then the sinister woman began to move towards the bed, gliding menacingly along the side of the mattress, holding out her long arms and talon-like fingers. As Diane shrank back against the headboard, the thin bony hands suddenly darted out, grasping her around the throat. As they tightened their grip, displaying frightening and unexpected strength, the air supply to Diane's lungs was quickly cut off and she began to choke. In her terror she clutched at the strangling wrists and, despite the horror of what was happening, was sickeningly aware of the icy coldness of the soft clammy flesh. As the old woman bore down, her forearms pressed heavily against Diane's chest, driving a desperate gurgling noise from her throat. Paralysed with fear, she managed to desperately scream out to her husband only inches away, but, unaware of his wife's dreadful ordeal, Isa remained deeply asleep.

The hands, clamped around Diane's throat, continued to squeeze with their iron-like grip, and she soon felt as though her life was gradually slipping away. Then, suddenly, came relief: the bony fingers relaxed their hold, the arms dropped back, and the terrifying apparition of the old woman, with a mocking smirk, drew away from the bed. As she did so, Diane began to hear the words: *'And now you will believe in ghosts, and now you will believe in ghosts,'* repeated over and over, almost as though the woman was taunting Diane's fear with an eerie and malicious mantra. The thin, weedy voice continued for some moments before the old woman glided back towards the bedroom door, and then she, as well as the jeering chant, faded away into the darkness and were gone.

Once the old woman had vanished, Diane began to cry out hysterically, waking her husband. Isa leapt from the bed and switched on the light. He saw his wife sitting up, clutching her throat, her face filled with terror. 'She was here, she was here!' Diane cried out. 'An old woman – she tried to strangle me!' Her husband managed to calm her and both tried to find a rational explanation for the incident. Diane was adamant it had not been a nightmare: she felt herself being throttled as the dreadful fingers tightened around her throat, and was sure that the old woman would have killed her had she not, of her own choosing, broken off the supernatural attack. They both were able to recall the stories they had been told shortly before they took on the lease of the flat: an old woman had lived there for over forty years, and had died there some time before the Samats had moved in. Her ghost was said to wander the building and Diane wondered if it had been her spirit, resentful of the new occupants, which had appeared and assaulted her.

Isa Samat listened to his wife's conjectures, but she noticed he wasn't nodding his head in supportive agreement with her. His sat with an odd, far off expression, as if his mind was not in the same room. His eyes stared vacantly past Diane. Coming back to the present, he asked her to describe the old woman's appearance and Diane, closing her eyes, reluctantly recalled the vision, reliving in detail the terrifying image of the apparition. Isa Samat shook his head in disbelief, and then quietly said, 'That was my grandmother.'

Isa Samat's parents had separated when he was two years old, and from that time he had been raised by his maternal grandmother. She had been a clinging, demanding personality, who dominated both the family and her husband. Even though she indulged her grandson, she was also insanely jealous and possessive of him. She died when Isa was six, yet her influence still overshadowed his childhood and adolescence. His grandfather believed that his wife's spirit continued to haunt the family home, watching, checking and prying, and he often dreamt that at night she returned to stand again by the side of Isa Samat's bed.

Thankfully, the sinister spectre of the old woman did not appear to Diane Samat again. However, in the years that followed, she and her husband continued to wonder if, from beyond the grave, Isa Samat's domineering grandmother still disapproved of their marriage, and that her insane and possessive jealousy had in fact been able to manifest itself to an innocent and unsuspecting woman in the form of a violent and sinister apparition…

Consult: Peter Moss, *Ghosts Over Britain* (Sphere Books Ltd, London, 1979).

Chapter Four

OUT OF THE EARTH

Ghosts of Woods, Fields and Highways

A Walk in Glydwish Wood (1930s)

One of the most remarkable and disturbing cases of an encounter with a haunting apparition is that claimed by English ghost hunter Robert Thurston Hopkins, a writer and countryman who was active as an investigator during the first half of the twentieth century. His account of meeting the ghost of a hanged man in an East Sussex wood reads like something from a ghost story, but Thurston Hopkins was adamant that every word was true…

'For centuries man has been fascinated by tales of haunted houses: houses in which ghostly figures walk, eerie voices cry out, and in which furniture levitates in the air and floats to and fro. Many people don't believe that such things really exist. But they are wrong!' So stated American psychical researcher, the late D. Scott Rogo, in the introduction to his *The Haunted House Handbook* (1978). For the general public, the most obvious and familiar association with the world of the paranormal is through the concept of the haunted house, which in Britain alone must number in the tens of thousands, from ordinary flats and council houses through to large private dwellings, stately homes and castles. However, the annals of organised paranormal investigation easily reveal that ghostly activity takes place wherever there exists or has existed the presence of man, and the natural world, like the built environment, is a strange and haunted realm: there are haunted lakes, rivers, caves, hills, moorland and mountains, but perhaps after the haunted house, dark woods and forests are the next places where it would seem most natural for ghosts and phantoms to dwell.

In the early 1980s, stories of strange happenings in Clapham Wood, an isolated area of woodland on the South Downs, three and a quarter miles north-west of the centre of Worthing, gained mainstream public attention following the publication of a series of articles in *The Unexplained* part-work magazine. Journalist Toyne Newton together with local UFO investigator Charles Walker, revealed a wealth of frightening and uncanny phenomena associated with the Friends of Hecate, a secret occult group that at the time used Clapham as a clandestine meeting place for Satanic rituals and animal sacrifice. Newton and Walker suggested that the disappearance of three local people during the 1970s, including the vicar of Clapham's small eleventh-century church of St Mary's, whose skeletal remains as well as the bodies of a police constable and another local man were later discovered in the wood and surrounding area, may have been linked to the group's sinister activities, and the researchers also reported a wealth of seemingly connected phenomena including the appearance of unidentified figures and shapes, the disappearance of dogs and other animals, strange footprints, as well as debilitating forces, levitations and numerous UFO sightings.

Across Britain, many forests and woods have similar strange associations with the world of the unseen and the supernatural: on the outskirts of Caddington near Luton in Bedfordshire, Badgerdell Wood, known for sightings of strange apparitions including a bizarre 'owlman' and a phantom black dog, was also the scene of Satanic rituals in the early 1960s; in Park Wood near the much haunted village of Pluckley in Kent, the ghost of the 'Colonel', a male suicide, walks among the trees; the site of Robin Hood's Grave in the woods at Kirklees in West Yorkshire is known for numerous ghostly experiences including the apparition of a white-robed woman and the sound of heavy footsteps; Black Dog Woods near Chapmanslade in Wiltshire seemingly gets its name from a huge phantom dog with blazing eyes said to haunt the area, and there are countless others. Perhaps, though, a candidate for one of the most frightening of supernatural woodland encounters is that associated with the haunting of Glydwish Wood, an iso-lated spot located one and a quarter miles south-east of the village of Burwash in East Sussex. Accounts of strange happenings here are based on two encounters that took place during the 1930s, although the origins of the case would appear to stretch further back to the first quarter of the nineteenth century and an interesting *cause célèbre* from the pages of English criminal history.

In the 1820s, the countryside around Burwash Weald was heavily wooded and the rural crime rate was high: highwaymen and footpads operated on the main toll road between the market town of Heathfield and the village of Hawkhurst over the county border in Kent, smuggling of contraband goods was prevalent and there were often robberies and thefts from local barns and from farmers' fields. One such local crook was Benjamin Russell, a farmer in his mid-thirties who, as well as running his home as an unlicensed public house, was an habitual thief and enjoyed a number of illegal pursuits including poaching and prize-fighting. In 1815, he was found guilty of stealing and six years later was sentenced to one month's hard labour for the theft of timber. Russell's wife, Hannah, worked as a baker but the couple were heavily in debt and as well as the returns from Ben Russell's smuggling and other illegal activities, they relied on the income from a lodger, Daniel Leney (also known as David Leany); like Ben, Leney was a thief and smuggler who local gossip suggested supplemented more than just the family finances. He may have been Hannah Russell's lover, possibly with her husband's approval. In 1825, Leney was caught with an accomplice practically red-handed while attempting to steal a catch of wheat from a barn but was acquitted, and was also implicated in the theft of an expensive scarf from a local public house, the Rose and Crown.

On the evening of Sunday, 7 May 1826, Russell and Leney left the house with a plan to relieve a local farmer named Holloway of several sacks of grain, a more than uncharitable operation as well as an illegal one: Russell's father William had borrowed an amount of money from Holloway some time before in order to buy his son a house and was at the time paying his mortgage. The route to the Holloway farm took them past nearby Glydwish Wood (also known as Gleddish or Glydish Wood, and later by Thurston Hopkins as Glad Wish Wood) and, after arriving at the barn under the cover of darkness, the two men went inside and filled up two large hessian sacks with corn. Soon after, and loaded down with their ill-gotten gains, Russell and Leney made their way unseen back the way they had come. One sack was much heavier than the other and after carrying it for a while, Daniel Leney asked his landlord if he would relieve him for the rest of the journey. Russell agreed, although for some time before he had been complaining of sharp pains in his chest. With the lighter of the two loads, Leney went off ahead and after reaching a suitable point along the way where it was unlikely he would be observed by a passing villager who might happen to be abroad at that late hour, he waited for Ben Russell to catch up. Time passed and with no sign of the other man, Leney stashed the sack away and went back through the field looking for him. He soon came upon Russell lying on his back in the middle of the footpath leading from Holloway's farm, with the stolen sack of corn in the grass next to him. Unable to revive him, Leney hurried back to the house to raise the alarm.

Around one o'clock in the morning, Hannah Russell, together with Daniel Leney, made their way to her father-in-law's house and awoke William Russell by throwing clods of dirt at his bedroom window. After Russell senior had hurriedly dressed himself, they went out across the fields to where the prone body of Ben Russell still lay exactly as Leney had left him, and it was quite clear as they knelt over him that the young poacher was dead. Leney admitted that they had been involved in theft from the Holloway farm and, despite his shock at the sudden death of his landlord, was quite earnest about keeping the circumstances a secret. No doubt the fact that his son had been stealing from the person to whom he was in the process of repaying a large debt was the incentive that persuaded William Russell to agree to conceal the crime and between them, Russell, Hannah and Leney carried the body and the corn sacks to nearby Glydwish Wood, where they hid the stolen corn amongst the undergrowth and concealed the body in one of the old bell-pits, covering it over with a layer of brambles.

Unfortunately for the three conspirators, their plans rapidly fell apart. Shortly before dawn, as they made their way from Glydwish Wood back home, the two men met a neighbour, Thomas Hawkins, and were forced to invent a story on the spur of the moment that they were fetching the local doctor as Russell's daughter-in-law was unwell. The same morning, Daniel Leney was also seen by another local man, John Woodsell, walking in the direction of the wood. In order to explain the circumstances of Ben Russell's death, or at least account for his body being discovered in Glydwish Wood, Russell and Leney had decided to spin a story of the younger man arranging to meet a man who promised to sell him a 'tub' of gin. Soon Leney, returning from Glydwish, met John Woodsell again and revealed he had found Ben Russell lying dead inside the wood. The two men returned to Burwash where Leney repeated the story he had told Woodsell concerning the cask of spirit, and later the same day the body was recovered by a group of villagers lying on a pathway inside the wood not far from the bell-pit from which Leney had dragged it out of hiding earlier that same morning. It was taken to the house of Dr Thomas Evans, a local surgeon who, together with two colleagues, Robert Meek and Samuel Newington, performed a post-mortem.

Two days later, on 10 May 1826, an inquest was opened in the presence of John Cobb JP and Dr Evans presented his findings. The cause of death was arsenical poisoning: sixty grains of arsenic had seemingly been detected in the body of Benjamin Russell which the doctor stated had been administered via the dead man's food. It transpired that just over a month before, Hannah Russell had bought 'white mercury' in the village shop, ostensibly for killing mice in the bakery. Several of those present found themselves recalling threats that Hannah had made against her husband on a number of occasions and Hannah and Leney were quickly arrested: Hannah was charged with plotting to murder her husband while Leney was indicted as her accomplice. The controversial and convoluted trial took place at Lewes Assizes on Friday 28 July. Twenty-one witnesses gave evidence for the prosecution, testifying to the acrimonious relationship between the accused and her husband; Thomas Evans repeated his professional opinion that Benjamin Russell had been poisoned to death. The trial lasted for the whole day and at seven o'clock in the evening, the couple were found guilty and sentenced to death.

At this point a local doctor, Gideon Mantell, became interested in the case. Mantell is now familiar as an early dinosaur hunter and pioneer in the then fledgling science of palaeontology, but he was trained in medicine and expressed an opinion that the evidence for arsenic poisoning given by Dr Evans was inconclusive, that the amount of arsenic in Russell's body had been overestimated, and that Benjamin Russell's death had in fact been due to a heart attack. Mantell petitioned the trial judge but by this time Daniel Leney, protesting his innocence to the last, had already walked to the scaffold. Fortunately for Hannah Russell, her defence counsel, Mr Platt, was able to obtain a stay of execution after lodging a technical objection that the trial judge, Sir Robert Peel, had misdirected the jury. Early in November 1826, the case was referred to the Twelve Judges and on 13 February 1827 they directed that Hannah be granted an unconditional pardon. Whether Gideon Mantell's petition had any effect in influencing Sir Robert's decision is unclear. In more recent times, a modern examination of the evidence for poisoning has suggested that Mantell was wrong and that poisoning by arsenic was in fact the most likely explanation for the poacher's death. If so, then Hannah Russell may well have got away with murder, and the unfortunate Daniel Leney, who may or may not have been an accomplice, took her rightful place on the gallows instead.

In 1953, author and journalist Robert Thurston Hopkins, a Sussex Downsman and ghost hunter with a penchant for investigating haunted and screaming skulls, gave a lecture to the London Ghost Club. Thurston Hopkins, a man who by his own admission saw the world as 'a place of mysteries and miracles', was well qualified where allegedly haunted skeletons and bones were concerned: his father had once owned the death's head of William Corder, perpetrator of the notorious Murder in the Red Barn, a relic which, according to Thurston Hopkins senior, was capable of creating debilitating psychic attacks and was ultimately haunted by the ghostly presence of a mysterious apparition wearing a furry top hat and a blue overcoat with silver buttons. Following the meeting, Thurston Hopkins spoke with Peter Underwood, who

was to take over the Ghost Club Presidency in 1960, and the two men discussed an incident that had been included in the book *Adventures with Phantoms* that the speaker had issued in 1946. Described by writer Antony Hippisley Coxe as 'one of the most frightening passages I have ever read', this is seemingly a collective night-time encounter within the dark depths of eerie Glydwish Wood by three men with the terrifying ghost of the tragic farm labourer, Daniel Leney. Despite the passage of many years (the full story was not published in its entirety until the mid-1980s), it remains one of the most unsettling and thought-provoking experiences in the history of British psychical research.

Today, organised ghost walks around the haunted sites in our

Ghost hunter Robert Thurston Hopkins in later life, examining one of the haunted skulls of Warbleton Priory, East Sussex. The frightening ghost man of Glydwish Wood remains his most astonishing and controversial case. *(Peter Underwood Collection)*

towns and cities are a familiar and popular attraction, but they are in fact not a modern phenomenon: Robert Thurston Hopkins had the idea way back before the Second World War and in conjunction with the Southern Railway and Southdown Coach Services, organised and led night-time excursions in and around haunted sites across the South of England for much of the 1930s. Taking advantage of his extensive knowledge of the South Downs (he was the founder of the Society of Sussex Downsmen) as well as his own practical experience as a researcher and writer on the supernatural, Thurston Hopkins was able to visit a number of interesting and allegedly haunted locations, including the Lepers Pathway near Burpham and Arundel's Mickelgrove tower. However, it was a friendship with the great Rudyard Kipling during the time that the writer was living at Batemans, his country home near Burwash, which was to introduce Robert Thurston Hopkins to the tragic story of David Leney and provide the ghost hunter with one of his most astonishing adventures.

Kipling knew Glydwish Wood as it was only a mile or so from his house, and used to walk there, tracing the source of the stream that arises amongst the trees and eventually joins the River Dudwell which flows through Batemans' grounds. He described it as an evil place, full of secrets and menace, where 'a sense of ancient ferocity' still lingered. Such a spot was an ideal location for a midnight ghost walk and Thurston Hopkins lost no time in arranging to lead a party of walkers there as part of a local meeting. Rudyard Kipling, it seems, was not the only person who found the quiet and brooding atmosphere of Glydwish unsettling. Village locals from Burwash, some of whom had knowledge of the events that took place there in 1826, considered the wood to be haunted and avoided the area after dark. It was said to be frequented by unsettling sounds and noises: strange grunting voices and moaning, as well as the distinct sound of pattering feet moving through the undergrowth quite unlike the usual movement of nocturnal animals and the stirring of roosting birds. The woodland itself was wild, overgrown and in places treacherous: medieval bell-pits abandoned centuries ago survived as deep pools filled with stagnant water amongst the brambles and fallen branches, waiting to trap the unwary visitor, and in places the trees grew close, filling the wood with deep shadows even during the bright light of day. When Robert Thurston Hopkins and a party of nearly thirty walkers first saw its line of trees fronting the Burwash road by moonlight shortly after twelve o'clock one summer night, it looked forbidding and uninviting and a place where it was quite easy to imagine unquiet spirits might well walk.

Normally Thurston Hopkins was enthusiastic about exploring haunted buildings and byways, but on this occasion he was disinclined to venture further and stated his intention to lead the party past the wood and navigate a less forbidding route back towards distant Burwash. However, under pressure from a journalist friend named Blunden who, sensing the germ of a story, was keen to spend some time by himself in the allegedly haunted wood, the ghost hunter finally agreed to take the walkers around the edge of Glydwish Wood and meet the newspaperman on the far side: he would cut straight through the middle and mark his progress by blowing a police whistle at regular intervals, guided by Thurston Hopkins who would signal to Blunden with a whistle of his own. The group of walkers watched as the journalist made his way through the hedgerow bordering the wood and after a minute or so was lost to sight amongst the dark trees. In the stillness the sound of his progress through the dense undergrowth came back to them and soon the reassuring sound of Blunden's whistle convinced Thurston Hopkins that they could move off. Aided by the bright moonlight, the party crossed the deserted road and began following the tree line downhill in the general direction of Burwash village.

After twenty minutes or so, Thurston Hopkins realised that the regular blasts from Blunden's whistle had stopped. At the same time, another of the walkers trailing behind suggested that he could hear the sound of movement and footsteps, as though someone was following the journalist through the darkness; at one point he and others in the group claimed they had glimpsed the outline of a dark figure crossing an open fern glade momentarily in the moonlight. Halting the party, Thurston Hopkins listened and agreed that something was moving around amongst the trees some distance from where they were standing. Convinced that it was the newspaperman who had managed to lose himself in the darkness, the ghost hunter blew a long note on his whistle and listened for Blunden's reply. Neither he nor any of the paranormalists with him were prepared for the response: a terrible moaning cry, as of 'utter despair', which hung in the still night air before fading into silence. Now certain that the journalist had injured himself somewhere inside the pitch black woods, Thurston Hopkins instructed a doctor friend to take charge of the group, and together with another walker, he forced his way through the surrounding thicket and made off in the direction from which the sound had appeared to come.

After ten minutes of thrashing around in the treacherous darkness the two men came across the missing journalist stumbling through the undergrowth in a highly distressed and confused state. Unable to speak clearly and at first unsure as to the identity of his rescuers, Blunden appeared to have suffered a severe mental shock, the origins of which were only made chillingly clear once he had been led clear of the dark heart of Glydwish. After joining the rest of the party on the outskirts of the woodland, he gradually regained his composure. As he stood listening to the newspaperman's story, Robert Thurston Hopkins quickly realised that one of the most impressive first-hand supernatural encounters of his ghost-hunting career had seemingly taken place only a short distance from where he and his party now stood: Blunden claimed that in the depths of Glydwish Wood he had encountered the apparition of a dead man, and it had been like something out of a nightmare…

In his 1985 book *The Ghost Hunters*, Peter Underwood recalled the description that Thurston Hopkins had given him, based on the journalist's own account of his frightening experience. As Blunden picked his way through the dense undergrowth, he became aware of the sound of movement coming towards him out of the darkness, accompanied by an eerie moaning noise. Before he had time to think what might be approaching, the blackness under the trees seemed to suddenly come to life and, without warning, a hideous human-like form was rapidly bearing down on him: 'It seemed to resemble the shape of a man and it coughed and choked and moaned as it walked…the flesh of the face around the protruding eyes was withered and decayed, and the neck, exceptionally long and thin, it seemed, was horribly wizened.' As the figure stumbled forward it clutched and pulled at its throat with long fleshless fingers, the cadaverous skull-like head on the impossibly extended neck – in Thurston Hopkins own words – bobbing and swaying 'like the head of a daffodil shaken by the wind'.

The journalist stood, stunned with horror, as the dreadful vision cast about from side to side, seemingly unaware of his presence only yards away. Finally, after what seemed an eternity but was in fact only a matter of seconds, Blunden overcame his initial fear and, assuming that one of Thurston Hopkins' party was playing a practical joke, stepped forward and with a shout struck out at the figure with his walking stick. If Thurston Hopkins' account is to be believed, the blow made physical contact with the skeletal head, there was a distinct impression of the skull *crumbling* or shattering under the force of the impact, accompanied by the sound of broken fragments dropping onto the woodland floor. At this point, the newspaperman appeared to black out; his next recollection was of being led out of the wood by the ghost hunter and his companion, and a circle of anxious faces in the moonlight as the reunited party stood on the edge of the trees listening to his astonishing experience, odd glances being cast back by several of the company into the now thankfully still and silent darkness of Glydwish Wood.

It is easy to dismiss an account such as that described by Robert Thurston Hopkins as nothing but a piece of sensationalist invention. Other investigators and writers in the field of the paranormal, such as Harry Price and Elliot O'Donnell, have had far less dramatic claims for supernormal phenomena dismissed out of hand by sceptical critics. In 1939, as part of his *Fifty Years of Psychical Research*, a half-decade survey of organised scientific investigation, Price published an account of a blackout séance held at an unnamed address in London, where the nude figure of a deceased six-year-old girl named Rosalie allegedly materialised in a closed and sealed room. Price, who was present as an invited guest and whose knowledge of séance trickery and the antics of fake mediums was immense, was able to observe the 'materialisation' by the glow from a luminescent plaque and carry out a physical examination. The experience remained one of the most intriguing and mystifying of his entire career in psychical investigation, but to the sceptics it was simply a tall tale inserted into a somewhat staid pseudo-academic textbook as a 'hook' to sell the work to the popular press. Over the years other researchers including Trevor Hall, David Cohen, Paul Tabori and John Randall have become fascinated with the enigma of Rosalie with varying degrees of success; a genuinely supernatural explanation seems unlikely but ultimately to date the case remains unsolved.

As with the paranormal journalism of Harry Price, similarly many of the hundreds of paranormal experiences claimed by the Irishman Elliot O'Donnell, a contemporary of Price who was described on occasion as 'the Champ' and 'the greatest ghost hunter of all time', have been called into question. O'Donnell, who died in 1965 at the age of ninety-three, wrote several dozen books chronicling his ghostly adventures in his native Ireland, as well as in England and America, in which he claimed to have seen the face of a phantom in a mirror, witnessed the apparition of a skeleton looking in through a window, as well as an account of staying in a spectral hotel that had disappeared when he went back to collect his bags, and interviewing a man who claimed to have been shaved by a ghostly barber. Although he never claimed to have ridden on the ghost train that he discovered was said to drive at express speed through an American railway station, O'Donnell was adamant that he had had his first paranormal experience at the age of five when a strange tall figure with yellow eyes, 'long arms, and a head too big for its body' drifted through his bedroom in the family home in County Clare.

When Robert Thurston Hopkins included the eerie phantom of Glydwish Wood in his *Adventures with Phantoms*, he knew that such an encounter was more at home in the ghostly fiction of M.R. James rather than the modern world or organised scientific psychical research. However, when Peter Underwood met the former banker turned author at the Ghost Club in the early 1950s, he felt that the elder ghost hunter was completely convinced that the journalist Blunden had had some incredible and quite horrifying experience on that moonlit night over twenty years before. Underwood was also absolutely confident that Thurston Hopkins was totally sincere when he also told him, in confidence, that he had in fact seen the terrible ghost of Glydwish for himself…

A month later, so Thurston Hopkins disclosed, he, together with Mr Blandish, the same man who accompanied him on the desperate search for Blunden on their first visit, returned to Glydwish Wood. Taking advantage of the bright moonlight, the two men, both equipped with torches and walking sticks, walked the same route the party had taken four weeks before and, again shortly after midnight, they crossed the Burwash road and entered into the dark and forbidding woodland using approximately the same route that the journalist had taken into the very heart of that sinister and ominously silent place. By torchlight, Thurston Hopkins and Blunden negotiated their way between the trees and through the dense undergrowth; nothing appeared to stir and after some time it appeared that they would walk through the wood without incident. However, as they pressed on, both men became aware of the sound of what appeared to be something large and powerful moving uninhibited towards them through the darkness: there was the cracking and whipping sound of twigs and small branches marking the progress of an unseen person coming nearer, accompanied, so Thurston Hopkins recalled, by an intensely disturbing and high-pitched moaning noise.

Instantly on their guard, the ghost hunter and his companion ducked down behind a fallen tree and waited, uncertain as to whether they were about to encounter a local poacher or something far more sinister. Moments later, in a chilling recreation of the events of a month before, a man-like shape suddenly appeared out of the darkness, which was instantly illuminated by the beams from the two ghost-hunters' torches. The revelation stayed with Thurston Hopkins for the rest of his life: it was 'a ragged man, choking and clutching at its scraggy long neck, his eyes bulging out of a withered and almost fleshless face'. Unfazed by the sudden torchlight, the apparition blundered past them, seemingly unaware of their presence, and disappeared between the trees; after a few minutes Glydwish Wood was still, dark and silent once more. The two men came out from their hiding place and made a hasty retreat. To the end of his life, Thurston Hopkins never went back.

It is easy to see why the writer omitted including this experience in his original account of the haunting – it is so fantastic that it would never have been believed. Yet Thurston Hopkins was adamant that both he and his friend Blandish saw the ghost of a hanged man, who was almost certainly, in the ghost-hunter's opinion, the unquiet spirit of the wrongly executed Daniel Leney. Thurston Hopkins researched the trial and was convinced that something from the tragedy of those times continued to live on there, and the haunting cannot be pure invention, as the witnesses to the first incident involving the journalist Blunden, which included other newspapermen, would have been easily able to denounce the story upon publication of *Adventures with Phantoms* if the ghost hunter had not reported the incident exactly as it had occurred.

Like the case of the ghost child Rosalie, the haunting of Glydwish Wood remains unexplained. There appear to be no further reported sightings of the zombie-like figure since those eventful and unnerving nights back in the 1930s and the exact location of the sighting of the apparition is also equally obscure; Ghost Club member Godfrey Godden made an examination of the case in the 1970s but was unable to say exactly where the three men had their encounters. Undoubtedly something strange happened at Glydwish Wood all those years ago, and, if something does indeed walk there still, it, like the ghosts in American novelist Shirley Jackson's famous Hill House, walks there alone…

Consult: Antony D. Hippisley Coxe, *Haunted Britain* (Hutchinson & Co. Ltd, London, 1973); R. Thurston Hopkins, *Adventures with Phantoms* (Quality Press, London, 1946); Harry Price, *Fifty Years of Psychical Research* (Longmans, Green & Co. Ltd, London, 1939); D. Scott Rogo, *The Haunted House Handbook* (Tempo Books, New York, 1978); Peter Underwood, *The Ghost Hunters: Who They Are and What They Do* (Robert Hale, London, 1985).

The Silent Hitch-Hikers (1970s)

Solid human figures that purposely walk into the paths of moving cars and then vanish, together with mysterious passengers who disappear from closed vehicles, rank as some of the most disturbing of all paranormal experiences. Here we feature two classic British cases.

The phenomenon of the phantom hitch-hiker, the mysterious spectral traveller who disappears into thin air after being picked up by a passing motorist or motorcyclist, is a category of paranormal encounter that is known the world over – countries as diverse as Sweden, Pakistan, Canada, Korea and South Africa all have their own individual and specific hitch-hiker tales. One of the most famous sites in Britain, made notorious due to several separate encounters with an eerie roadside ghost over several years, is a section of the A229 between Maidstone and Chatham in Kent, more familiar to ghost hunters and paranormalists as Blue Bell Hill. Here the apparition of a young woman of indeterminate age has been encountered by several motorists beginning initially from incidents dating from the mid-1960s. As well as the original by-passed section, known as the Old Chatham Road, the modern dual-carriageway that later replaced it, as well other roads in the area, have been the scenes of eerie and inexplicable incidents.

The first investigator into the mystery of the Blue Bell Hill Girl, as the phenomenon is popularly known, was Tom Harber, a hospital switchboard operator, who collected several accounts from a dozen members of the public, tracing and interviewing the witnesses personally. In the early hours of the morning of 13 July 1974, Maurice Goodenough, a thirty-five-year-old bricklayer, was driving along the old A229 road at Blue Bell Hill when, without warning, the figure of a young woman suddenly appeared in the car's headlights as though she had risen up out of the roadway in front of him. As Goodenough desperately braked to avoid a collision, the car skidded, but he was unable to stop quickly and by the time the frightened motorist managed to pull his car to a halt he had registered an impact with the girl in the road. Getting out he ran back to where the crumpled figure lay in the middle of the carriageway and saw that the girl, who he estimated was around ten years of age, had cut knees and was bleeding from the head. Taking a rug from the car, Goodenough wrapped it around the prone and unresponsive girl and, carrying her to the side of the road, tried unsuccessfully to flag down several passing cars, all of whom proved to be either oblivious to the seriousness of the situation or unwilling to stop and help. Today, help would have been a simple mobile phone call away, but in the mid-1970s, alone on the lonely stretch of night-time road and with no public call box in sight, Maurice Goodenough found himself in a desperate situation. Unsure as to the severity of the victim's injuries, he decided against moving her again into the car and, leaving her wrapped in the travelling rug, he got back into his car and drove directly three miles further north to Rochester police station, where he informed the sergeant on duty about the accident. Soon police officers were back at Blue Bell Hill but the only thing which confirmed Maurice Goodenough's version of events was the travelling rug, now soaked by heavy rain, which still lay in the spot where the driver said he had left the prone and unmoving figure – of the young girl there was no sign, and enquires made at all the casualty departments of local hospitals in the area were unsuccessful in tracking down the injured pedestrian. Either the young girl had come to and wandered off by herself, or she had been seen and picked up by another motorist who had let the incident go unreported – or Maurice Goodenough had seemingly knocked down the ghostly Blue Bell Hill Girl.

In 1992, two more motorists had strange and disturbing experiences in the same area and within a fortnight of each other. Shortly before midnight on Sunday 8 November, Ian Sharpe, a coach driver from Maidstone in his mid-fifties, was driving his own car down the dual-carriageway section of the A229 at Blue Bell Hill when he saw in the distance ahead a figure standing in the middle of the road on his side of the central barrier. As he got closer he saw that the person was a woman who, to his utter horror, suddenly ran forward directly into the path of his vehicle. Like Maurice Goodenough nearly twenty years before, Sharpe was unable to stop and as he came upon the woman, travelling around 50mph, she turned and looked straight over her shoulder at him, went downwards and disappeared from view under the front of the car. Ian later described the woman as having a round face with shoulder-length fair hair, wearing a white-coloured coat over a roll-neck woollen sweater or jumper. Sharpe braked to a halt but on going back along the carriageway he was stunned to find no sign of the woman, either lying in the road or sprawled on the hard-shoulder or in the grass by the side of the road. As in the 1974 incident, there was no damage to the front of his car and police officers, who accompanied the distraught driver back to the scene of the 'accident', could find no evidence of either a collision or a casualty.

The section of the A229 at Blue Bell Hill, Kent, where coach driver Ian Sharpe encountered the apparition of a phantom woman in the early 1990s. *(Sean Tudor)*

Exactly two weeks later, on the evening of Sunday, 22 November 1992, nineteen-year-old Chris Dawkins was returning home after spending the afternoon watching the motor racing at Brands Hatch near Swanley. As he passed the Robin Hood Lane junction on the old Blue Bell Hill road, approximately a mile and a half north of the spot where Ian Sharpe had his encounter, the figure of a young woman suddenly ran out from between a line of parked cars directly into the path of his vehicle. Unable to react in time, Dawkins saw the woman stop in the road, turn and look directly at him and smile before dropping down and vanishing below the level of the car's bonnet. Like Sharpe a fortnight before, the teenager was horrified, not only at the violence of the collision but also finding, on getting out of the car, that the woman had seemingly vanished into thin air. Graham Dawkins, who answered his son's frantic call for help from a telephone box further up the road, found his son in a state of shock and convinced that somehow the woman was still under his car. Mr Dawkins, like the police who were called to the scene, could find no one…

Who is the eerie Blue Bell Hill Girl who has terrified motorists intermittently for the past forty years on these seemingly ordinary stretches of road, and what causes her to appear and disappear in such a startling and disturbing way in this particular part of the peaceful Kent countryside? Is she, as several people, including early researcher Tom Harber and local reporters and journalists have suggested, the unquiet spirit of a young twenty-two-year-old girl who lost her life only hours before her wedding in a fatal car accident that took place at this spot on the Old Chatham Road during the early winter of 1965? On the evening in question – Friday, 19 November 1965 – a Ford Cortina carrying four women returning home from a hen night celebration collided with a Jaguar motor car on a bend of the original A229 road at Blue Bell Hill. The two occupants of the Jaguar survived but three of the soon-to-be wedding party were killed, one at the scene, the other two dying shortly afterwards in hospital. Not surprisingly, such a violent tragedy as this soon became connected with ghost stories that began to circulate in the area soon after, and a number of accounts of an actual female hitch-hiker apparition picked up by passing motorists that were collected by Tom Harber have a direct connection to the 1965 accident. One witness, who Harber knew well and who he was able to interview within twenty-four hours of his experience, claimed to have picked up a female hitch-hiker who asked to be taken to an address in Maidstone. During the journey, the passenger, who appeared to be a solid flesh and blood person, spoke about her forthcoming wedding, which was due to take place the following day. The motorist dropped the woman off close to where she said she lived, but something about her demeanour caused suitable concern for the driver to make a specific trip a day or so later to check on her wellbeing. On arriving at the given address he found that a young girl matching her description had been killed in a car accident the previous year on the eve of her wedding, a year to the day that the unsuspecting motorist had given a lift to her phantom…

An urban legend or something more complex and far more sinister? Accounts of incidents such as this – which took place in 1966 – seem too good to be true and more suited to the realms of supernatural fiction than convincing and verifiable evidence for genuine paranormal phenomena. But is it possible for someone to actually give a lift to a ghost? Where the phenomenon of the ghostly vanishing hitch-hiker is concerned, the experience of Bedfordshire motorist Roy Fulton ranks as one of the most compelling and thought-provoking examples of this particular roadside phantom and the case is chilling and fascinating in equal measure.

Late on the evening of 12 October 1979, Fulton, a twenty-six-year-old carpet fitter from Dunstable, was driving home after playing in a darts match at a pub in Leighton Buzzard. It was a cold, misty Friday night and notions of ghosts and the supernatural were far from Fulton's mind: being an avid Liverpool FC fan, he was casting his thoughts ahead to the following day's match and the prospects of his favourite team. Driving along an unlit section of Station Road on the outskirts of Stanbridge, Fulton saw in the glare of the Mini van's headlights the figure of a young man standing on the nearside pavement thumbing for a lift and, guessing he was either going to Totternhoe or Dunstable, decided to pull over. Slowing down, he stopped in front of the hitch-hiker, who responded by walking along the pavement towards the van. He was casually dressed in dark trousers and wore a dark-coloured jumper with an open white-collared shirt. Nothing seemed out of the ordinary; the man looked pale but the only thing

Station Road, Stanbridge, Bedfordshire: Paul Adams stands on the spot where, one night in 1979, Dunstable carpet-fitter Roy Fulton picked up a phantom hitch-hiker. *(Isa Adams)*

that struck Fulton as slightly unusual was the shape of the youth's face, which he later described as being 'unusually long'. The hiker opened the van door and got in but when asked where he wanted to go, his only response was to point ahead further down the misty road. Fulton let in the Mini's clutch and the van pulled away.

The journey continued in silence for some minutes until Fulton decided to offer the youth a cigarette. It was the point where what had been a completely ordinary situation suddenly crossed over a threshold into the strange and frightening world of the unknown. As Fulton later recalled: 'I leant forward and picked up the packet of cigarettes [and] turned round to offer the lad one, *and that man or boy was not sitting there.*' Stunned, Fulton pulled the Mini to a halt and, turning on the interior light, looked into the back, thinking that the youth had somehow climbed into the rear of the van. There was nothing there – Roy Fulton was completely alone. Now terrified, Fulton drove 'like a bat out of Hell' to his local pub, The Glider in Lowther Road, Dunstable, where his entry into the bar, shaking and ashen-faced, was greeted initially with some levity by the landlord, Bill Stone, who asked jokily, 'What's the matter, Roy? Have you seen a ghost, or what?' '*I have,*' Fulton replied, 'I have seen a ghost,' and, after a large Scotch, proceeded to tell this strange and disturbing story.

Two things haunted Fulton about his experience – that the pale-faced youth was somehow part of an earlier traffic accident which had not been reported to the police, and secondly, in the tradition of fictional ghost stories, that the silent figure would somehow follow him home. In order to address these issues, later the same night Roy Fulton went to Dunstable police station, where Inspector Rowland was told the same account. Accustomed to hearing all manner of unusual stories, Rowland was unable to offer any explanation – no accident involving a hitch-hiker had been reported on that section of Station Road or nearby Peddar's Lane, either that day or in the proceeding weeks; neither, to the policeman's knowledge, had a similar account to Fulton's about a disappearing figure been local knowledge in the area. Fulton went home with his wife Sheila, the experience still weighing on his mind, to the point that the couple slept with the bedroom light on in order to alleviate the carpet-fitter's fear that the ghost would return.

Fulton's story made both local and national headlines – the *Dunstable Gazette* and later the *Sunday Express* picked up the story. All those who came into contact with Roy Fulton and heard him describe his experience were impressed with his sincerity, making the idea that he was perpetrating an elaborate hoax an unlikely one. Fulton was later interviewed by writer and researcher Michael Goss (who subsequently published what is to date the most complete and detailed account of the incident) and in 1985 took part in the respected television documentary series *Arthur C. Clarke's World of Strange Powers,* where he was interviewed on camera and featured in a reconstruction of his experience; on both occasions he told the same story without any deviations or embellishments – that one night in October 1979 he took a ghost for a ride. 'There's

Roy Fulton, photographed during the early 1980s. His encounter with a phantom hitch-hiker remains one of the most convincing on record. *(Michael Goss)*

obviously someone [*sic*] got in that motor,' Fulton would later state, 'and I do not know to this day what it was.'

Can we explain Roy Fulton's compelling and eerie experience? Was the person who climbed inside his Mini van the spirit of a dead pedestrian, some paranormally-induced hallucination, or a figment of his imagination? In the 1940s, British mathematician and psychical researcher George N.M. Tyrrell developed a theory of apparitions based on data collected as part of the Census of Hallucinations, the first large-scale questionnaire into sightings of ghosts and associated paranormal experiences carried out by the then fledgling Society for Psychical Research (SPR) in the closing decade of the nineteenth century. As part of his thesis – delivered as the seventh Myers Memorial Lecture before the Society in 1942 – Tyrrell devised a concept that he termed the 'Perfect Apparition', an imaginary collation of the many reported aspects (nineteen in total) of ghostly figures and forms that had been reported (and are still being reported to this day) as being experienced by members of the public over many years. These characteristics included the complete three-dimensional reality of the apparition, its ability to pick up real objects and open and close doors, touch people, be visible in mirrors, appear unexpectedly and ultimately suddenly vanish without trace, as well as have some aspect to it that on reflection strikes the person seeing the ghost as slightly odd or not quite right.

Although Tyrrell's creation was simply a way of demonstrating the bizarre and seemingly unknowable rules behind the numerous well reported and documented sightings of apparitions, many aspects of his theoretical 'perfect ghost' seem to apply to the strange silent man that got into Roy Fulton's van that October night in the late 1970s: the living 'flesh and blood' quality of the figure, the way it opened and closed the van door, its visibility in the vehicle's headlights, as well as the figure's curiously long and pale-looking face. Did the young carpet fitter encounter the 'Perfect Apparition' on the misty byways near Dunstable all those years ago, and what actually caused his experience?

In looking for parallels between the Stanbridge and Blue Bell Hill cases, it is interesting to note the presence of high-voltage power lines in the vicinity of the area where the apparitions were encountered, which suggests that somehow electrical fields generated in their immediate vicinity can possibly, under the right conditions, stimulate the appearance of phantom figures. At Stanbridge, a row of transmission-line towers crosses Station Road at exactly the point where Fulton said he picked up his mysterious silent passenger, and at Blue Bell Hill a similar line of pylons passes over the dual carriageway section of the A229 close to where the eerie woman ran into the path of Ian Sharpe's car. Here, however, the similarities stop and it is a fact that the spot where Chris Dawkins had his encounter was actually a mile and a half further north of these particular power lines. It must also be said that there are hundreds of locations where electricity pylons cross over British roads and only a handful of road ghost cases as convincing and eviden-tial as those of Blue Bell Hill, Stanbridge, as well as the next case at Stocksbridge in Yorkshire, where electricity towers are in close proximity to the allegedly haunted area. Where the Stanbridge case is concerned, what actually happened on the lonely roads of Bedfordshire that night we will now never know for sure – Roy Fulton died in December 2002 at the age of forty-nine, taking the secrets of the phantom hitch-hiker with him.

Consult: Paul Adams, *Haunted Luton* (The History Press, Stroud, 2012); John Fairley, *Arthur C. Clarke's World of Strange Powers* (Collins, London, 1984); Michael Goss, *The Evidence for Phantom Hitch-Hikers* (The Aquarian Press, Wellingborough, 1984); Damien O'Dell, *Paranormal Bedfordshire* (Amberley Publishing, Stroud, 2008).

Stocksbridge Bypass: The Road to Nowhere (1987-Present)

One of the most compelling and persistent British highway hauntings of the last quarter of the twen-tieth century concerns a section of newly constructed single-lane road crossing the lonely Pennine Hills between Sheffield and Manchester. The building of the A616 extension in the mid-1980s appeared to precipitate a series of strange incidents involving the sighting of frightening phantom figures that continues to the present day.

The South Yorkshire town of Stocksbridge lies eight and a half miles north-west of Sheffield on the eastern edge of the Peak District. Through traffic crossing the Pennines between Manchester and Sheffield originally passed through Stocksbridge and neighbouring Deepcar to the east, but in the mid-1980s, the A616 corridor route was created north of Sheffield heading west from the M1 motorway, with a bypass being constructed through the hills above the town's sprawling steelworks. The new road, built by civil engineering contractors McAlpine, was opened by the then Transport Minister, Paul Channon, on 13 May 1988 and has since garnered a some-what chilling reputation. Within three months, the first of many fatal accidents took place on this new section of highway – by 2002, twenty-five people had lost their lives on what quickly became known as the 'Killer Road'. Mixed with the tragedy were other stories, some of which had begun to circulate during the time that construction work was taking place in 1987: that the bypass route was haunted by the apparition of a mysterious monk-like figure that had been seen and had terrified several credible witnesses, including two serving policemen.

Shortly after midnight on 8 September 1987, two men, Steven Brookes and David Goldthorpe, both from the Constant security company, made what was for them a regular visit to the McAlpine construction site along the route of the new and still unopened Stocksbridge bypass. As they drove along Pearoyd Lane, a farm road above the town which now crossed the bypass cutting on a new concrete bridge, the security guards' attention was drawn to one of the large metal electricity pylons which, then as now, ran parallel with the line of the A616 road, fifty yards further up the hillside. As their Landrover approached the bridge (which was still under construction and impassable), Brookes and Goldthorpe saw what appeared to be a group of children moving around in a circle at the base of the nearest transmission line tower. Pulling the vehicle to a halt, they both got out and retraced their route, but by now the figures had disappeared. The men went up to the base of the tower and inspected the area by torchlight but there was no sign of the children, and strangely, although the mud around the metal columns was freshly turned over, they could find no footmarks or prints of any kind. Convinced that they had not been mistaken, the security guards stopped off at the temporary caravan site where several of the construction workers were living and enquired if anyone had seen children playing around the site that evening. Although no one had seen anything, Brookes and Goldthorpe were told that on several occasions, children's voices and the sound of singing had been heard, often late at night, along that section of the new road.

A short while later, the two security men completed another patrol of the construction site and again drove their Landrover up to the base of the Pearoyd Lane bridge. As they approached, both men could see the clear outline of what appeared to be a monk-like figure standing on part of the bridge structure that, to their knowledge, was completely inaccessible to members of the public. Convinced that someone was playing a trick, Steven Brookes got out of the Landrover and asked his companion to drive the vehicle onto the entrance ramp so that the headlights would shine directly along the length of the bridge and allow them to see what was going on. As David Goldthorpe swung the Landrover around, he was astonished to see revealed in the vehicle's headlights the tall figure of a man dressed in brown robes which looked almost identical to a monk's habit with a large cowl pulled up obscuring the head and face; even more disturbing was the fact that the powerful beams from the headlights seemed to pass straight through the figure. Before the security man had time to notice anything further, the apparition vanished. Terrified, Steven Brookes got back into the Landrover and they drove to the Constant company office where they telephoned the duty manager, Peter Owens. When he arrived, he found the two men distraught and both convinced that they had seen a ghost on the bypass construction site.

The haunted A616 Stocksbridge Bypass, South Yorkshire, where a phantom monk-like figure has been regularly seen since the late 1980s. *(Richard Bramall)*

First thing the following morning, Brookes and Goldthorpe went to Stocksbridge police station where they spoke to PC Dick Ellis, who knew both men through his dealings with the Constant security company. As nothing had been reported stolen and no crime had been committed, Ellis was unable to help and suggested, somewhat light-heartedly, that the men visit a priest who might be able to offer some form of guidance. Taking the policeman at his word, the two security guards, desperate for some kind of protection from what they considered was a force of evil on the Pearoyd Lane bridge, drove immediately to a nearby church, where their haranguing of the vicar and subsequent refusal to leave prompted a call to the police station, with the result that PC Ellis was sent to request the men to go home, and also to find some explanation for their unusual behaviour.

Three days later, on the evening of Friday, 11 September 1987, PC Dick Ellis accompanied by a Special Constable, John Beet, drove up to the Stocksbridge bypass construction site in their Vauxhall Astra patrol car. Their intention was to spend some time around the Pearoyd Lane bridge in the hope that whatever had spooked the two security guards, and which they believed had a perfectly natural explanation, would happen again. PC Ellis was convinced that the two Constant employees had been the victim of a practical joke, and as such was hoping to catch the culprits, if they showed up again, red-handed. On purpose, the two policemen had told colleagues that they were going to nearby Oughtibridge in order that some of the other policemen at the station wouldn't be tempted to come up and play a trick themselves. It was a warm evening with a clear sky and a bright full moon. Arriving from Deepcar, Ellis and Beet parked the car so that they had a good view towards the unopened bridge across the new cutting, and settled down to wait.

After a while, both policemen thought they could see something moving up on the bridge structure but an inspection on foot revealed nothing out of the ordinary. A short time later there appeared to be further movement and, taking a torch, PC Ellis climbed up a ladder onto the bridge deck, where he found that a sheet of polythene over a stack of concrete blocks had come loose and was blowing about in the breeze. Fixing it down, Ellis returned to the patrol car and the two men continued to sit in silence with the windows on both sides wound down. Not long after, Dick Ellis suddenly became intensely cold and had the frightening impression that a person was standing alongside the Astra with part of its body pressed through the window opening only a few inches from the side of his head. Ellis froze and found himself unable to speak. The sensation lasted only a few seconds when, suddenly, the figure alongside the car vanished and the policeman found himself able to move again. As he made to turn to speak to his colleague, John Beet let out a loud cry and recoiled away from his side of the car. Ellis jumped out and ran round to the far side of the Astra but there was nothing there. Beet claimed that at that moment, a figure had been pressed up against his side of the patrol car in the same fashion that Ellis had experienced only moments before. Dick Ellis fetched a torch and searched around and under the vehicle and also inspected the embankments in the immediate vicinity, but the two men were quite alone. He was convinced that, despite the darkness, no one could have approached the car and then got away without being seen by either Constable Beet or himself. Tellingly, both officers could see the tyre tracks of the Astra together with their own footprints in the mud where they had both walked up to previously inspect the Pearoyd Lane bridge, but there was no other physical sign of anything that would correspond to the experience that they had had only minutes before.

Unable to explain what had happened, both policemen got back into the Astra and Ellis drove up into Pearoyd Lane overlooking the new road cutting where, as before, they sat in the car with the engine and lights switched off. Suddenly, there came from the back of the vehicle what seemed to be a flurry of blows, as though the Astra was being struck violently by someone wielding a heavy stick or club. Both men jumped out but the noises ceased and it was clear that there was nothing in the vicinity of the patrol car that could have caused the disturbance. Now feeling decidedly uncomfortable, Ellis and Beet drove back to the Stocksbridge police station, where Dick Ellis entered a full report of their experiences in the station log. Subsequently, in the mid-1990s, PC Ellis was interviewed on camera for two paranormal-themed television programmes, Michael Aspel's *Strange But True?* (1994) and William Woollard's *Ghost Hunters* (1997); on both occasions he described the incident in considerable detail and maintained that both he and his companion experienced something that night that they could not explain.

As construction of the Stocksbridge bypass continued, there were further reports of strange and frightening happenings. One evening, a local builder, Graham Brooke, who at the time was training for a marathon, was running along the old road close to the construction site with his son, Nigel. As the two men made their way along the side of the road, they both became aware of a figure walking towards them in the roadway with its back to the oncoming traffic. As the figure got closer, Brooke was astonished to see that the person appeared to be walking *in* the road itself – about a foot length of both legs gave the impression of being buried or submerged in some way into the tarmac, as though the person were walking along a line that was now below the current level of the ground. The runner was able to describe the figure in some detail: dressed in old-fashioned-looking clothes, brown in colour, with a cape buttoned up with eyelets down the front, and carrying a large bag that trailed in the ground behind it; most disturbing of all was the face, or lack of it; featureless and black 'like a chap who comes out of the mine'. Both men saw the figure, and each was aware of an unpleasant musty smell that seemed to accompany it. As Brooke turned to speak to his son and then looked back, the man had gone.

Once the new bypass was opened, reports of a bizarre monk-like figure, seen by both drivers and pedestrians in the vicinity of the A616, began to appear with disturbing regularity. One afternoon, a young couple, David and Judi Simpson, were returning to Stocksbridge from a visit to relatives. As they drove along Pearoyd Lane and over the newly built road, both became aware of what appeared to be a grey featureless figure hovering in a field alongside the highway. As they watched, the apparition seemed to scuttle up the side of the grassy embankment and move across into the road and into the path of their oncoming car, where it instantly vanished. On another occasion, a local bus driver claimed to have seen what he described as a brown monkish figure running and moving at great speed around a field adjacent to the new bypass cutting, while lorry drivers parked up in the vicinity of the new bypass also reported seeing the apparition of a monk dressed in brown robes, and accompanied, as Graham and Nigel Brookes noted, by a rank and nauseating smell, akin to stagnant water or rotting rubbish.

Not surprisingly, the monkish appearance of the Stocksbridge ghost has resulted in attempts to find an explanation for the origins of the haunting in the local religious history of the area. In a similar scenario to the Black Monk of Pontefract case, which we will encounter in detail later on in the present book, it has been suggested that an answer may lie in a local legend that, centuries before, a monk from a local Cistercian order had broken his vows and as a result, on his death had been buried in un-consecrated ground in the vicinity of the new A616 highway. However, this historical angle, although seemingly a logical way of providing some framework in which to set the eerie Stocksbridge haunting, may be wide of the mark, and perhaps the true answer lies in the, at present, unknowable physics of the paranormal. A large number of British hauntings involving the appearance of ghostly monks and similar-looking apparitions have been reported from sites and locations with no previous monastic or ecclesiastical history.

In 1985, Sharon Grenny, a council tenant, was forced to flee with her family from their house in Sutcliffe Avenue, Grimsby, after several encounters with a faceless apparition that she described as being a monk-like person with a wide hood drawn up, obscuring its features. Two cases involving a similar monkish figure were researched by Paul Adams from separate locations in Luton, Bedfordshire. In the late 1970s, Jennifer Davies reported experiencing poltergeist phenomena accompanied by appearances of a frightening monk-like figure with a disfigured face in a 1960s-built tower block in the Hockwell Ring estate; while on the other side of the town, a haunting of a semi-detached house (built by construction firm Laings in 1977) that again features a hooded figure in a brown habit-like costume, seen regularly in the vicinity of the staircase and first-floor landing, was on-going at the time of writing. In all three cases, there is no previous history of monastic buildings or activity in the area, which seems to suggest that these monk-like ghosts owe their continuity of appearance to whatever forces or phenomena creates the paranormal hallucination, in the same way that the vast majority of haunting apparitions are described as being faceless or have their features obscured in some way.

As such, rather than being the spirit of a long-dead and seemingly wayward religious ascetic, the ghostly monk of Stocksbridge seems likely to be an incorrect interpretation of a common and countrywide paranormal manifestation. Why the haunting only commenced with the construction of the new bypass road, like the phenomena itself, remains a mystery.

Consult: Paul Adams, *Haunted Luton* (The History Press, Stroud, 2012); Peter A. Hough & Jenny Randles, *Strange But True?* (Piatkus, London, 1994).

Chapter Five

DISTURBING THE PAST

Haunted Stones and Other Strange Objects

On the Wings of the Pharaohs (1936)

The curse of the mummy's tomb is perhaps the most familiar of all extreme hauntings. Here we examine two famous cases of vengeance from beyond the grave associated with the land of ancient Egypt that involve a blending of both fact and fiction.

In early 1972, German writer Philipp Vandenberg carried out an interview with Dr Gama ed-Din Mehrez, at that time the Director of the Department of Antiquities at the Cairo Museum. Vandenberg was researching for a book that examined the claims for the strange deaths of persons associated with the excavation of royal remains in Egypt over the previous fifty years, and one of the most high-profile of these 'mummy's curse' cases was, and still is, the events surrounding the discovery by English archaeologist Howard Carter of the tomb of the boy king Tutankhamun in 1922. *Der Fluch der Pharaonen* was published the following year and an English translation, *The Curse of the Pharaohs*, was issued by Hodder and Stoughton in 1975. Dr Mehrez told Vandenberg that he had no belief in the curse and, citing his own lifelong association with tombs and mummies, suggested that coincidence and the will to believe were behind a catalogue of unusual happenings associated with King Tut which stretched back over the preceding half century. Four weeks later, in March 1972, Mehrez supervised the loading of over fifty of the Tutankhamun treasures, including the iconic gold burial mask, onto an RAF Vulcan in order for them to be flown to London where the British Museum was holding a major exhibition. While the plane was in the air, Dr Mehrez collapsed and died of a heart attack at the age of fifty-two...

Stories of vengeful ghosts associated with the curse of the mummy's tomb undoubtedly began with the death of George Edward Herbert, 5th Earl of Carnarvon, on

5 April 1923, five weeks after the official opening of the tomb of Tutankhamun. Lord Carnarvon had become interested in Egyptology in 1907 while taking winter holidays at a resort in Luxor, where the warm dry air alleviated breathing problems associated with a car accident that took place in the spa town of Bad Schwalbach, Germany, six years before. Carnarvon began funding exploration work in the Valley of the Kings in the hope of discovering a hidden tomb containing a hoard of valuable antiques and employed Howard Carter, an artist and archaeological draughtsman who had come to Egypt as a teenager, as his adviser. Carter was a former employee in the Antiquities Service and had gained experience as a practical Egyptologist through working as an assistant to high-profile archaeologists Edouard Naville and William Flinders Petrie, the first incumbent of the chair of Edwards Professor of Egyptian Archaeology at University College, London. He worked for Carnarvon for fifteen years and on 4 November 1922, in an untouched area of the Valley of the Kings, made the momentous discovery that was to radiate around the world: a small flight of stone steps that led to the unrifled tomb of the boy pharaoh, Tutankhamun.

Lord Carnarvon arrived in Egypt at the end of the month and on 26 November the two men entered not only the last resting place of the 18th Dynasty king but also the pages of history. Four months later, after quarrelling bitterly with Carter, Carnarvon suffered a mosquito bite on the face; the wound became infected and he developed blood poisoning. The Earl lapsed into a coma and died at the relatively young age of fifty-seven in his suite at the Continental Savoy Hotel in Cairo shortly before two o'clock on the morning of 5 April 1923: at the exact moment the electric lights in the hotel and across the city flickered and went out, while over 2,000 miles away, at Highclere Castle, the family seat in Hampshire, Carnarvon's fox-terrier, Susan, howled mournfully and died like her master. Newspaper editors quickly fanned the flames of the paranormal and despite the claim (made many years later by one of Howard Carter's security guards) that the archaeologist had invented the story of a curse to keep sightseers and thieves away, the revenge of the mummy's tomb had seemingly begun.

By the beginning of the Second World War, over the course of a fifteen-year period, over a dozen persons who were involved in some way with the opening of the tomb of Tutankhamun, either as invited guests or members of Carter's and Carnarvon's team, were dead. They included Arthur Mace, Howard Carter's assistant who died of arsenic poisoning in 1928; the Hon. Richard Bethell, Carter's secretary, who Harry Price invited to a ghost hunt at Borley Rectory in 1929, the same year that Bethell was found dead of a heart attack in the bedroom of his London club and whose father committed suicide a few weeks later; railroad executive George Jay Gould, who died of pneumonia in 1923 after spending a day visiting the tomb; Sir Ernest Budge, Keeper of Egyptian Antiquities at the British Museum, found dead at home in 1934; and Howard Carter himself, who died of cancer at his Kensington apartment on 2 March 1939 at the age of sixty-four. Writing about the mysteries of Egypt for *The Unexplained* magazine in the early 1980s, journalist Humphrey Evans summed up the tantalising ambiguity of the case when he wrote: 'Perhaps that is all it was, the curse of Tutankhamun, a hoax that suddenly acquired a serious focus at Carnarvon's death. Perhaps public attention itself has produced an artificially heightened awareness of every incident that has apparently confirmed the existence of the curse. Or perhaps Tutankhamun should have been left undisturbed…'.

Not surprisingly, Victorian novelists with a penchant for ghost stories and Gothic fantasy had found inspiration in the dusty tombs of the Pharaohs long before the strange events in the Valley of the Kings in 1923. In his post-*Dracula* novel *The Jewel of Seven Stars* (1903), filmed by Hammer seventy years later as *Blood from the Mummy's Tomb* (1971), Bram Stoker resurrected the ancient mummy of Egyptian Queen Tera, and the footsteps of vengeful cloth-wrapped feet echoed through similar stories and screenplays for much of the twentieth century including the 1966 film novelisation of *Curse of the Mummy's Tomb* (also by Hammer Films) of John Burke, horror master Guy N. Smith's 1983 novel *Accursed*, and Anne Rice's *The Mummy, or Ramses the Damned* (1989).

Fourteen years after the death of Lord Carnarvon, an article in the edition of *The Scotsman* for 10 April 1937 showed that perhaps there was more truth to stories of strange happenings associated with the disturbed tombs and mummies of Ancient Egypt than most people would give credit. Under the headline 'Curse of the Pharaohs', the newspaper gave details of a meeting held at the Edinburgh Psychic College the previous evening during which Mrs Boardman, a clairvoyant from London, gave a chilling prediction to the guest speaker who a short time before had delivered a lecture at the college. That person was Sir Alexander Seton, and the medium's warning related directly to the subject of his talk, a mysterious haunted bone that Sir Alexander claimed was possessed with eerie psychic powers. 'I feel that that bone should be got away in the next six weeks,' Mrs Boardman told reporters. 'It has come very strongly and most emphatically that if it is not got away by six weeks, blindness will come upon those who touch it.' The psychic saw a dark beckoning hand wearing a ring and it was several minutes before the sinister presence left her and she was able to continue with the scheduled platform demonstration. When told by reporters of the medium's warning, the Baronet was non-committal. 'I am absolutely and entirely open-minded… I refuse to be drawn into any controversy, because things have taken place which I cannot explain.' As we will see, the experiences of Sir Alexander and Lady Seton read like something from the pages of supernatural fiction, but this is an extreme haunting that many have claimed proves that the sinister curse of the Pharaohs is chillingly real.

Sir Alexander Hay Seton, the 10th Baron of Abercorn and Armour Bearer to the Queen, and informally known as 'Sandy', was born in 1904. The Setons were an ancient Scottish family and the Baronetcy can be traced back to Sir Walter Seton in 1663 during the reign of King James VI. The family at one time owned a large estate of land in Linlithgow but by the early twentieth century much of this had been sold, with the result that the title was little more than an echo of a once rich and historic past. In 1927, Sir Alexander married Zeyla Sanderson and the couple lived for a time at Prestonfield House, Duddingston, before moving to a modest three-storey terraced house, No. 15 Learmonth Gardens, in the Craigleith district of Edinburgh. In 1936, the Setons went on a sightseeing tour of Egypt and Sir Alexander sold an account of his journey and travels to a Glasgow newspaper. The Setons visited the temple at Luxor and also spent a day in the Valley of the Kings where they toured a number of tombs including that of Tutankhamun. The harsh barren valley was something of an anti-climax and although Seton found the famous tomb of the boy king interesting, he and his wife were glad to return to the more luxurious surroundings of the Mena Hotel on the edge of the desert only a short walk from the Sphinx and the Great Pyramid. There, the Setons learnt from Abdul, one of the hotel workers, that a recently uncovered tomb was in the process of being excavated quite close to the pyramids, and for an extra fee, the Egyptian's brother could arrange for them to be shown around the inside out of hours before the archaeologists and their workers arrived. Following his experiences in the Valley of the Kings, Sir Alexander was nonplussed about spending more time inside another dusty burial place, particularly as the tomb was historically of little importance, but Zeyla Seton eventually persuaded her husband to accompany her and, putting aside the vague feelings of disquiet, the couple agreed to make the visit on the following morning.

After an early breakfast, the Setons accompanied their guide out to an area within the shadow of the Great Pyramid where the non-descript tomb of a nameless but wealthy Egyptian woman was in the final stages of being cleared. At one time in the distant past, the tomb had been flooded by the River Nile and the excavation of the underground chamber had involved digging out large quantities of solidified mud which had caused widespread damage to the interior. The couple were shown down a narrow flight of some thirty stone steps cut into the floor of the valley and into a small, cramped and airless room where the remains of the occupant still lay *in-situ* on a stone slab on the floor. Sir Alexander looked with fascination at the fragile skeleton whose skull, leg bones and spine stood out against the dark centuries-old mud and, as he glanced around the interior of the tomb, the Scottish lord had a sudden and immediate sensation of the past. After a while, the couple felt the need to re-join the twentieth century and made their way back up the flight of stone steps and into the bright morning sunlight. While he stood smoking a much-needed cigarette, Zeyla Seton, who was clearly enthralled by the experience, went back into the tomb for a final look round, after which she posed for a photograph and the couple went back to their hotel.

That evening after a bath and evening meal, Zeyla Seton admitted to her husband that she had obtained a unique souvenir of their visit to the mysterious tomb that morning and produced a small object. During her brief return to the underground chamber she had removed a small bone from the crumbling skeleton on the slab and now handed it to her husband. 'She showed it to me and to my eyes it looked like a

Sir Alexander and Lady Zeyla Seton examining the family coat of arms in the Seton Collegiate Church at Longnidry, East Lothian, Scotland. Both felt that the haunted sacrum bone exerted an evil influence on their lives. *(Peter Underwood Collection)*

digestive biscuit,' he later wrote, 'apart from it being slightly convex and the shape of a heart.' The relic was actually a sacrum, a triangular pelvic bone located at the base of the spine. After a cursory examination, the bone was packed away into one of his wife's travelling trunks and for the rest of their holiday and during the return journey, Sir Alexander never gave the object another thought. However, their trip to the tomb and Zeyla Seton's removal of the bone was to be a sequence of actions that the Earl would later come to seriously regret...

One evening shortly after returning to Scotland, the couple were entertaining some friends at Learmonth Gardens, and during their meal as part of her reminiscences of their recent holiday, Lady Seton produced the sacrum for the inspection of their guests. The relic was looked on with some amusement and Sir Alexander, as part of the light-hearted atmosphere, decided to improvise a display case for the bone using an empty glass-fronted wooden case that had once contained a carriage clock. The small cabinet was placed on a table in the dining room and the party subsequently retired to the drawing room without giving the sacrum bone another thought. An hour later the Seton's guests were leaving when, at the moment they were about to walk down the short pathway from the front door to the street, a section of stone coping from the roof parapet over one of the first-floor windows came loose and fell with an enormous crash into the garden below, narrowly missing the departing guests. 'Whether this can be connected with the

Bone or not is difficult to say,' Seton reflected, 'but it certainly scared us and was hard to explain.' Coincidence or not, a short while afterwards a chain of strange and inexplicable happenings began to take place inside the house in Learmonth Gardens.

One night during the following week after the household had retired to bed, the Seton's live-in nanny, Miss Clark, who was employed to look after their five-year-old daughter Egidia, came to their bedroom door and with some alarm claimed she had heard what she assumed was a burglar moving about in the drawing room downstairs, where by this time the sacrum bone complete with its display case had been moved and now stood to one side on a small table. Taking a poker from the fire grate, Sir Alexander went down to investigate but found nothing out of place and the lower floor of the house empty. Heavy rain at that moment was beating against the front windows of the house and, deciding that this was what the nanny had heard, he went back to bed. The following morning, the couple made an unusual discovery: the corner table on which the sacrum was kept was found overturned on its side and the case together with the bone lay scattered on the floor. Seton recalled that during the night he had had a vague dream-like recollection of hearing a brief noise that may well have been the table falling, caused by, to his mind, the vibration from passing traffic, although Zeyla Seton was more inclined to put the incident down to her husband's seeming clumsiness while moving about the darkened house investigating the non-existent burglar.

Soon strange noises and other unusual happenings began to be a regular occurrence inside the house in Learmonth Gardens. The Setons became disturbed at night by sounds they could not explain. On one occasion when alone in the house, the couple both heard the sound of someone walking on the stairs which Zeyla Seton concluded was their nanny returning early from an evening out; when she went to see if everything was alright there was no one there and the nanny came back at her pre-arranged time a short while later. A few days after the incident of the footsteps on the stairs, Alasdair Black, a nephew of the Setons, spent a few days with the couple in Edinburgh and was put up in a spare bedroom. One night while coming out of the downstairs toilet into the hallway, the young man saw a figure dressed in what he later described as unusual-looking clothes walking up the stairs into the upper part of the house. At this point, although unable to explain both the footsteps and the sheeted figure, the Earl was more inclined to believe that the disturbances were due to someone attempting to steal items from the house, including a valuable collection of snuff boxes kept in the drawing room, rather than a haunting presence; but, convinced that something out of the ordinary was taking place, Seton decided to hold a vigil the following night in the hope of seeing something for himself.

After the rest of the household had retired, Sir Alexander took up a position on the upstairs landing and settled down to wait. Downstairs the drawing-room door and windows were locked and Seton had a clear view of the wide hallway and staircase where much of the unexplained activity had been concentrated in recent days. Several hours passed with not the slightest disturbance, by which time the Scotsman began to feel slightly foolish and, with a last glance at the drawing-room door, finally went to bed in the early hours of the morning. He had not been asleep long when he was shaken awake by his anxious wife: both she and the nanny had heard noises and were convinced that somebody was moving about downstairs.

Snatching up a loaded revolver from his bedside drawer, Seton quickly went downstairs, but there was no sign of an intruder in any of the rooms leading off the hallway and the door to the drawing room was still locked shut as the Earl had left it several hours before. Calling up to his wife, who fetched the key from her husband's dressing-gown pocket, the room was unlocked and, calling out a challenge, Seton threw open the door and switched on the lights. Neither he nor Zeyla Seton was prepared for the sight that greeted their eyes. The room had been ransacked: furniture overturned, books and papers swept from bookcases onto the floor, and ornaments disturbed; but incredibly there was no sign of a forced entry from outside – the sash windows were unbroken and remained securely fastened, access through the chimney was impossible, and the room door, for which Sir Alexander had the only key, had been locked the entire time. As he surveyed the damage and began righting fallen chairs, the Scotsman came to the only conclusion he could make (and perhaps one that had been in the back of his mind for some time) that some psychic or supernatural force had been unleashed inside the room, and that the enigmatic sacrum bone, which remained untouched inside its glass case in the centre of the chaos, was its focal point.

Over the course of several weeks following this watershed incident, the Setons continued to experience irregular disturbances, and all the time these inexplicable happenings took place in the immediate vicinity of the mysterious Egyptian bone. After periods of inactivity lasting several days, noises and the sounds of movement would disturb the family during the night hours and items of furniture were subsequently found moved or overturned. At one point, the sacrum together with items that were found to be regularly affected by its presence were moved to another part of the house, but despite the change of location, the regular phenomena continued to take place: on one occasion, Sir Alexander found that one of the legs of the ornamental table on which the case containing the sacrum bone rested was cracked and distorted, as though it had been subjected to an immense pressure or force. Now tired of the sinister object's continued presence in the house, Seton decided to get rid of it, but this provoked a storm of disapproval from Zeyla Seton, and was the instigator of several heated arguments that were now regularly afflicting what was an already strained and difficult relationship.

The momentous events in the Valley of the Kings in 1923 went on to create a wave of Egyptomania in Britain during the 1920s and in a post-Tutankhamun environment, the strange happenings associated with the Seton sacrum were unsurprisingly of great interest to the sensationalist side of the country's press. For a time both the story and the bone itself became the province of first the Scottish, and later, the

English and American newspapers, with the resultant publicity creating a mythology very reminiscent of the stories associated with the alleged happenings connected with Lord Carnarvon and Howard Carter. A reporter from the *Daily Express* who borrowed the relic for a week was later involved in a car accident, while another journalist from the Scottish *Daily Mail* who again took possession of the sacrum in order to have it photographed for the newspaper, needed an emergency operation for peritonitis only days after returning it to its owners. Although the Earl was initially amused by the press reaction, it coincided with events that would ultimately lead to the breakdown of his marriage to Zeyla Seton, and in the increasingly strained atmosphere of Learmonth Gardens, the continued press sensationalism soon became intolerable.

At the same time, the seemingly haunted sacrum bone was still making its eerie and unwelcome presence felt in the house. One day shortly before Christmas 1936, the couple quarrelled bitterly in front of their daughter's nanny with the result that Zeyla left with Egidia to stay with her parents. Following this 'domestic scene', Seton decided to cool off at his club and returned to the house later that evening to find the nanny, Janet Clark, in a state of shock. Around six o'clock she had been terrified by violent sounds of disorder coming from the drawing room including the crash of breaking glass, and had been so frightened that she had locked herself in the kitchen and had not had the courage to come out until her employer's return. Expecting to find that the room had again been trashed by a psychic attack, Seton was suitably amazed to see that all was in order and that the disturbance was centred solely on the mysterious bone itself: the ornamental table had been over turned and broken as had the former clock case, and lying amongst the shattered glass was the sacrum, itself now broken into five separate pieces.

Over the Christmas period, the couple affected a reunion, but the sudden and violent disturbances continued unabated. During a Boxing Day dinner party, the sacrum gave the Setons' guests a chilling display of its supernatural power. 'Whilst we were talking, and a fresh round of drinks were being served, the entire bone, table and all, went hurtling onto the wall opposite, with a terrific thump. No one was standing near it, nor did anyone see it happen – it just happened!' Seton later wrote. A maid and one of the female guests fainted; Sir Alexander left the bone where it had fallen and the party moved to another room.

By the time Sir Alexander Seton stood before an audience at the Edinburgh Psychic College in Heriot Row, just over three months later on the evening of Friday, 9 April 1937, with the sacrum on the table in front of him to discuss the experiences of both himself and his family, the catalogue of unsettling experiences and incidents had expanded still further to include two mysterious fires and further sightings of the eerie robed apparition; a surgeon friend of the Setons who had taken the pieces of the bone away to cement them together, claimed that the first night the relic lay in his house, a maid had broken her leg running away from a ghostly figure; while at Learmonth Gardens, both the Earl and his wife had succumbed to sudden and uncharacteristic periods of ill health; so much so that even before that evening's impromptu warning of impending danger, the couple had already given notice of their agreement that the sacrum had to go. 'I believe my family has been haunted by a sacred bone, part of the skeleton of a Pharaoh, that we acquired while on holiday in Egypt last year,' Seton had told a reporter from the *Daily Mirror* the previous week. 'That bone is going to be replaced in the tomb we took it from as quickly as possible. Lady Seton is making the trip herself to ensure that it gets there. This ghastly business has got to stop, and we are taking no chances.'

Despite the steadfast talk of action, this proposed pilgrimage to the nameless tomb at Giza was never made. Although the most likely reason is that the financial outlay for another trip abroad was beyond the couple, it seems clear that despite the horrors associated with its keeping, Zeyla Seton was reluctant to part with the mysterious relic, and for a time it continued to remain with the Setons at Learmonth Gardens. The Earl received many letters in connection with his strange experiences offering supposed explanations and advice, one of which Seton claimed was written by Howard Carter himself. '[He] asked me to respect his confidence by not publishing its contents, but he assured me that things quite inexplicable like this could happen, indeed had happened and will go on happening.'

Eventually things came to a head and a resolution was made that rather than return it to its original resting place, the bone would be destroyed completely. It seems that this was not a joint decision and that Sir Alexander Seton took it upon himself to rid the family of its unnatural and harmful effects. 'Zeyla could not forgive me for destroying the Bone and it did not help our already rocky marriage at all,' he later wrote, but the Earl had made up his mind that the sinister relic had to go and taking advantage of his wife's absence from the house, he put his plan into effect. Having obtained permission from the Roman Catholic authorities, Seton's uncle, a priest at St Benedict's Abbey at Fort Augustus on the south shore of Loch Ness, visited the house and performed a service of exorcism on the bone; the sacrum was then taken into the kitchen and in front of Janet Clark, Seton placed it in the fireplace and they both watched it burn. Eventually its charred remains were broken up and thrown out with the ashes from the grate.

Sir Alexander and Lady Zeyla Seton were divorced in 1939. Both remarried, Sir Alexander twice, although their lives apart seemed to be filled with ill-health, financial problems and unhappiness. Seton married Julia Clements, a noted writer and expert on flower arranging, on 30 July 1962 but the couple were only together for a few months; the 10th Baronet of Abercorn died on 7 February 1963 aged fifty-nine, the same year as his former wife, Zeyla. Seton himself appears to have had a premonition of his own death and advised the new Lady Seton on their honeymoon that he didn't have long to live; Julia Clements outlived her husband for many years and died on 1 November 2010, at the age of 104.

Although the curse of the stolen sacrum was played down by other members of the Seton family, particularly the actor Sir Bruce Seton, who succeeded to the title on his brother's death, Sir Alexander Seton came to believe that contact with the relic had exerted an evil influence on his life and was at the root of much of his later ill-fortune. In an unpublished autobiography *Transgressions of a Baronet*, extracts of which have appeared on the Internet in recent years, Seton had cause to reflect on the many incidents following the eventful trip to Egypt in 1936. 'I can give no answer as to what caused these mysterious happenings but to my mind, there was some strange power released that we humans are apt to laugh at, but which was [so] very real! Looking back… I still think it was one of the most horrible experiences that I have been through, happening as it did both in the daytime and the night. My own interpretation of the matter is that through some uncanny power of religion it was brought under destructive control but if – and I emphasise the word "if" – it really did carry a curse, as many people thought, the curse certainly did not end when I destroyed the Bone by fire, and from 1936 onwards trouble, sometimes grave, seemed to be always around the corner… and altogether life was very difficult.'

Did the modern-day representatives of a distinguished Highland family bring a curse upon themselves by stealing part of an ancient Egyptian skeleton, or is this 'curse of the Pharaohs' a tall tale that got out of hand? It is true that in order to bring in additional funds, the Earl did sell accounts of his foreign trips to the Scottish news-papers, and it has to be considered whether in fact the legend of the haunted sacrum started life as a 'silly season' story pitched as a light-hearted piece of money-raising that became fanned by the flames of media hype and sensationalism. Today all the players in this bizarre drama are gone and, as with two other cases in our survey – the haunt-ings at Cheltenham and Hinton Ampner – we have to rely mainly on a single narrative as the primary source of evidence in the case, an unsatisfactory situation where alleged hauntings and paranormal phenomena are concerned.

However, in instances such as this, the quality of the material and the integrity of the person presenting it can make up for a lack of independent testimony, and there seems no reason to doubt the sequence of events as presented in Sir Alexander Seton's manuscript. Although very young at the time, Egidia Seton, who later married the publisher Norman Haynes (died 2007), always believed that the sacrum was an evil object, while the Setons' former nanny, Janet Clarke, who was interviewed in 1965, two years after the death of her old employer, confirmed a number of the happenings as reported by Sir Alexander, including the destruction of the bone in the kitchen fireplace at Learmonth Gardens. Perhaps a way of assessing the integrity of the story of the haunted Seton sacrum is to compare it with another instance of an allegedly cursed Egyptian relic, one whose notoriety stretches back beyond even the discovery of Tutankhamun and the death of Lord Carnarvon…

Among several disparate news articles on the front page of the *Daily Mirror* for Friday, 2 September 1904, which included reports of two whales stranded on a beach at Blackpool, the suicide of a music hall artiste from Stoke Newington, and the escape of the eldest daughter of King Leopold II of Belgium from a lunatic asylum, was an unusual photograph, the report of which the day before in the same newspaper had sent crowds of several hundred sightseers on a bizarre pilgrimage to the First Egyptian Room of the British Museum. The object of curiosity was what the *Daily Mirror* described as being a 'haunted' mummy case, whose history 'from its discovery to the time of its housing in the Museum, is one of death and disaster'. A few weeks before, a London photographer, Mr W.A. Mansell, had cause to photograph the case on behalf of a client interested in Egyptology, and a series of personal accidents involving both himself and his family during and after the visit seemed to prove that the mysterious relic was living up to its dangerous and unenviable reputation. 'Can scientists or spiritualists offer any possible explanation of [*sic*] this extraordinary series of disasters?' the *Daily Mirror* asked its readers. Today, nearly 100 years later, the answers are more forthcoming than they were for Londoners at the time, who quickly became enthralled by another mysterious mummy mystery.

By the time ghost hunter and author Peter Underwood included an account of what is now commonly referred to as the 'Unlucky Mummy' in his 1973 gazetteer *Haunted London*, the first book of its kind to record the capital's supernatural history, the story was easily '[one] of the most interesting cases of haunting in London'. The object of this attention, as well as the focal point for allegedly paranormal forces is, then as now, a wooden coffin lid that was made to cover the mummified body of a high ranking and unidentified Egyptian woman, most likely a priestess from the temple of the sun god Amen-ra, and which dates to around the end of the 21st Dynasty, some 2,900 years ago. The coffin lid was discovered at Thebes sometime in the latter half of the nineteenth century and was presented to the British Museum in Bloomsbury in July 1889 by Mrs Warwick Hunt on behalf of the owner, Arthur F. Wheeler. The whereabouts of the mummy to which it belongs is unknown – it is said to have remained in Egypt but conceivably could have been sold for use at an 'unwrapping party', a society event that became something of a craze in Victorian Britain.

The coffin lid was placed on display soon after its acquisition by the Museum and during the course of only a few brief years, judging by the contents of the *Daily Mirror* article, a macabre history of unnatural happenings was quickly established:

> The gentleman who bought it from its Arab finder in 1864 lost his fortune within two weeks, and shortly afterwards died. Two of his servants, who handled the coffin, died within twelve months. A third has lost his arm, owing to a gunshot wound. On being transferred to London the case brought unmeasured misfortunes to its new owner. Then came a startling development, which suggested a connection between these disasters and the mummy case.

The development, possibly with a factual basis, came via a photographer commissioned to take a photograph of the coffin lid and on whose camera plate appeared the face of a

living Egyptian woman whose features 'wore an aspect of horrid malignity'. So disturbed
was the man by this discovery that he is said to have returned home and committed suicide shortly afterwards, and a photograph, purported to be this very image, 'confirmation
of one of the most curious details of the story', was included in the museum display case
with the coffin lid at the time the original *Daily Mirror* story appeared in 1904.

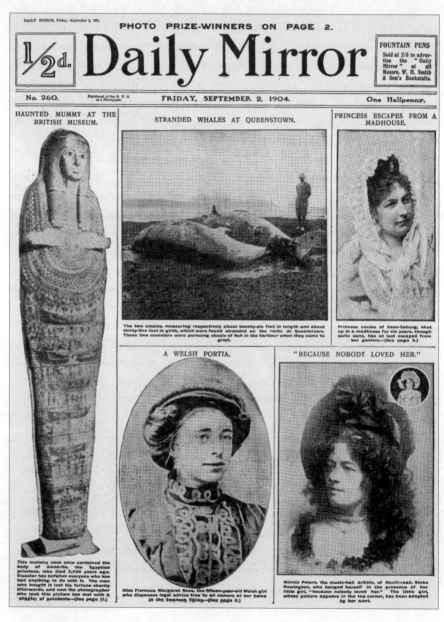

The British Museum's famous 'Unlucky Mummy', making the front page of the *Daily Mirror* for
2 September 1904. (*UKpressonline*)

As well as being the alleged cause of accidents and personal misfortune, the mummy case itself seemingly became the haunt of sinister apparitions and phantom figures, with the result that several English ghost hunters have become interested in the case. Robert Thurston Hopkins, who we have already encountered in connection with the Corder skull and the haunting of Glydwish Wood, claimed to have interviewed a British Museum keeper who admitted to seeing a figure with 'a horrible yellow face' rise up out of the bottom half of the coffin lid one evening while alone in the First Egyptian Room, and that other members of the museum staff reported hearing sobbing sounds and knocking noises coming from the vicinity of the exhibit on occasions. Another Englishman, James Wentworth Day, the 'sporting ghost hunter' who died in 1983 and whose investigations included the Theatre Royal, Drury Lane, Glamis Castle, the much haunted chapel at St Peter's on the Wall at Bradwell-on-Sea, and the ruins of Borley Rectory, was another researcher who became fascinated with the Amen-ra mystery. Wentworth Day was convinced that Sir Ernest Wallis Budge, a noted Egyptologist and former Keeper of Egyptian and Assyrian Antiquities at the museum between 1894 and 1924, sincerely believed that the mummy case had sinister powers and that the Arab who made the initial discovery dropped dead as soon as he removed the inner coffin lid and touched the mummified body lying inside. It was during his time as Keeper of the Department that the photographer W.A. Mansell cut his face severely while handling the glass plate negative that contained the chilling impression of a living face, and whose son fell through a glass cold-frame during the same assignment. Although Budge publicly denied that the coffin lid was haunted, and issued a statement on behalf of the British Museum in 1934, the year of his death, that many of the stories associated with it were false, in private he was less sure. He is known to have had a long interest in ghosts and hauntings and through his translation into English of an Egyptian funerary text known as the *Book of the Dead*, came to believe in the power of ancient magic.

Today, the most well-known 'victim' of the curse of the 'Unlucky Mummy' is the famous passenger liner the RMS *Titanic* whose maiden voyage ended in disaster when, on the night of 15 April 1912, the ship struck an iceberg in the North Atlantic Ocean and sank with the loss of 1,514 lives. According to the mythology, Sir Ernest Budge, keen to relieve the British Museum of its troublesome relic, sold the mummy case lid to a wealthy American philanthropist who arranged to have it shipped to America on the White Star Line's famous new ship. However, the curse of Amen-ra ensured that the luxury liner was doomed – a member of the *Titanic*'s crew was bribed to allow it to escape destruction by stowing it away in a lifeboat (an alternative account has it being recovered after being found floating in the sea) and the mummy case eventually ended up in Montreal where it caused even more havoc before being sold and sent back to England on another ocean liner, the RMS *Empress of Ireland*. Early on the morning of 29 May 1914, a few hours into its voyage from Quebec City to Liverpool, the vessel struck a Norwegian cargo ship in dense fog and sank; over 1,000 people died, but again the 'Unlucky Mummy' survived and was brought back to England on another ship to be returned to its former home in the Egyptian collection at the British Museum, where it remains on display to this day, exhibit number 22542.

Although writers such as Dan Farson and Hans Holzer have written enthusiastically about the princess's curse, much if not all of the relic's dangerous and sinister history can be dismissed as being palpably untrue. Since its acquisition in 1889, the coffin lid in fact remained on public view in the British Museum throughout the whole of the twentieth century, apart from periods during both world wars when, along with other artefacts, it was moved to a temporary location in the basement of the building as a precaution against damage from air raids. Only in recent years has the mummy case of Amen-ra been part of travelling exhibitions: in 2003 and 2004 it was part of the museum's 'Treasures of the World's Cultures' exhibition that visited several locations in Japan and Korea including the Tokyo Metropolitan Art Museum and the Busan Museum of Art, and in September 2007 was shown for three months in the Hong Kong Museum. The mummy case was never sold to buyers in either Canada or America, and the famous *Titanic* connection clearly stems from an interest shown in the relic by William Thomas Stead, a journalist and prominent Spiritualist who, along with associate Douglas Murray, attempted to hold a rescue séance in the Museum's Egyptian Room in order to lay to rest what they felt was the tormented soul of the coffin's former occupant. Early in 1912, Stead accepted an all-expenses-paid invitation to visit America to speak at a religious congress being held at New York's Carnegie Hall, and his subsequent death on the RMS *Titanic* was the catalyst that fuelled later rumours of an ancient Egyptian curse being behind the disaster. It seems likely that the two Spiritualists became interested in the mummy case of Amen-ra after reading the *Daily Mirror* article in September 1904, by which time, as we have seen, a sizeable body of mythology had already grown up about the relic. This may well have its source in the activities of English anthropologist and folklore collector Margaret Murray, also a noted Egyptologist mentored by Flinders Petrie, who admitted to Peter Underwood shortly before her death (at the age of 100 in 1963) that a fictitious story related by her during the course of an interview was later retold, much to her astonishment, as a factual account of the mummy case's history.

If the extreme haunting of the 'Unlucky Mummy' of Amen-ra can now be discarded with relative ease, the story of the Seton sacrum bone remains as a strange glimpse into the dark side of human existence. The supernatural destruction that formed part of the mysterious phenomena at Learmonth Gardens is a familiar and chilling aspect of the next group of extreme hauntings in our survey: the modern age of the poltergeist is one that has its roots firmly in the pages of history…

Consult: Peter Underwood, *Gazetteer of Scottish & Irish Ghosts,* (Souvenir Press, London, 1973); Peter Underwood, *Haunted London* (George G. Harrap Ltd, London, 1973); Philipp Vandenberg, *The Curse of the Pharaohs* (Hodder and Stoughton, London, 1975).

The Curse of the Caves (1940s & 1974)

This account of strange happenings associated with an underground system of limestone caverns near Wells in Somerset is an interesting combination of haunting and a series of sinister events connected with a collection of buried artefacts recovered at the location. It is based on recollections of events given to one of the present authors by the principal experient.

In early May 1974, writer Gerry Davis was asked to contribute a new story for the twelfth season of the long-running BBC television science-fiction series *Doctor Who*. Davis had been script editor on the programme in the mid-1960s and, together with Dr Christopher 'Kit' Pedlar, a medical scientist with an interest in both sci-fi and the paranormal, had created the Cybermen, a fictional race of cybernetic creatures that, along with Terry Nation's famous Daleks, had become popular adversaries for the show's eponymous time-travelling central character. Keen to achieve a ratings boost by including favourite monsters in his debut season, recently appointed producer Philip Hinchcliffe commissioned Davis to write a new four-part Cybermen story which, due to budgetary constraints, was initially envisaged as being an entirely studio-bound production. However, as work on the serial progressed, additional money became available and the programme's then current script editor Robert Holmes asked Davis to amend his scripts to include extra story elements that could be filmed on location.

Production on Davis' story 'Revenge of the Cybermen' began in November 1974 and assigned to direct the serial was former actor and television director Michael Briant who had already helmed a number of episodes of the programme in the preceding two years. In realising the fictional asteroid Voga, which played a central part in the drama, Briant eschewed the customary quarry locations regularly used by the BBC to portray alien worlds, and decided to set the action at a specific locale in the West Country he had visited with his family during the summer and that he now quickly realised would be particularly suitable for the purpose. Wookey Hole, a small village on the southerly edge of the Mendip Hills, one and half miles north-west of Wells in Somerset, is also the name of a series of impressive limestone caves close by, part of which today has become a popular tourist attraction owned and managed since 1973 by Madame Tussauds. Created by the erosion of the River Axe, whose waters were used to power the oldest known paper mill in the country, founded on the site in the early seventeenth century, the Wookey caves have been used by man since the Iron Age and Roman lead working is also known to have taken place in and around the surrounding area.

On 12 November 1974, Briant supervised a day's special effects filming at the BBC Television Centre Puppet Theatre where several sequences involving model spacecraft were recorded, following which he travelled down to Somerset in order to carry out a reconnaissance of parts of the Wookey Hole caverns so that a shooting schedule for the imminent location work could be drawn up. On arrival, Briant found that the caves were still open to the public and that access was restricted; however, after speaking with the Tussauds staff, the cave manager was willing to accommodate the director once the attraction was closed for the day and arrangements were made for him to spend time there on his own later on in the evening. Before leaving for a nearby hotel where Briant planned to have an evening meal before returning to the caves, he took a brief walk around and it was during this period that the director made a curious discovery: in the sandy floor of one of the underground chambers were several stone artefacts – a number of arrowheads and a stone scraper – which appeared to date back to Iron Age times. Intrigued by the finds, Briant decided to keep the artefacts as a memento of the visit and soon after left, unaware that what would prove to be a series of strange and frightening incidents connected with the Wookey Hole caves were about to be set in motion…

A few hours later Michael Briant returned to Wookey Hole. Meeting up with the cave manager it was agreed that he could spend the rest of the evening on his own inside the caverns to plan out the filming of the *Doctor Who* story. The underground lighting would be left on and the entrance and exits locked to ensure that members of the public were not able to get inside; the manager agreed to stay on out of hours and once the director had finished working he simply had to ring a bell at the entrance in order to be let out. Soon Briant was alone and, working with a copy of the script, began drawing up the shooting schedule.

Around eleven o'clock, as he was finalising his plan and preparing to leave, the director became aware that a person was coming towards him along the passageway leading down from the cave entrance. Assuming it was the cave manager arriving to see how he was getting on, Briant was surprised to see what he took to be the figure of a diver dressed in spelunking gear pass by him in the shadows and continue walking on towards the first of the deep underground pools. Aware that Wookey was often explored by cave divers, the only thing that seemed out of place was the lateness of the hour, but assuming that like his own visit the activities had to be undertaken out of hours, Briant finished up and made his way to the entrance where, after a short wait, the manager came to open up the door, and it soon became clear that the BBC man had had a strange experience: no cave dives were planned for that night and the Wookey Hole staff had not arranged for anyone other than the director to be present in the caverns that evening. Several people, however, so it transpired, had had similar experiences in the past which, as Briant learned, seemed to be an echo of a tragedy that had taken place several years before.

On 9 April 1949, two men, Robert Davies and James Gordon Ingram-Marriott, were part of a group of divers exploring the underwater cave system inside Wookey Hole. Ingram-Marriott, an ex-Royal Marine, was an experienced diver who at that time had spent 500 hours under water, but his experience of caving was limited. After visiting a remote part of the flooded caves, known as the Ninth Chamber, the two divers began returning along a guide line with Ingram-Marriott in the lead. At one

A cave diver re-enactment at the Wookey Hole Caves, Somerset. Several people have claimed to have encountered a similar phantom figure in the underground caverns, including BBC director Michael Briant. *(Wookey Hole Ltd)*

point, Robert Davies thought that his helmet light had gone out, but in fact it had only become obscured by thick mud. Davies expected his companion to have carried on ahead but, on reaching the Third Chamber along the line, it became clear that Ingram-Marriott had lost contact with the line and was missing. His body was found a short while later facing upstream and an examination of his equipment showed that a fault in his test pressure gauge had caused him to run out of oxygen. In December 1955, Davies himself escaped death by seconds after becoming detached from a guide line in difficult conditions in one of the flooded sumps, but Ingram-Marriott became British cave diving's first fatality, and over the years the rumour that Wookey is haunted by his ghost has persisted. Michael Briant's strange experience on the eve of the filming for the BBC programme seems to confirm this…

On 18 November 1974, Briant was joined by the rest of the BBC crew, including producer Philip Hinchcliffe and principal actors Tom Baker, Elisabeth Sladen and Ian Marter, for the beginning of a four-day location shoot at Wookey Hole. It was to prove, even for a show that normally dealt with the weird and the fantastical on a regular basis, one of the most eventful in the programme's history, and the director later came to believe that the raft of strange happenings that took place were in some way connected to the disturbing of the Iron Age tools earlier on in the week and which he still kept as a souvenir. As filming began, the production soon became beset with problems. Two small boats equipped with outboard engines that were used in several key shots on the underground pools, despite being in perfect working order on a previous job, kept breaking down which caused Briant several periods of delay, while several members of the film crew themselves seemed to be affected by the strange atmosphere inside the caves: Jack Wells, the film unit's armourer, became sick and had to be replaced, while Rosemary Hester, the assistant floor manager, was overcome by an attack of claustrophobia, necessitating another member of the crew standing in which again caused the director delays. Briant finally began to get the shooting back on track, but there was more to come.

As well as stories of the ghostly diver, the Wookey caves had another alleged connection with the supernatural whose origins were said to be far older. Due to its unusual human-like profile, one particular stalagmite formation had become known

The stalagmite formation known as the 'Witch' of Wookey Hole', long regarded as possessing mysterious powers. *(Wookey Hole Ltd)*

as the 'Witch' and about whom a number of colourful stories had been put forward, the principle one being that, like The King's Men circle at Rollright, it was the petrified remains of a sinister old woman with magical powers who had been turned to stone centuries ago by a young monk from nearby Glastonbury. The 'Witch' was often pointed out to visitors by the cave tour guides (a smaller mound of limestone at the base of the stalagmite being described as a frozen familiar spirit) and, treated to a certain amount of superstitious respect, it was an unwritten rule that the formation was to be left alone and not disturbed. However, during the third day's filming, one of Briant's crew decided to break the taboo and dressed the 'Witch' up with a number of suitable items from the BBC prop store, including a black cloak and pointed hat. Almost immediately the problems that had beset the production in the early stages returned with a vengeance.

While filming a scene on the lake inside the 'Witch's Parlour' cave, the boat containing actress Elisabeth Sladen suddenly went out of control and sped away towards the far side of the cavern. Realising she was about to slam into a dangerously shelving section of the cave wall, Sladen leapt out of the boat and was only saved from drowning by stuntman Terry Walsh who jumped into the flooded sump and pulled her out. Soon after, Walsh himself became ill and had to go back to the crew's hotel to recover. Not long afterwards, another of Briant's production staff, an electrician and the person who earlier in the day had dressed up the 'Witch', was setting up a lighting effect when he fell off a ladder and suffered a broken leg. He too had to be taken out of the caves on a stretcher. Finally, on 21 November, more delays ensued when visual effects assistant Tony Harding encountered problems with a number of pyrotechnic effects that at the BBC studios in London had worked perfectly in rehearsal.

The BBC film crew departed from Wookey Hole the next day and the remaining studio-based scenes were filmed at Television Centre in London the following month. Away from the caves, production continued without any further problems and 'Revenge of the Cybermen', now a highly regarded story from the original *Doctor Who* series, was finally broadcast in April 1975. However, for Michael Briant, the presence of the mysterious Iron Age arrowheads seemed to create a continuing series of personal problems that lasted for several weeks following the end of the filming in Somerset. Finally, uneasy about their presence in his house, Briant disposed of the items, following which things quickly went back to normal. 'I had the "tools"… for about a couple of months or maybe six weeks,' he recalled many years later to Paul Adams. 'I am not a very superstitious person but the filming problems followed by other problems at home made me wonder. In the end I put them in the dustbin, back in the days when they were emptied weekly, knowing they would end up in [a] landfill and one day somebody else might find them… Within a week I started to become a "lucky" person again although I was sad to have disposed of such interesting and precious things.'

A curious footnote, or perhaps more correctly a prequel, to these strange events are the supernatural happenings which occurred within a property situated on the Wookey estate in the years immediately following the end of the Second World War. In 1927, Wing Commander Gerard Hodgkinson, whose family had owned the Wookey caves and the surrounding land for generations, began to develop the 'Witch's lair' as a public attraction. Gardens leading up to the caves were created, and a museum, shops and restaurant added. However, in 1948, a cottage on the Wookey estate, which would eventually be used by the caves' catering staff, became the scene of a series of paranormal incidents which gave rise to the idea that they were in some way linked to the malign influence of the Wookey Hole 'Witch'.

During excavations of the caves in 1912, the remains of a young woman were uncovered together with a dagger, knife, weaving comb and a ball of white stalagmite resembling a witch's crystal; beside her were the bones of two goats. Whether this was indeed the celebrated 'Wookey Witch' is unclear, but the discovery and subsequent removal of the remains led many to believe that the paranormal activity reported within the caves and the estate cottage was in some way connected with her despoilment. The cottage was built in 1870 and curiously had had no previous haunted history. For almost seventy years, it had been lived in by one woman. In 1947, aged eighty, she died and it was decided thereafter to open up the building to lettings. Throughout her residence the woman had eschewed the need for electricity, preferring to find her way about the building at night by candlelight. In 1948, the cottage was modernised with the installation of running water and power. It was after these improvements that strange incidents began to be reported.

The first tenants were a couple with a young son and the early months of their residence past uneventfully. However, one evening the eight-year-old boy, who had gone upstairs to bed, came hastily back down looking very frightened, and asked his mother, 'Who is the old lady upstairs?' His mother looked at him mystified. 'There is no old lady upstairs,' she replied, but her son was adamant that he had seen an old woman wearing a cap and a white apron standing in his bedroom. His puzzled mother went up to investigate and on reaching the top of the stairs was astonished to see the apparition of an old woman walk across the landing. So much was the young boy's fear at what he had seen that he refused to sleep on his own. Throughout the following months, the family heard the sound of phantom footsteps going up and down the stairs, and the spectre of the old woman was seen a number of times. Eventually, the haunting became too much for them and they moved out, but strange happenings continued to be reported by subsequent tenants. As well as the phantom footsteps, the interior doors of the cottage were seen to bulge with unnatural pressure and flew open and shut by themselves. Electric lights switched themselves on and off during the night hours and the ghost of the old woman continued to walk, accompanied by a wave of intense cold and a rotten, foetid smell that one witness described as that of a decayed body in a coffin.

In early 1950, the cottage, together with the one adjoining (which had not experienced any paranormal happenings) were converted into accommodation for the restaurant staff. Despite the modernisation, the haunting continued. One night a female employee awoke and was terrified to see the apparition of an old woman emerge through one of the walls and walk into the bedroom. The catering manageress, concerned that her staff were reluctant to sleep in the cottage, agreed to spend a night alone there. She had no belief in ghosts and was sure that the whole hysterical story had a rational explanation. However, after only after a short time in the building she began to feel uneasy and found it hard to sleep. Inexplicable noises and whisperings sounded in the room, and the manageress had the eerie feeling she was not alone. Eventually the tension became too much and she fetched an assistant manageress; both women searched the cottage but could find nothing out of place. The two women parted and the manageress went back to bed but the uneasy feeling persisted. Just after two o'clock in the morning, she awoke with the chilling sensation that a cold, bony hand was being placed on her shoulder. She quickly sat up and, putting on the side lamp, looked around the room. To her horror the figure of a woman stood across from her bed, seemingly having entered the bedroom through the closed door. The manageress screamed in terror as the apparition drifted across the floor and disappeared through the wall opposite. Not surprisingly, the previously sceptical woman fled from the cottage and refused to enter it again.

By the summer of 1952, the haunting in the cottage had continued at intervals for nearly five years. During that time twenty-three people had experienced unusual happenings inside the house, seven of whom had seen the apparition of the old woman. By this time the disturbances had come to the attention of local spiritualists, and vigils were held at the cottage in the hope of establishing a reason for the haunting. These were to prove fruitless and in 1954, following an exorcism ceremony undertaken in the house by the local vicar at the request of the Hodgkinson family, the haunting seemingly came to an end.

Strange and mysterious happenings connected with seemingly innocent and innocuous objects from the past are a phenomenon that features in several of the cases in the present work. For director Michael Briant, the 'curse' of the caves was shockingly real, but perhaps the most 'extreme' haunting of all connected with sinister buried objects is the next to feature in our survey; indeed, it may be the most chilling of them all…

Consult: Michael E. Briant, *Who is Michael E. Briant?* (Classic TV Press, Cambridge, 2012).

Tooth and Claw: The Sinister Story of the Hexham Heads (1971)

The appearance of a werewolf-like apparition seemingly precipitated by the discovery of two stone heads in a Tyneside town in the early 1970s remains one of Britain's most mysterious and controversial paranormal cases. The bizarre haunting of the eerie Hexham Heads, like the strange objects themselves, has never been fully explained.

The Northumberland market town of Hexham lies on the south bank of the River Tyne, twenty miles due west of Newcastle, and the surrounding area has a turbulent history that stretches back over the centuries. The Viking chieftain Halfdene was one of the first to carry out raids on Tyneside in the latter quarter of the ninth century when Hexham church was plundered and burnt. In 1297, during the Wars of Independence, the Scottish knight William Wallace attacked Hexham following his victory at the Battle of Stirling, and fifty years later an invasion by King David II saw the destruction of the original monastery that was founded nearly 700 years before by Saint Wilfrid and which replaced the building destroyed by the Danes; today only the crypt of this building survives. During the Wars of the Roses, John Neville, 1st Marquees of Montagu, defeated the Lancastrian resistance of Henry Beaufort, 3rd Duke of Somerset, in a battle that took place near the town on 15 May 1464; the Duke was beheaded in Hexham marketplace the same day. During the first Jacobite rising of 1715, the same market square saw James Radclyffe, 3rd Earl of Derwentwater, raise the standard for the House of Stuart, but like Henry Beaufort he suffered a similar fate and was executed for his treason on Tower Hill in February 1716 following the Battle of Preston. The marketplace at Hexham again saw bloodshed in 1761 when fifty-one local people protesting over military conscription were shot and killed by soldiers from the North Yorkshire Militia.

In pre-Roman times, Hexham and the area along the length of the Tyne valley formed part of the most northerly territory of the Brigantes, a Celtic tribe whose kingdom, known as Brigantia, covered a huge area of Northern England with its centre on what is now the county of Yorkshire. It is widely believed that these Celtic people venerated the human head above all other symbols, and that the 'cult of the human head' played a significant part in their religious life. Although academics have debated its importance, it is clear that Celtic warriors did sever the heads of fallen enemies and place them as trophies on display, most often at the entrances to hill forts and shrines. In 1923, during the excavation of a Celtic sanctuary at Roquepertuse in Velaux, seventeen miles north-west of Marsailles in southern France, a portico or entrance doorway was discovered in which human skulls had been placed inside specially carved niches in the stonework. In Celtic Britain, this veneration was also reflected in the creation of carved stone effigies that may have been used as charms to ward off evil spirits or as fertility symbols; and many of these stone heads have been found across the North of England in areas corresponding to the former kingdom of Brigantia. With these historical facts in mind, the periodic recovery of such stone artefacts at Hexham, an area where the Brigantes are known to have dwelt centuries before, although interesting it itself, would not normally strike as being anything but less than remarkable an event. However, just such an incident that took place in the early 1970s, for reasons which are still beyond our knowledge, has transcended the world of archaeology to become one of the most intriguing and controversial happenings discussed by paranormalists today. It is known simply as the case of the Hexham Heads.

Rede Avenue, a short road in an estate of early post-war council houses, lies just under half a mile south-east of the main town centre. Built on farmland originally known as Bogacres, the estate houses are functional if unspectacular with nothing outwardly to separate the individual dwellings, either from each other or from the countless other similar developments erected by local authorities across the country in the second half of the twentieth century. In 1971, the Robson family moved into No.3

Rede Avenue, a two-bedroom house on the western end of the street, and nothing remotely out of the ordinary took place until early the following year. Around the end of May 1971 (or possibly early in June – the actual date is unclear), eleven-year-old Colin Robson was digging in the small back garden when he made an unusual discovery. Buried in the earth was a curious round object slightly smaller than a cricket ball; as the boy scraped away the soil clinging to it, it revealed itself to be a small stone head with a human-like face. Colin called to his younger brother Leslie and the two boys decided to see if they could find another of the strange trophies. Shortly afterwards, Leslie Robson came across what proved to be a second stone head.

The brothers took the objects inside where they were cleaned up and it became clear that both were man-made out of a heavy greenish-grey sandstone-type material which contained traces of a quartz-like crystal. The slightly larger of the two skull-like heads became known as the 'girl' due to its rounded witch-like face; there had been a clear attempt to sculpt hair on the reverse side which appeared as though combed back, while a yellowish-red pigment present on this side of the stone gave it an additional colouring. The second head had a clearly masculine personality with again stripes running over the top and around the back in a hair-like pattern; this 'boy' head had more pinched-looking features and the principal photograph that survives of both heads together shows this individuality as well as their decidedly sinister expressions.

Most accounts of the case acknowledge that, almost immediately, the discovery of the stone heads coincided with an escalating series of strange and disturbing incidents that began to take place inside the small house in Rede Avenue, and all of which were seemingly focused around the two curious objects. Paul Screeton, a regional journalist with an interest in folklore and the paranormal who first began examining the case in 1977, reported a catalogue of incidents: 'The heads would turn around spontaneously,

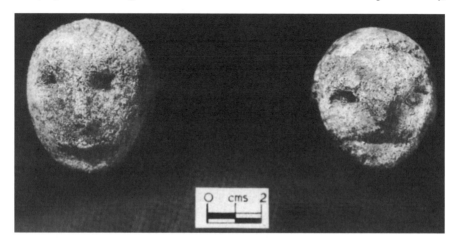

The original Hexham Heads. Linked with strange stories of the appearance of a sinister werewolf-like apparition, their origins remain a mystery. *(Authors' collection)*

Rede Avenue, Hexham, where seemingly haunted stone relics were discovered in the early 1970s. *(Paul Screeton)*

objects were broken for no apparent reason – and when the mattress on the bed of one of the Robson daughters was showered with glass, both girls moved out of their room.' However, this poltergeist-type phenomena was not limited to either the Robsons themselves or the house in which they were living – the family's immediate neighbours, the Dodds, also experienced bizarre happenings.

After several disturbed nights during which her children complained of being touched by something moving around their bedroom, Ellen Dodd had cause to sleep in their bedroom in order to look after one child who was ill. Mrs Dodd had dismissed the complaints as simple bedtime pranks and became irritated when ten-year-old Brian Dodd insisted that, as on previous nights, something was pressing against him through the bedclothes as he lay trying to sleep. Deciding to lay down the law once and for all, she raised herself up in the bed and was shocked to see a tall dark shape in the middle of the room which, as she watched, started to move towards her. When the 'creature' touched her on the legs, Mrs Dodd screamed and the sinister apparition dropped on all fours and quickly scampered out of the bedroom. The commotion was heard by the Robson family next door and, on investigation, the front door of the Dodd's house was found to be standing open. Ellen Dodd was the first to describe a frightening part-animal, part-human figure in connection with the Hexham Heads; she claimed it had been a man-like creature with a face similar to that of a sheep, and was so upset by her experience that Hexham Town Council agreed to move her and her family to another property.

The Robsons continued to live on at Rede Avenue and although they apparently never reported seeing the wolf-like creature, the family claimed that strange things continued to take place during the time that the stone heads were present in their house: this included witnessing a mysterious glowing light in the garden on the spot where the heads had been dug out of the ground, and over the Christmas period, a 'strange flower' appeared growing in the same place. Finally, the heads were passed to Newcastle Museum and the absence of the objects seemingly brought peace to the household – to date there have been no further accounts of unusual happenings connected with the property. Later, a subsequent tenant, concerned with stories connected with the house, arranged for an exorcism ceremony to be carried out.

However, the story of the Hexham Heads does not end there and in fact the supernatural mystery surrounding the strange objects was about to deepen. At Newcastle, the museum staff were unable to shed any light on the origins of the heads and Dr David Smith quickly arranged for them to be examined by Dr Anne Ross, a leading Celtic scholar at Southampton University, where they were sent and subsequently photographed by Professor Frank Hodson, the university's Professor of Geology and Dean of the Faculty of Science. In her professional capacity as an archaeologist, Dr Ross, who received the heads in November 1971, felt that they were both examples of Celtic head worship and dated them to around the second century AD. Despite the sober academic environment of Southampton being nearly 300 miles away from Rede Avenue and the bizarre experiences of the Robsons and their neighbours, this distance together with a change of ownership, seemed to have no effect on the paranormal forces connected with the eerie artefacts, and much of the published accounts of strange happenings connected with the Hexham Heads involves the experiences of Anne Ross and her family.

In 1978, Peter Underwood carried out a tape-recorded interview with Dr Ross at her Southampton home and subsequently included an account of their discussion in his autobiography *No Common Task* (1983). Anne Ross claimed that immediately she took possession of the stone heads she felt an intense dislike for them, despite there being little difference between the objects found at Rede Avenue and the numerous similar Celtic heads she had examined during the course of her career. Due to her teaching commitments at the university, she had taken the heads home in order to study them at her leisure, and within hours of them being present in the house, unusual things began to happen. In the early hours of the morning, Dr Ross came awake in a state of panic to find the bedroom filled with an intense and unnatural feeling of coldness quite unlike the normal atmosphere of the house. As she looked across the room, like Ellen Dodd, she was horrified to see a large black figure only feet away in the action of moving across the room towards the bedroom door: 'It was about six feet high, slightly stooping… half-animal and half man.' The upper part of the creature appeared to be distinctly wolf-like, while the lower limbs had the proportions of a human being; the whole apparition appeared to be covered in very dark, almost black hair or fur, and as it moved out of the room, appearing momentarily as a solid physical shape against the whiteness of the door, Dr Ross experienced an overpowering compulsion to follow.

Getting out of bed she moved quickly out onto the landing where the upper hallway light was always kept on as a comfort for her five-year-old son. The nightmarish figure was at that moment half-way down the staircase and clearly visible in the bright artificial light. As she watched, it vaulted over the balustrading and landed on the hallway floor with a distinct heavy sound, then turned and scurried out of sight towards the rear of the house. Anne Ross followed to the bottom of the stairs, at which point the unnatural feeling urging her forward disappeared and she suddenly became very frightened. Her husband, a commercial artist, had been woken by the sound of his wife moving down the stairs and immediately searched the house thoroughly but there was no sign of anything out of the ordinary, or indication that an animal of some kind had gained entry into the house. At this point, the academic did not connect her startling experience with the presence of the stone heads from Hexham, but this was to change.

Four days later, both Anne Ross and her husband spent the day in London and arrived back in Southampton around six o'clock in the evening. Although their fifteen-year-old daughter was responsible enough to look after her younger brother, the family had a prearranged signal so that she knew when to answer the door. On this occasion, however, when their daughter let them in, it was clear that shortly after returning from school, the teenager had had an unnerving experience which had left her in a state of shock. About an hour before, as she had let herself into the house, she had been confronted by an almost identical creature to that seen only days before by her mother. Crouching halfway up the stairs was a solid black semi-human figure which immediately sprang over the stair rail and padded animal-like on all fours along the passageway into a part of the house at the back used by Dr Ross and her family as a music room. Anne Ross' daughter had a distinct impression of the creature's wolf-like character – she described it as being 'as near a werewolf as anything' – and again there was an unnatural fascination that immediately made her both temporarily fearless of the 'animal's' presence as well as curious as to where it had gone. On looking inside the music room, she found the strange figure had completely vanished, and spent the time waiting for her parents' return in a state of increasing anxiety.

Where the case of the Hexham Heads is concerned, it is clear that a substantial body of mythology has grown up in the ensuing years concerning the objects which today is extremely difficult, if not impossible, to substantiate. Peter Underwood, a highly experienced researcher, was impressed by the first-hand testimony he obtained from both Dr Anne Ross and her husband, and it seems clear that for the time that the stone heads were in their possession, several incidents of a paranormal nature, which may or may not have been connected with the stones, took place in their house. All members of the Ross family either heard or sensed the presence of what appeared to be the same man-beast creature that was seen initially by both Anne Ross and her daughter – all three children later claimed to have seen the apparition – and loud crashes and other noises were heard, while several room doors in the Southampton house seemingly began opening and slamming shut by themselves. In 1973, Dr Ross published an account of her experiences with the Hexham Heads as part of an article written for the book *Folklore, Myths and Legends of Britain* issued by *Reader's Digest* (second edition 1977), and three years later, in February 1976, she was one of several people interviewed about the case for an edition of the BBC's popular magazine programme *Nationwide*, by which time the heads themselves had disappeared.

Experiences said to have taken place in the presence of a number of other people who at one time or another are alleged to have had the stone heads in their possession are more problematic. In a similar way that strange phenomena and unpleasant happenings are said to have charted the travels of the haunted British Museum mummy case, similar inexplicable happenings and unusual accidents are described as accompanying the transfer and temporary ownership of the stone heads from Rede Avenue. They are said to have been buried and then dug up again at least once, with unusual happenings accompanying their recovery and temporary ownership, although exact details such as places, dates and names of persons involved are lacking, such as the un-named scientist who supposedly took charge of the heads for a time and who is said to have had 'too many accidents' while the stones were in his car that he became uncomfortable about keeping them.

One person who did possess the Hexham Heads for a period knowing full well their sinister reputation was Dr G.V. 'Don' Robins, an inorganic chemist from the Institute of Archaeology and author of the book *Circles of Silence* (1985) who during the 1970s was the physical consultant for the Dragon Project, a wide-ranging study of the earth energies and similar properties associated with standing stones and other ancient sites around Britain using a combination of both psychic and scientific means. Robins suggested in his book *The Secret Language of Stone* (1988) that the 'stone tape' theory of paranormal phenomena propounded by researchers such as Tom Lethbridge had its basis in the ability of minerals to store information (in the form of electrical energy) within their crystalline structure (the Hexham Heads contained a high proportion of quartz) and that this created a fluctuating energy network that gave rise to the sounds and images associated with haunted buildings and other places. Through Anne Ross, with whom he later co-authored a book on the Lindow Man bog body, Robins became interested in the Rede Avenue heads and for a period kept them under observation in his own home. Although the werewolf creature seen by the Ross family did not make an appearance, Robins was aware of what he described as a 'stifling, breathless' atmosphere intimately connected with the witch-like 'girl' head, and on the day he collected the heads to take them home, his car's electrical system suddenly failed although up until that particular moment there had been no previous problem.

Despite much study, two questions concerning the mysterious Hexham Heads remain unanswered to this day: the exact age of the stones as well as their present whereabouts. Dr Anne Ross suggested that both heads were around 1,800 years old, but this dating was challenged in late 1972, a year after the sinister stones first began to spread their strange influence inside the Hexham house. Desmond Craigie, a Northumberland lorry driver who had lived in No.3 Rede Avenue for many years prior to the Robsons, claimed that he had made the heads himself and they were in fact only a mere sixteen years old. Craigie, whose father had moved out of the house in 1971 before the arrival of the Robsons, suggested that the heads were two of an original three that he had made in 1956 out of reconstituted stone while working at a local factory as simple toys for his daughter Nancy. One became broken and was thrown away; the remaining two eventually were lost in the garden and were eventually dug up by Colin and Leslie Robson. Despite the apparent debunking, a definite date was never established by any of the persons who at any one time had access to the heads, and the fact that they have now not been seen for many years contributes to the enigma. The belief that the heads were finally buried in a secret location in order to prevent any further supernatural activity taking place is an unsatisfying end to an extreme haunting that continues to fascinate the paranormal community forty years after their initial discovery.

Is there an explanation for the eerie phenomenon of the Hexham Heads? The paranormal activity that is alleged to have taken place at Rede Avenue in 1971 – the movement of objects, noises and the sighting of phantom figures – is little different from many reported poltergeist outbreaks, and as we shall see, there is an interesting similarity between the experiences of the Robsons at Hexham and the Hodgson family at Enfield in North London a mere five years later. Poltergeist cases are described as 'person-focused' hauntings, but what sets Hexham apart from cases such as the Enfield Poltergeist is that rather than being focused on an adolescent child (although they were present in the house) the strange happenings seemed to be firmly centred around the inanimate stone heads themselves.

An interesting precursor to the case is a newspaper sensation that took place in the same area nearly seventy years earlier that has become known as the 'Beast of Allendale'. In December 1904, sightings of a large dark-coloured wolf became linked with the slaughter of farmers' livestock around the village of Allendale, seven miles south-west of Hexham. The carcasses of several sheep were found partly eaten and mutilated, while other animals showed signs of having been worried or bitten about the legs, and in one incident, a group of women and children came across the animal which was scared away by their screams. The *Hexham Courant* reported in several editions on the efforts of large numbers of local people, who at one point had formed into an armed hunting party over 100 strong, in an effort to run the creature to earth, but despite a large wolf being found dead on a railway line at Cumwinton, thirty miles away, it appears that the 'Hexham Wolf' was never caught, and the attacks seemingly came to an end in the early weeks of 1905. Perhaps it should be no surprise that this unusual but nevertheless natural occurrence should be linked with the werewolf aspects of the much later Hexham haunting. Whatever its origins, the strange story of the Hexham Heads remains very much an enigma and as such, the potential rediscovery of the sinister relics promises to be one of the most potentially momentous occurrences in twenty-first-century paranormal research…

Consult: Reader's Digest Association (Ed.), *Folklore, Myths and Legends of Britain* (Reader's Digest, London, 1973); Don Robins, *Circles of Silence* (Souvenir Press, London, 1985); Don Robins, *The Secret Language of Stone: A New Theory Linking Stones and Crystals with Psychic Phenomena* (Rider & Co., London, 1988); Paul Screeton, *Quest for the Hexham Heads* (CFZ Press, Bideford, 2012); Peter Underwood, *No Common Task: The Autobiography of a Ghost Hunter* (Harrap Ltd, London, 1983).

Chapter Six

TALES OF DESTRUCTION

The Poltergeist Enigma in Britain

Mary Ricketts' Legacy: The Ghosts of Hinton Ampner (1764-71)

The eighteenth-century haunting of the original Tudor manor house of Hinton Ampner occupies a unique position in the haunted history of Britain. For a period of nearly eighteen years, various occupants reported a wealth of strange and unnerving phenomena including footsteps, door slamming, eerie noises and the sighting of apparitions. It remains one of the country's greatest extreme hauntings of all time.

In his last published work, the substantial 100,000-word *Poltergeist Over England* (1945), written during the dark days of the Second World War, English ghost hunter Harry Price stated with confidence that '[one] of the most detailed, convincing, and best-documented stories of Poltergeist haunting is that of the manor house at Hinton Ampner'. Of all the many and varied manifestations of the paranormal that Price studied during the course of his long and controversial career, poltergeist phenomena was the one aspect of the supernormal that attracted him the most and, given the many instances of fraudulent mediumship that he discovered and exposed during the inter-war years, it was perhaps the one that he found the most convincing, and the Hinton case one of its most notable examples.

The small Hampshire village of Hinton Ampner lies nine miles east of Winchester on the western edge of the South Downs, and it was here some time around 1620 that a large mansion house was constructed by Sir Thomas Stewkley, who, together with his descendants, lived at Hinton for many years. The building stood until the early 1770s when it was demolished and a new manor house was built close by; this still stands and today is in the care of the National Trust. Although the old Hinton Ampner manor house stood for around 150 years, it was in the last two decades of its life that it acquired a formidable reputation locally as a haunted house, and in time this knowledge was to achieve a much wider audience. Sir Walter Scott included a brief account of the case in his *Letters on Demonology and Witchcraft* (1830) and forty years later, in 1870, a more detailed but nonetheless incomplete account was published as part of a biography (written by the writer's son) of Richard H. Barham (*Life and Letters of Richard H. Barham*), author of *The Ingoldsby Legends*. Two years later, the *Gentlemen's Magazine* presented the full story of the haunting as a two-part article entitled 'A Hampshire Ghost Story', while in 1936, 'The Haunting of Hinton Ampner' formed a chapter of *Lord Halifax's Ghost Book*, a classic collection of allegedly true accounts compiled by Charles Lindley Wood (1839-1934), 2nd Viscount Halifax, and published with a foreword and annotations on the contents by his son. All these accounts of the Hinton ghosts, including the later version by Harry Price, are a presentation of an original account of the haunting by Mrs Mary Ricketts who, like Rosina Despard at Cheltenham, was the case's principal experiant and sole chronicler.

Mary Ricketts and her husband William, who was born in Canaan, Jamaica, took a furnished tenancy of Hinton Ampner in December 1764 and moved in during the January of the following year. They were to stay at the house for nearly seven years, finally leaving in the autumn of 1771. The couple had married in 1757 but William Ricketts' business affairs required frequent visits overseas and for a large part of the period that they were living at Hinton he was away in the West Indies. Mary stayed at the house accompanied by the customary servants, and for a period she was joined by one of her brothers, Captain (later Baron) John Jervis and Earl St Vincent, who, like his sister, experienced a number of strange and seemingly inexplicable incidents during his time there. In July 1772, by which time she was staying temporarily at Hinton Parsonage, Mary Ricketts compiled a written account of her experiences at Hinton Ampner which she addressed to her children in the hope 'that the truths which I have so faithfully delivered shall be as faithfully transmitted to posterity'. Two manuscript copies were prepared by Mrs Ricketts and remained in the family for many years: a great-granddaughter, Mrs William Henley Jervis, owned one which was used as the basis for the ghost story that appeared in the *Gentlemen's Magazine* while an aunt, Mrs Edmund Palmer, retained the other. Later, Lord Halifax was given one of the original copies by Dr Harold Browne, the Bishop of Winchester, and presented an edited version as part of his book. The account given by Harry Price in his *Poltergeist Over England* is the most complete of all the various versions of the story. After leaving Hinton, Mary Ricketts and her family moved to the old palace at Wolvesey, Winchester; later she stayed in the London home of the Bishop of St Asaph before finally renting a house in Curzon Street.

Although the haunting of Hinton Ampner is extremely well detailed, its origins are obscure, but appear to date from several years before the occupancy of Mary Ricketts and her children, to a time when the Stawell family were in residence. Edward Stawell (who was elevated to the Peerage in 1742) married Mary Stewkley, a descendent of Sir Thomas Stewkley, the builder of Hinton, in May 1719 and the couple lived there for several years with Mary's younger sister, Honoria. After Mary Stewkley's death in July 1740, Honoria continued to live on at the house with her brother-in-law, an arrangement which soon fanned the flames of local village gossip, with allegations of a liaison between the couple and the supposed birth of a bastard child which was said to have been killed and buried somewhere within the building in order to cover up the affair. Lord Edward Stawell was sitting alone in the parlour at Hinton on 1 April 1755 when he suffered an apoplectic fit and died the following day; he was in his mid-fifties and the estate of Hinton Ampner passed to the Right Honourable Henry Bilson Legge, who only stayed at the house for one month a year during the shooting season. The small retinue of domestics who had served Lord Stawell, which comprised a bailiff cum house steward, a housekeeper, coachman, a housemaid, a dairymaid, a cook, a butler, a groom and a gardener, some of whom had been resident at Hinton for over forty years, continued to live on in the house during this time.

The first reported incident of paranormal phenomena at Hinton Ampner appears to date to the period immediately following Edward Stawell's death when his former groom, Mr Joseph, claimed to have seen an apparition of the dead man one night standing in his bedroom. Joseph claimed the figure was quite solid and real and in the bright moonlight streaming in through the window he described his old master as being dressed in a drab-coloured coat. How many times the ghost was seen is unclear and in fact it may well have been restricted to this one occurrence; between 1755 and the time of Henry Legge's death in August 1764, the servants continued to live on peacefully and without disturbance in the house, and Hinton was in no way regarded as being a notably haunted residence during this time. This, however, was to change...

The ownership of Hinton Ampner passed to Henry Legge's daughter who, at the time of her father's death, was married to the Earl of Hillsborough. As the house and its grounds were surplus to her requirements, the decision was made to let the estate and shortly before Christmas 1764, the Ricketts came to Hinton, unaware of the strange happenings that were to become an integral part of their stay. By this time, Edward Stawell's coachman, Thomas Parfait, was dead and once the tenancy was agreed, his widow Sarah, together with Elizabeth Banks, the former housemaid, gave their notice and left. Subsequently, when William and Mary Ricketts and their three children moved into the house from London, they brought their own servants with them, with the result that the only person from the former household still present on the estate was Lord Stawell's gardener, Richard Turner, who was kept on by William Ricketts, although he appears not to have lived in the house and in fact resided in the village close by. This arrangement goes some way to dispelling the notion that the incidents of ghostly activity described by Mary Ricketts in her written statement were wholly or in part due to the activities of Lord Stawell's former employees who may have resented the presence of the new tenants and created phenomena, either by suggestion or fraudulent activity, in order to either drive them away or make their time at Hinton as unpleasant as possible.

The activities of the new occupants seemed to stir up strange and sinister forces within the old rooms and passages of Thomas Stewkley's former residence, and though their origins are obscure, the ghosts of Hinton Ampner soon began to make their unnatural presence felt. Not long after William and Mary Ricketts had settled themselves and their children into their new home, Mrs Ricketts began to be disturbed at night. Strange noises, as though an unknown person was walking about the house beating or slapping the doors 'with vehemence' became a frequent and disturbing occurrence, and although her husband immediately went to investigate, he could never find anything untoward or any indication that an intruder had forced a way inside. Assuming that one of Lord Stawell's old servants had a duplicate set of house keys that enabled him or her to enter the building at night, William Ricketts arranged for the locks on all the external doors to be changed, but despite this precaution, the strange door slamming continued to afflict the household after dark.

Six months after the Ricketts' arrival, in July 1765, apparitions began to be seen at Hinton. One warm evening, the family's nursemaid, Elizabeth Brelsford, was sitting in the nursery watching over Mary Ricketts' eldest son Henry as he lay sleeping, when she saw through the open doorway a man dressed in a drab-coloured suit of clothes pass by and enter into the yellow bedchamber opposite. Assuming this to be a visitor, she continued to watch over the sleeping child until, on enquiring with the housemaid, Molly Newman, who sometime afterwards brought up a tray of supper, who the gentleman was, it became apparent that no one matching the description had called at the

The manor house at Hinton Ampner, photographed from the site of the much-haunted former Tudor building where Mary Ricketts made her extraordinary record of poltergeist phenomena in the 1760s. *(Peter Underwood Collection)*

house that evening. The two women went and searched the yellow bedroom, whose only door was the one visible from the nursery, but the room was empty and Elizabeth Brelsford was adamant that no one had come out again. Some weeks later, the figure was seen again, this time by George Turner, the son of the Ricketts' gardener, who was working at Hinton as a groom. As he crossed the hall to go to bed one evening, he saw a man wearing a drab-coloured coat standing at the far end of the room who he took to be the newly arrived butler, who had a suit of a similar colour. On going up to the dormitory where all the male servants slept, he was alarmed to find the butler and all the other male staff settled in their beds. A search was made of the ground floor of the house but nothing out of place was discovered.

In July of the following year, four of the Ricketts' staff including the postilion, Thomas Wheeler, and Mary Ricketts' own maid, Ann Hall, were sitting in the kitchen around seven o'clock in the evening when they heard the sound of a woman 'whose clothes rustled as of the stiffest silk' come down the back staircase and approach along the kitchen passage. Looking up, they all saw a woman wearing dark-coloured clothes pass quickly by the open doorway, while at that moment the cook, Dame Brown, who was coming into the house through the yard door, saw the same figure rush past her; before she had time to see who the person was, the apparition had vanished. A workman, who at the same time was following Mrs Brown into the house from the yard outside, saw no one.

Strange noises continued to plague the inside of the house at night. Mary Ricketts often heard the sound of an unseen person moving about her bedroom, accompanied by a rustling as though someone wearing a silk dress was passing through the doorways in and out of the apartment, and several of the domestics claimed to have similar experiences; one woman, Susan Maidstone, became particularly distressed 'with the most dismal groans and rustling' around her bedside as she lay trying to get to sleep. Although unwelcome, the disturbances appear to have been accepted by the Ricketts' household and in her account, Mary Ricketts does not claim that any of her staff left her employment due to ghostly activity. Staff did come and go during the time that she and her husband held the tenancy of Hinton and by the time the couple left in 1771, 'I had not one servant that lived with me at my first going thither, nor for some time afterwards'.

Towards the end of 1769, William Ricketts left Hinton Ampner for an extended spell of business in Jamaica and his wife continued to live on in the house with their three children, a company of eight servants and the strange and unknowable haunting force that began to gradually increase in frequency and power. During the time that her husband was away, Mary Ricketts had a number of personal and alarming experiences. One summer night, as she lay 'awake and collected' in the same bedchamber in which, five years before, the figure dressed in brown had been seen by Elizabeth Brelsford, Mrs Ricketts was alarmed to hear clear and heavy footsteps as of a man 'with plodding step' walking towards the foot of the bed. Terrified, she jumped out of the bed and fled into the nursery where Hannah Streeter, the nursemaid, was watching over the sleeping children. Lighting a lamp, the two women went back into the bedroom but the chamber was empty, the only way out being the door into the nursery through which she had made her escape. Strange music, described by Mary Ricketts as unusual 'sounds of harmony', was heard by her on at least two occasions in the bedroom over the main hall, while in the early months of 1771, a strange hollow murmuring sound seemed to fill the entire house; quite distinct from the wind in the chimneys, it was heard 'on the calmest nights' and was never explained. Knocks and raps continued to sound in the house during the night hours; on one occasion Mrs Ricketts was disturbed by a violent hammering as though someone were beating on one of the servant doors with a heavy club.

Elizabeth Godin, Mary Ricketts' personal maid, shared a number of her mistresses distressing and inexplicable experiences while at Hinton Ampner. One night in early April 1771, which happened to be the sixteenth anniversary of the death of Lord Edward Stawell, the two women became disturbed by a series of noises, as though someone was moving about behind the door leading into the yellow bedchamber. Suspecting a burglar, Mary Ricketts summoned the coachman, Robert Camis, who went to investigate armed with a length of timber, but he found the bedroom empty and the outer door of the room bolted as usual on the inside. Earlier the same year, Elizabeth Godin had experienced the haunting in her own bedroom, when one moonlit night 'the most dismal groans and fluttering' sounds had disturbed her sleep to the point that her distressed state was noticed the following morning by Mary Ricketts herself.

Around the beginning of May 1771, the haunting seemed to gather strength to the point that 'the noises became every night more intolerable'. The knocks and murmuring sound began in the early evening and continued until after daybreak. Mary Ricketts, who by this time had arranged for her maid to sleep in a single bed in her own room, heard voices in the night, one a shrill female voice, as though invisible people were speaking inside the bedroom. The bed curtains rustled and moved on their own, knocks sounded on the bedroom door, footsteps crossed the bedchamber, while the 'opening and slapping of doors' became a nightly occurrence. A terrible crashing sound, followed by 'a shrill and dreadful shriek' which came three or four times before fading away as though sinking down into the ground, frightened Mrs Ricketts' nursemaid so much that she gave her notice and left the house. She confided that on most nights, footsteps came and went outside her bedroom door accompanied by the sound of someone trying to force their way inside the room.

By now concerned about the detrimental effect that the noises were having on the household, Mary Ricketts decided to confide in her brother, Captain John Jervis, a distinguished naval officer stationed at Portsmouth, and invited him to stay at Hinton. Jervis was initially sceptical about tales of haunting but that morning a family friend, Captain Luttrell, happened to call at the house and on being taken into the Ricketts' confidence, persuaded Mary Ricketts' brother that they should carry out an investigation. That evening, Captain Luttrell returned to the house accompanied by John

Bolton, Captain Jervis's manservant, and the three men carried out a complete search of the building including the roof spaces and attics. Nothing out of the ordinary was discovered and it was decided to divide the night hours up into a series of watches and to control the upper part of the house in such a way that should the disturbances be due to intruders, they could be found and dealt with. The door leading into the back staircase was locked and all of the bedrooms were occupied by members of the household – Mary Ricketts, Elizabeth Godin, Captain Jervis and the three children – so that, due to the way that the bedchambers led off one another, the only way for anyone to pass through the whole first floor of the house was via the main staircase and through the lobby room, where Captain Luttrell kept a solitary vigil armed with a pistol.

Almost immediately, the strange phenomena of Hinton Ampner began to stir. As she lay down on her bed, Mary Ricketts heard an eerie rustling sound as though someone was moving around behind the closed bedroom door. At the same time, Captain Luttrell became aware of footsteps walking across the room opposite and, jumping to his feet, he pulled open the door and called out a challenge. As he did so, he had the impression of an insubstantial shadowy figure moving past him in the gloom which almost instantly disappeared. John Jervis, who lay awake in the adjacent bedroom, also heard the sounds and, getting out of bed, he and Captain Luttrell searched the upper part of the house together including the servants' quarters in the attics, but were unable to find anything out of place or the slightest sign that someone had managed to get into the house through the windows or outside doors. Mystified, the two men sat up together for the rest of the night and only retired just before daybreak. Around dawn, Mary Ricketts was disturbed by two loud crashing noises, as though doors downstairs on the ground floor were being slammed shut with the utmost force that seemed to shake the very house.

For the rest of the following week, John Jervis continued to stay at Hinton, during which time he held vigils throughout the night hours and phenomena continued to take place: the sound of a pistol shot followed by groaning noises as though a wounded person was moaning in agony was heard in her bedroom by Mary Ricketts, while Captain Jervis himself was disturbed by a tremendous noise, as though a heavy object had fallen through the ceiling of the room and struck the floor with incredible force. Initially sceptical of the supernatural, Jervis became convinced by his own experiences that the house was unfit for the family to live in and advised his sister to move out. Such was his concern that, being forced to return to Portsmouth, he arranged for an old family friend, Lieutenant Nicholls, to stay at Hinton Ampner until Mary Ricketts was able to find alternative accommodation. Jervis left Hinton on 9 August 1771 and his sister followed a few weeks later, finally persuaded to vacate the house she had occupied for nearly seven years by an experience for which she gives only the scantest of details: 'I was assailed by a noise I never heard before, very near to me, and the terror I felt not to be described,' as though the recollection was almost too painful and upsetting to revisit in detail.

The departure of Mary Ricketts and her family from Hinton Ampner in the autumn of 1771 ended one of the most impressive first-hand accounts of a poltergeist haunting in Britain, and the case remains a classic of its kind. The following year the house was let to the Lawrence family who, according to Harry Price, also reported phenomena including the sighting of a female apparition. It is clear that by then Hinton had gained a local reputation as a haunted house as the Lawrences, perhaps under pressure from Lady Stawell for whom continued ghostly stories made the future letting of the house difficult, took pains to stop their servants from talking about their experiences in the village, making it clear that the haunting was not solely focused around the Ricketts family, although it is possible that they, and in particular Mary Ricketts' young children, were a catalyst for the bizarre happenings that took place during their stay there.

The phenomena reported during poltergeist hauntings or 'infestations' as Harry Price and some modern authors like to describe them, are remarkably consistent and although many years and great distances may separate individual cases, an examination of the reported evidence shows that there is in fact much similarity. In the early 1990s, over 200 years after the happenings at Hinton Ampner, Yasmin Adams, the ex-wife of the present co-author and then a dental student at Southampton City College, was living with another female student in a small terraced Victorian house in Boulton Road, Portsmouth. During the six months that the two women were present in the house, a number of inexplicable incidents took place that are almost mirror-images of the happenings as described by Mary Ricketts in her manuscript: footsteps were heard walking down the stairs when either of the two students were alone in the house and on several occasions loud crashing noises were heard for which no cause could be found; these were described as sounding as though the upper doors in the house were being slammed with incredible force, but an immediate examination of the first floor (made with much trepidation) revealed that all the doors were exactly as they had been left. These crashing noises took place during both the day and night and when all the outside doors and windows were closed.

Although poltergeist activity has been reported with much regularity stretching back over hundreds of years, the serious scientific examination of the phenomena is a relatively recent happening. In 2010, Dr Barrie Colvin published (in the *Journal* of the Society for Psychical Research) the results of an examination of the sound patterns of several audio recordings of alleged poltergeist raps from cases both in Britain and abroad. The poltergeist cases, ten in number, covered a period of forty years – the earliest was a recording made by a Scottish doctor at Sauchie in Aberdeenshire in 1960, while the most recent was from an investigation carried out at a house in Euston Square in London in 2000 – and in all of the separate recordings, Colvin discovered that the sound envelopes of the disparate rapping sounds in each of the incidents (one of which took place in Germany) were of an identical nature, and also dissimilar to the envelope of a rapping or knocking noise produced in a normal way.

The implication of Colvin's research is that the knocking or rapping associated with poltergeist hauntings are caused by a sudden release of tension or alteration in the substance of an object, rather than by the physical action of striking one object with another. Colvin was encouraged to study the phenomenon after personal experience of a rapping poltergeist at a house in Andover for which it was clear that no normal explanation could be found.

The Lawrences left Hinton Ampner in 1773 and the house remained empty. It was eventually pulled down and a new building erected in 1793. During the demolition, the contractors are said to have discovered within the floor space of one of the rooms the remains of a monkey's skull, although those villagers whose memories stretched back to the time of the tales of the bastard child of Edward Stawell suggested a more sinister identity. This story brings to mind aspects of the haunting of Athelhampton Hall in Dorset where a spectral monkey, known as Martyn's Ape, a former household pet, is said to have been seen on a number of occasions. The origins, however, of the Hinton skull remain a mystery. The new manor at Hinton Ampner was built approximately fifty yards from the site of the haunted house, which is now part of the handsome landscaped garden. Its demolition and lack of redevelopment means that today the only record we have of this vivid and convincing haunting is the extraordinary legacy of Mary Ricketts.

Consult: Charles Lindley, *Lord Halifax's Ghost Book* (Geoffrey Bles Ltd, London, 1936); Harry Price, *Poltergeist Over England* (Country Life Ltd, London, 1945); Sir Walter Scott, *Letters on Demonology and Witchcraft* (J. Murray, London, 1830); Peter Underwood, *Hauntings: New Light on the Greatest True Ghost Stories of the World* (Dent, London, 1977).

'There's evil here...': The Black Monk of Pontefract (1966-69)

Two hundred years separate the strange happenings at rural Hinton Ampner and the first of three twentieth-century poltergeist hauntings included in the present survey. The extraordinary and at times violent phenomena experienced by a working-class family in a house in West Yorkshire in the mid-1960s is a landmark case now often overlooked.

The fear of the unknown is the driving factor that makes stories of hauntings and encounters with ghostly figures unpleasant and a taboo subject for many people: most of us enjoy a good ghost story when it is presented as fiction, but when the ghost story steps off the printed page and enters the real world of human experience, it can be too much to bear. Although what we recognise and classify today as poltergeist activity has a recorded history in England that dates back at least to the end of the sixteenth century (a case at North Aston in Oxfordshire in 1592 – see *Poltergeists* (1979) by Alan

Gauld and Tony Cornell), the sudden outbreak of violent physical phenomena, including the movement and destruction of objects and furniture and even assaults on human beings by paranormal forces, in ordinary modern suburban settings involving ordinary everyday people as opposed to remote rural manors and estates populated by the titled gentry of history, makes the poltergeist the most frightening and extreme haunting of all. Earlier in this book we described the contemporary paranormal scene as being the 'age of the poltergeist' and the first of our three examples, covering a period of forty years, comes from the North of England during the time of the 'Swinging Sixties', an iconic era of modern Britain.

The market town of Pontefract in the West Riding of Yorkshire, with a recorded history dating back to the end of the eleventh century, lies twelve miles south-west of Leeds city centre. In 1090, a Cluniac monastery (i.e. subservient to the Benedictine Cluny Abbey at Saône-et-Loire in France) was founded by Robert de Lacy and survived until the Dissolution in 1540. During the Civil War, Pontefract Castle was a Royalist stronghold and was subjected to a fifteen-month siege by Parliamentarian forces that began on Christmas Day, 1644. Despite heavy bombardment and attempts by Cromwell's men to tunnel under the castle walls with explosives, the siege ended on 1 March 1645, when a superior force led by Sir Marmaduke Langdale routed the besieging army at the Battle of Chequerfield, an area of high ground a mile south-west of the centre of the town. Three hundred years later, the same area was assigned as a blueprint for a post-war housing development and by the early 1950s, much of the Chequerfield estate had been laid out. Number 30 East Drive, a three-bedroom semi-detached house on a corner plot opposite a wide circular green, was no different to the dozens of other council properties built on the estate at the time, and in 1966 it was occupied by the Pritchard family: Joe Pritchard, the owner of a pet shop in Pontefract town centre, his wife Jean, and their two children, fifteen-year-old Phillip and twelve-year-old Diane. Despite the domestic normality, the August Bank Holiday week was to prove a watershed for the unassuming family as it marked the beginning of one of the most astonishing cases of poltergeist haunting recorded in Britain up until that time, and one which remains a classic of its kind.

For the Pritchards, the 'first rumblings of the coming storm', as Alan Gauld has described the onset of the poltergeist phenomenon, began on Thursday, 1 September 1966. Joe and Jean Pritchard, together with their daughter Diane, were spending the week on holiday in the West Country, while at East Drive, Mrs Pritchard's mother, Sarah Scholes, was staying over to look after the teenage Philip who, like most adolescents of his age, was more interested in doing his own thing than spending a week in Devon with his parents. Shortly before midday, the East Drive Poltergeist announced its presence with a gust of wind which, seeming to appear from nowhere, chilled the air inside the house and slammed the back door shut. Mrs Scholes, who had spent the morning knitting a cardigan, assumed the weather was changing, but outside it was a warm and sunny day. When Phillip Pritchard went to bring his grandmother a cup of tea a short time later, it became clear that something very strange had started to happen inside their ordinary family home: everything in the small living room – the carpet, furniture and ornaments – was becoming covered with a greyish-white chalk-like powder that could be seen drifting down like falling ash. What was more astonishing was the fact that the dust appeared to begin on a plane halfway up between the floor and the ceiling which, even given the incredible variety of reported poltergeist phenomena collected by researchers through the years, remains one of the most singular and unique happenings in the history of psychical research.

Not surprisingly, Sarah Scholes immediately suspected that her grandson was playing a trick on her, particularly as a short while later, and with the dust continuing to float down in the living room, round pools of water began to appear one after the other across the kitchen floor. As fast as she and her other married daughter, Marie Kelly, who was fetched from her own house on the opposite side of the road, could wipe them up, the puddles of water reappeared in another part of the kitchen. Marie lifted up the lino but the concrete floor underneath was dry and there was no sign of rising damp. By this time another neighbour, Joe Pritchard's sister-in-law, Enid Pritchard, had been called in to look at the flooding: suspecting a water leak she turned off the stopcock under the sink, but it made no difference and in desperation Mrs Kelly called the local water board and requested they send someone to investigate the leak. Later that afternoon an engineer arrived at East Drive and examined the Pritchard's kitchen floor, coming to the conclusion that the problem was due to condensation. Neither Mrs

East Drive, Pontefract: the poltergeist house. *(Colin Wilson)*

Scholes or her daughter were particularly convinced by the explanation, but a short time afterwards both the mysterious dust storm and the water patches ceased, and after tidying up the house, Mrs Scholes tried to forget the incident and get things back to normal. Unfortunately for the Pritchards, normality was gradually fading away from the house in East Drive: later that evening the poltergeist returned…

As Sarah Scholes and her grandson sat watching television, ordinary household objects and even the very house itself seemed to suddenly start coming to life. In the kitchen, an old-fashioned loose tea dispenser began working by itself, showering tea into the sink; the hall light began turning on and off and, as Mrs Scholes went to investigate, she found a pot plant lying discarded in a ball of soil halfway up the stairs. Then, from the direction of the kitchen again, came the sound of plates and cups shaking and rattling inside the crockery cupboard, while upstairs, loud hammering noises, like a mallet pounding against a piece of timber, began to vibrate down through the building. Sarah again went to get her daughter and they both stood listening to the knocking sounds. Assuming it was their immediate next-door neighbour, the Mountain family, causing the disturbance, Mrs Scholes went round to check but found May Mountain had also heard the same noises and had assumed that it was the Pritchards carrying out some building work. Not long afterwards, the hammering noise stopped and the house became silent. Uncertain what to make of the noises, Marie Kelly went back home and Philip Pritchard got ready for bed.

A short time later, as Mrs Scholes looked in on him as she began to get ready to retire, they were both stunned to see the wardrobe in Philip's bedroom start to rock and sway from side to side as though an invisible person were trying to manhandle it out of the corner into the centre of the room. Now frightened by the continuing disturbances, Sarah Scholes decided to spend the night at her daughter's, and with Philip in his dressing gown and pyjamas, they went across to Vic and Marie Kelly on the other side of East Drive and went to bed in the spare room. Mrs Scholes' son-in-law, who up until then was inclined to put the disturbances down to subsidence or some other natural cause, now felt that things had got out of hand and decided to put a call through to the local police station. An inspector and two constables arrived within a few minutes and, together with the Kellys, they went across to No.30 and made a search of the house: all was quiet, nothing seemed out of place and there were no indications of where an intruder might have got in.

After the police had left, Vic and Marie Kelly sat talking about the happenings in their kitchen and the subject of ghosts came up. A friend of Vic Kelly, named O'Donald, who lived further down East Drive, was interested in the supernatural and despite the lateness of the hour, the couple decided to see if he was still awake. Fortunately, Mr O'Donald had not gone to bed and just before midnight, the amateur ghost hunter accompanied them back to the Pritchards' house. O'Donald, who was sufficiently knowledgeable to deduce that the Kellys were describing poltergeist activity, looked over the house and they all sat downstairs for some time waiting to see if anything would happen, during which time he described some of the phenomena he had read about, including knocking and drumming, and the movement and breaking of objects. After around an hour and a half, and with no sign of any further disturbances, they decided to call it a night and Mr O'Donald went back to his own house. As the Kellys were going down the hall to the front door, there was a crash from the living room. On investigating, they found some small framed paintings and a photograph – the Pritchards' wedding portrait – had been knocked onto the floor: the photograph had been vandalised and seemingly cut from top to bottom. Only a short time before, Vic Kelly's friend had mentioned that one phenomenon he had heard in poltergeist hauntings was the way photographs were sometimes attacked and torn up…

After staying at her daughter's house for most of the day, Sarah Scholes and her grandson plucked up the courage to return to No.30 East Drive later in the afternoon: there was no sign of a recurrence of the bizarre knocking or any of the other unnerving happenings which had driven them from the house the previous evening, and the calm remained into the weekend when the Pritchards arrived back in Pontefract after the long drive back from Devon on the Saturday afternoon. Soon the family were all sitting in the living room where two days before the mysterious dust had begun appearing from nowhere, and Mrs Scholes described as best she could the sequence of events that had taken place on that eventful Thursday. As if to reinforce her account, the temperature in the room suddenly dropped several degrees and almost like a replay of the beginning of the haunting, the same sudden cold wind swept through the house accompanied by several loud knocks from somewhere upstairs. Then, almost as suddenly as it had occurred, the atmosphere in the room righted itself and the house became quiet. In fact, the storm had receded, and for the Pritchards there was to be two years of calm. Then, during the last week of August 1968, the psychic storm clouds began gathering again, heralding what would be a gruelling nine months filled with the most astonishing and frightening paranormal phenomena ever recorded.

The East Drive Poltergeist haunting is noted for some of the most remarkable manipulations of physical objects ever reported in a case of its kind. Following the August Bank Holiday (26 August 1968), Jean Pritchard spent the remainder of the week decorating her daughter's bedroom. One afternoon, as she and her mother sat drinking tea in the living room, they both heard a noise from out in the hallway, and when Mrs Pritchard went to see what might have caused it, she found a bed quilt from Diane's room lying at the bottom of the stairs. A short time later, she was interrupted from her wallpapering by a loud clatter: now the counterpane from Phillip Pritchard's bed was lying in the downstairs hall accompanied by several upended plant pots. The seventy-two-year-old Sarah Scholes, who had been in the living room all the time, recognised the tell-tale signs all too well and began to cry – she knew that the events of two years before were beginning all over again.

That night, unable to sleep due to the warm weather, Jean Pritchard got up and decided to make herself some tea. Out on the first-floor landing she found the temperature had suddenly dropped, and at the same time she became aware that her decorating tools, which she had moved out of her daughter's bedroom, were starting to move on their own: a pasting brush and bucket appeared to come to life and jumped up, striking the wall near where she was standing, while a rolled length of wallpaper became animated and began rocking on its end in the middle of the hallway. Mrs Pritchard made to snatch it up, but it instantly became lifeless and dropped to the carpet. Before she realised what was happening, the poltergeist had transferred its power to a carpet sweeper leaning against the banister rail: it upended itself and swung round menacingly towards her. Jean dropped to the floor and in a state of abject terror managed to crawl back into the bedroom, where her screaming instantly woke her husband and their two children. In a state of incomprehension, the family watched as a psychic storm seemed to tear across the landing and through into Diane Pritchard's bedroom, hurling loose items and the remainder of the decorating tools about. Then, with an incredible show of paranormal strength, a length of wooden pelmet covering the curtain rail in the bedroom was wrenched from the wall and hurled out of the open window into the back garden below. Joe Pritchard slammed the bedroom door shut and they retreated back into the main bedroom. From Diane's room came the sound of objects hitting the inside of the closed door, but shortly afterwards the activity subsided and the family managed to go back to bed, with Diane sleeping in her parents' room.

If the overture to the haunting in 1966 had briefly drawn its energy from the presence of the then fifteen-year-old Philip Pritchard, it soon became clear that the main act of the supernatural drama at East Drive was firmly focused on his teenage sister, now aged fourteen. Almost all of the phenomena was to take place in Diane Pritchard's presence, and she was to bear the brunt of the most remarkable and frightening episodes of physical attack and disturbance. Despite being one of the landmark British poltergeist cases of the second half of the twentieth century, the appearance of the Black Monk of Pontefract – as the East Drive incident is most commonly referred to today – may have totally slipped off the radar as far as organised psychical research is concerned if it had not been for the activities of a local Yorkshire historian named Tom Cunniff. In 1979, ten years after the haunting had ceased, Cunniff read about the Pritchards' ordeal in archive copies of two Yorkshire newspapers that had briefly covered the story in September 1968, during the early weeks of its second and most violent phase. Tom Cunniff went to No.30 East Drive and spoke with the Pritchards. Despite the passage of a decade, their memories of the events were vivid and Cunniff, who felt that the origins of the haunting lay in the alleged activities of one of Pontefract's

Diane Pritchard, photographed in the early 1980s, the focus of the extraordinary Black Monk of Pontefract. *(Colin Wilson)*

Cluniac monks from centuries before, wrote up an account of the poltergeist's activities.

By the end of the 1970s, stories of haunted houses and possessed buildings were very much in vogue, due in no small part to the publication in 1977 of American writer Jay Anson's bestselling book, *The Amityville Horror*. In November 1974, twenty-three-year-old Ronald 'Butch' DeFeo had shot to death six members of his own family at their home, No.112 Ocean Avenue, in Amityville, Long Island, New York, claiming that a mysterious black-handed 'demon' had handed him a 336 Marlin rifle and sinister voices in the house had told him to kill. Fifteen months later, the Lutz family gave up the same house that they had moved into only a few weeks before, claiming that the Colonial-style mansion was a gateway to Hell populated by a violent retinue of evil ghosts and spirits. In 1978, writer Colin Wilson had issued *Mysteries*, a sequel to his landmark book *The Occult* (1971), and was known as a former sceptic who now accepted that there was as much evidence for the paranormal as conventional scientific claims for atoms and other sub-atomic particles. Tom Cunniff sent his report on the Pritchards' experiences to Wilson with the proposal that here was the British 'Amityville Horror' waiting to be written. In August 1980, fourteen years after the beginning of the first disturbances, Colin Wilson went to Pontefract and interviewed the family himself; he also spent time familiarising himself with the local history that the Yorkshireman suggested was at the root of the phenomena. However, the UK version of Jay Anson's famous book was not to appear. 'I... decided that it would be pointless to dramatise it,' Wilson later wrote. 'The facts themselves are already as sensational as anything in the recorded history of poltergeist hauntings.' Instead, the material formed a lengthy chapter in the writer's full-length international study of the phenomenon, *Poltergeist!*, which appeared in 1981, and it is from this work that all subsequent accounts of the case, including the present study, are based.

Unlike Joseph Procter at Willington Mill, or Lionel Foyster at Borley Rectory, no contemporary record or diary of the events at East Drive were made at the time by the Pritchard family, with the result that specific dates of a number of incidents are lacking. Despite this, although a local ghost-hunting group from Doncaster (who looked into the case in 1969) had suggested that Philip Pritchard had faked some of the phenomena, Wilson was convinced that the Pontefract poltergeist was genuine. 'As soon as I went into the Pritchards' home, I became convinced that… they were obviously discussing something they had all lived through. And every one of them remembered some slightly different aspect of what had taken place. No group of conspirators could have made up such a story and then told it so convincingly.' It was a story that was tantamount to a nine-month reign of terror.

Soon evenings in the house in East Drive became filled with strange and bewildering happenings. Lights would turn themselves on and off, clothes and household items – ornaments, books and food items – were found scattered down the stairs, while one of the most prolific phenomenon, loud and incessant knocks and raps, started up once Diane Pritchard had returned home from school and, continuing on occasion for hours, could be heard up and down the street outside. Like Tom Cunniff, Colin Wilson found the Pritchards' story was supported by contemporary evidence. Two reporters, one local and one county, from the *Pontefract and Castleford Express* and the *Yorkshire Evening Post* respectively, visited No.30 and both ran stories on the haunting, with the result that the Pritchards' home quickly garnered minor celebrity status in the town: passers-by would linger on the pavement outside and listen to the knocking noises, while on several occasions 'amateur ghost hunters' and sensation seekers camped out on the green opposite the house, hoping to catch sight and sound of the phenomena. Thankfully, Joe and Jean Pritchard and their family escaped the national media frenzy, that as we will see, plagued the Hodgsons at Enfield ten years later, but it is a loss to psychical research that no competent researcher was able to visit the house during the height of the disturbances and carry out a contemporary investigation.

Early in September 1968, the Pritchards invited a local Christian minister, the Revd Davy, to visit them at East Drive in the hope that he could perform an exorcism and rid the house of its unwanted visitor. The vicar came one evening and although noncommittal about performing a ritual ceremony, was to be one of several people outside of the Pritchard family to witness the phenomena. Unfortunately for Joe and Jean Pritchard, exorcisms, then as now, require sanctioning by a bishop following presentation of a substantial body of evidence, and in the late 1960s, Church authorities were reluctant to give the go ahead: in 1966, a Swiss girl who claimed to be possessed had been beaten to death during an exorcism ceremony, and a wave of church desecrations involving pseudo-Black Magic rites in Britain, beginning with the vandalisation of a seventeenth-century tomb in a ruined church at Clophill in Bedfordshire in 1963, had created an uneasy atmosphere that was likely to be exacerbated by further associations with poltergeists and haunted houses.

In the living room of No.30 East Drive, the Pontefract vicar suggested that natural causes were no doubt at the root of the Pritchards' problems: noises and the movement of objects were caused by subsidence, while stories of ghosts and similar happenings created a heightened atmosphere in which people mistakenly attributed supernatural origins to ordinary and easily explainable events. As the Revd Davy continued to speak, the knocking noises started up and an ornamental brass candlestick flipped off of the mantelpiece and landed on the floor at the church man's feet. Less than a minute later, a second candlestick moved, but this time it *rose up* off the shelf, drifted horizontally a short distance across the room, and then fell to the carpet. Almost immediately afterwards, there was an incredible noise that sent the Pritchards and the local vicar hurrying to the dining room: there all the crockery from the kitchen cupboard was lying scattered and unbroken over the floor. The formerly sceptical Davy was instantly sobered and declared that there was an evil presence in the house. His advice was that the family should move to another property, but both Joe and Jean Pritchard were completely against the idea.

Later the same evening as Diane Pritchard was about to go upstairs to bed, the temperature in the downstairs part of the house began to drop, the signal that another wave of activity was about to begin. As if in a power cut, all the lights in the house suddenly went out by themselves, plunging the family into darkness. On previous occasions, Joe Pritchard had found that the poltergeist had switched the power off at the meter under the stairs, and as he went to investigate, there was a sudden movement in the downstairs hallway: an oak hall stand, a family heirloom, together with an electric sewing machine that was resting on it, became animated and slid forward, cornering Diane at the foot of the staircase. As she made to push it away, the teenager tripped and fell backwards and was instantly pinned to the angle of the stair flight by the stand and the sewing machine. At the same time the lights all came back on by themselves, and when Joe and Philip Pritchard tried to pull the furniture off the frightened girl, they found it was completely immovable as though the animating force had placed the stand over her and then locked it into position. Both men struggled to get the girl free with no success, but when Diane forced herself to relax, the power lessened and the hall stand became an ordinary piece of furniture again and was dragged back to its normal location. Shaken, the teenager went upstairs but the same supernatural coldness was permeating her bedroom and it was clear that the ordeal was not over. Soon her bedclothes were being pulled away by invisible hands and the mattress flipped itself over, dumping Diane onto the bedroom floor. On this particular occasion, the family estimated that this took place at least four times on that one night.

A number of visitors to the house in East Drive were to witness similar astonishing happenings. Vic Kelly's married sister, Rene Holden, a natural clairvoyant, paid a number of visits, and felt that the poltergeist was drawing energy from both Phillip and Diane Pritchard in order to manifest: both often complained of stomach ache during periods of physical phenomena, in much the same way that sitters in a physical mediumship séance claim to experience a pulling sensation on the solar plexus as the energy is drawn out and channelled towards the medium. Mrs Holden was a witness to more than one of the 'psychic storms' which regularly blew through the Pritchard house, leaving scattered furniture and household objects in its wake. One Saturday evening in the early winter of 1968, she and Jean Pritchard went to a Ladies' Night at Joe Pritchard's local working men's club, and on the way home accompanied them back to the house for a coffee. While she was there, the East Drive poltergeist gave her some special attention. As Mrs Pritchard prepared the coffee in the kitchen, the room light blinked off and a chair cushion struck Rene Holden in the face; then the room seemed to erupt into pandemonium. Again the electricity had been knocked out at the fuse-board, and when Mr Pritchard turned on the lights they found that the living room had again been ransacked. Rene Holden suggested that the family should try and communicate with the ghost, but when the Pritchards held an impromptu séance in the hallway, standing in a circle with their hands joined together, they were pelted with items from the bedrooms upstairs – sheets, clothes, even a mattress – and the attempt at contact was abandoned. Similarly, when Vic Kelly tried to perform his own exorcism using holy water provided by his local Catholic priest, his efforts were rewarded with loud banging noises and the appearance of streams of water coming through the living room ceiling.

In his book, *Poltergeist!*, Colin Wilson describes many more astonishing incidents that are easy to dismiss as being too preposterous or fantastic to take seriously: a full jug of milk floating out of the kitchen refrigerator and upending itself over the head of Maude Preece, Joe Pritchard's sceptical sister; Mrs Preece's fur gloves floating in the air, seemingly filled with invisible hands, and beating time as Aunt Maude (a devout member of the Salvation Army) valiantly sang a rendition of 'Onward Christian Soldiers' in an attempt to ward off evil; a grandmother clock lifted off the wall and thrown down the stairs; enormous wet footprints, larger than a man, appearing in the hall carpet overnight; a brass crucifix jumping off the kitchen mantelpiece and sticking to Diane Pritchard's back like a magnet; a shower of house keys falling down the kitchen chimney; eggs dematerialising out of a closed box and reappearing in mid-air in the centre of the living room before exploding into fragments. The testimony of the Pritchard family, like Mary Ricketts at Hinton Ampner, the Setons at Learmonth Gardens, and the Hodgsons at Enfield, joins a body of alleged paranormal happenings that support the often-cited maxim of the noted Victorian scientist Sir William Crookes, who defended his own experiences of the supernatural by stating: 'I did not say it was possible, I said it happened'. For the Pritchards, the most disturbing and frightening of their claims for the existence of the Black Monk of Pontefract was to take place in the spring of 1969 when, as the phenomena began to ramp up to its climax, the ghost itself began to materialise inside their house in East Drive.

One night after they had both retired, Joe and Jean Pritchard were lying in bed with the light off when the bedroom door swung open by itself. In the streetlight filtering in through the landing window, they saw the solid outline of what appeared to be a tall, hooded figure: Joe immediately turned on the bedside light but the figure had disappeared. A few days later, May Mountain, the Pritchard's next-door neighbour, claimed that a similar apparition appeared to her while she was alone in her own kitchen. As she stood at the kitchen sink, she had the impression that someone had come up close behind her, and assuming it was her nephew playing a joke, turned round to scold him. She was astonished to see what she took to be a tall monk-like figure dressed in full-length black robes with a large cowl which hung down obscuring the face, standing within arm's reach. Although she was quite familiar with the happenings that were taking place in the Pritchards' home and had first-hand experience of the loud and insistent knocking and drumming sounds that filled their house, on this occasion Mrs Mountain found the sudden appearance of the figure startling more than terrifying – she told Colin Wilson she was more curious than afraid – and after a few seconds, the tall silent figure vanished.

The Black Monk, as the apparition soon came to be known, was seen on at least two further occasions. One evening, after Jean Pritchard and Rene Holden had spoken about their experiences to members of the local Pontefract Spiritualist church, the two women returned to East Drive and Mrs Pritchard invited the driver who had brought them back into the house for a cup of coffee. As they sat in the living room, the lights suddenly went out and Mrs Holden felt a hand being placed on the back of her head. As she turned round, she saw in the dim light from the street lamps outside the figure of a tall man wearing a long flowing robe-like garment standing immediately behind her; the vision lasted a few seconds until the room light came back on by itself and the figure was nowhere to be seen. Diane and Phillip Pritchard also witnessed the appearance of the Black Monk. As they sat in the living room watching television, both became aware that a person was standing on the other side of the interconnecting glass door leading through into the dining room. Assuming that it was one of the neighbours calling round, Phillip got up to check: he found the dining room empty but as he turned to look through the doorway into the kitchen, he saw the same figure – tall and featureless and clad in black drapery – seemingly in the act of sinking down through the kitchen floor and disappearing.

The haunting of No.30 East Drive, Pontefract, reached its peak in May 1969 with one final and shocking outburst of violence directed at the young Diane Pritchard. As she went along the downstairs hallway towards the kitchen one evening, the poltergeist again knocked out the overhead light, plunging the house into a supernatural half-light (it was still dusk outside), and there was a loud shriek from Diane. When her mother and brother rushed out into the hall they saw in the gloom the horrific sight of the teenage girl being forcibly pulled up the stairs as if by an invisible assailant: Jean Pritchard and her son could clearly see her cardigan stretched out in front as the girl fought against an overwhelming force that was dragging her crying and screaming up the staircase. As they rushed forward and began pulling her back, the 'Black

Monk' suddenly released the struggling girl, and all three fell back in a heap on the hall floor; Diane's throat was disfigured with red marks, as if the ghost had been pulling at her clothes with one hand and clawing at her neck with the other. It was to be one last frightening display of paranormal strength that effectively brought the incredible Pontefract case to a close: peace returned to the home of Joe and Jean Pritchard and there have been no further reports of disturbances in the house on East Drive.

Where do the origins of the Black Monk of Pontefract lie? Were the Pritchards haunted, as historian Tom Cunniff suggested, by the ghost of a long-dead Cluniac monk, supposedly executed for the rape and murder of a local woman in the first half of the sixteenth century; was the poltergeist an externalisation of physical energy created by the subconscious minds of firstly Phillip Pritchard, and then to a much greater extent two years later by his younger sister; is the very ground on which the Pritchards' unassuming council house was built, and on which the same building stands today, a powerful psychic battery that has retained, for a period of nine months during the winter of 1968/69, and suddenly and spontaneously released a cumulative build-up of psychic impressions – a possible solution put forward by Colin Wilson; or was the Pritchards' home infested by something far more sinister, something that was to return to menace another ordinary English suburban home in another part of the country, 150 miles away and less than a decade later? By 1977, for the Pritchards at Pontefract, the 'age of the poltergeist' was over – for the Hodgson family in Enfield, it was just about to begin…

Consult: Alan Gauld & Tony Cornell, *Poltergeists* (Routledge & Kegan Paul, London, 1979); Colin Wilson, *The Occult: A History* (Random House, New York, 1971); Colin Wilson, *Mysteries* (Hodder & Stoughton, London, 1978); Colin Wilson, *Poltergeist!: A Study in Destructive Haunting* (New English Library, London, 1981).

The House of Strange Happenings:
The Case of the Enfield Poltergeist (1977-78)

The story of the Enfield Poltergeist is not only an account of one of the most important paranormal investigations of modern times, but also that of its chief investigator, Maurice Grosse, an astute and practical researcher who spent over a year painstakingly documenting a wealth of remarkable and disturbing phenomena. The results of his efforts, together with those of fellow investigator Guy Lyon Playfair, have produced what is in effect a classic of psychical research.

With his committed practical approach to paranormal investigation and distinctive handlebar moustache, Maurice Grosse became one of the most respected and easily recognised of late twentieth-century ghost hunters and, despite the strong association with the 1977 Enfield Poltergeist, he read widely about and had a strong interest in

Maurice Grosse, the lead investigator in the case of the Enfield Poltergeist. *(Guy L. Playfair)*

psychical research all his life. Grosse was born into a North London Jewish family in 1919. After local schooling he went to the Regent Street Polytechnic and subsequently began an apprenticeship as a commercial artist and designer, but his career was interrupted by the war, during which time he served in the Royal Artillery. Following demobilisation, Grosse married (in 1944) and began raising a family, abandoning his earlier career in favour of a position with his family's retail business, while at the same time developing his own natural talent for electrical and mechanical design. Over the next thirty years Grosse became a successful inventor, filing many world-wide patents (the first in 1945 for a clockwork toy) and opened his own business as an engineering and display consultant in the early 1960s. His designs included dental equipment, newspaper dispensers, vending machines, as well as the rotating advertising hoardings familiar in every town and city in the world, and he became a member of both the Royal Institution and the Institute of Patentees and Inventors. Despite the success, personal tragedy was to alter not only the direction of much of Maurice Grosse's later life, but also the contemporary attitude that many people have to paranormal phenomena, from the general public through to psychical researchers themselves.

On 5 August 1976, Grosse's daughter Janet, the youngest of his three children, was critically injured in a motorcycle accident in the centre of Cardiff, South Wales. The inventor and his wife Betty were holidaying on Jersey but managed to get to the hospital to see her before she died the same day without regaining consciousness. Although beside himself with grief, Grosse became aware in the ensuing days of what he could only assume were some forms of psychic or paranormal incidents that seemed to be connected in some strange way with his daughter's death. They included a humorous birthday card sent by Janet the day before to her brother Richard (whose birthday was 5 August) whose cartoon figure seemed to predict some form of accident and injury; an unpleasant feeling experienced by Betty Grosse, again the day before her daughter's death, while she and her husband were lying on the beach which lasted for around an hour and never returned; Grosse's attendance at a Jersey synagogue in the evening of the same day to attend a mourning ceremony for the Fast Day of the Ninth of Av; a clock in the house of Betty Grosse's sister Miriam which stopped at 4.20 a.m., the exact time of Janet's crash, and the behaviour in Grosse's house of several Jewish mourning candles which, despite being designed to burn constantly, persisted in going out during the night. Grosse compiled a report of these incidents and sent it to the Society for Psychical Research (SPR) and, shortly afterwards, joined the organisation himself. He soon began attending public meetings and persistently started lobbying the Society with requests to take on investigative work within reasonable travelling distance of his Muswell Hill home.

On Monday, 5 September 1977, Maurice Grosse took a telephone call at his London office from the then SPR Secretary, Eleanor O'Keeffe, who told him she had received a request from a senior reporter on the staff of the *Daily Mirror* newspaper to look into unusual happenings being experienced by the Hodgson family (given the pseudonym Harper in contemporary and subsequent publicity) in a small terraced house in a suburb of North London. Grosse accepted and immediately drove to Enfield to begin what was to become one of the most famous paranormal investigations of modern times.

The Enfield Poltergeist occupied Grosse almost continuously for an entire year and out of all the people connected with the case, it was he who was to spend the most time in the house, both recording and experiencing apparently incredible paranormal phenomena. This included the violent projection and movement of objects and furniture, knocks and banging sounds, the apparent levitation of family members, apparitions (including bizarrely on one occasion an apparition of Grosse himself) as well as spontaneous fires and paranormal graffiti. Grosse also famously recorded what appeared to be the voice of the poltergeist manifesting through one of the young children, eleven-year-old Janet Hodgson, by attaching a specialist microphone to the child's throat. The eerie croaking voice claimed to be the ghost of the former owner of the house who had died there several years before the Hodgson family moved in. Later Grosse would offer £1,000 to anyone able to successfully duplicate the ghost voice by normal means, either by trickery or ventriloquism.

Writer and psychical researcher Guy Lyon Playfair, whose association with the Enfield Poltergeist investigation has spanned over thirty-five years. *(Darren W. Ritson)*

For most of the investigation, which lasted until the September of the following year and made, both during and afterwards, sensational newspaper and radio headlines, Grosse was assisted by freelance photographer Graham Morris (who took many of the iconic Enfield photographs including several of the famous 'levitations') and fellow psychical researcher and SPR member Guy Lyon Playfair who became sympathetic after witnessing Grosse ask for assistance during the discussion period of an SPR lecture at the Kensington Central Library and, shortly afterwards, hearing him talk about the case on the BBC Radio 4 news programme *The World This Weekend*. Playfair himself had experienced several incidents of poltergeist phenomena while working as a translator in Brazil during the early 1970s and, like Grosse, was convinced the case was genuine. He later recorded his and Grosse's many experiences in a book *This House is Haunted*, published in 1980.

Other members of the Society for Psychical Research visited Enfield at the time but were not so impressed. Former SPR President John Beloff and Council Member Anita Gregory spent time with the Hodgson family but were unconvinced. They felt the Hodgson children were play-acting and creating much of the 'phenomena', and that Maurice Grosse himself, due to his recent bereavement, was not critical enough in his investigation and too willing to believe in paranormal explanations for the happenings. Gregory later wrote: 'It is my opinion that Guy Playfair and Maurice Grosse may perhaps have experienced genuine paranormal happenings, particularly towards the beginning of the case. However, neither anything I saw, or experienced, when I visited the house, nor the content of either Mr Playfair's book or Mr Grosse's defence of it suggests to me that there is evidence here for anything other than a chaotic – and at times distressing – state of affairs'. In the years that followed, both Grosse and Playfair were forced on occasions to robustly defend their stance on the Enfield case – Grosse for example appeared on an edition of the Channel 4 programme *Right to Reply* following a personal attack on his investigation methods by psychologist Nicholas Humphrey.

For the Hodgson family – Peggy Hodgson, a single parent in her mid-forties together with her four children, thirteen-year-old Rose, eleven-year-old Janet, Peter aged ten and his seven-year-old brother Jimmy – what was to escalate into an intense and increasingly frightening encounter with the paranormal began soon after bedtime on the evening of 30 August 1977, a fortnight after the death of rock and roll legend Elvis Presley. The Hodgsons lived in a modest early 1930s semi-detached council house in Green Lane, Enfield. The house was laid out to a simple plan: a living room and kitchen on the ground floor with three bedrooms upstairs, while the bathroom and toilet was located off the kitchen below in a small back-addition. Mrs Hodgson had lived there since the mid-1960s. On this particular Tuesday evening, both Peter and Janet Hodgson were disinclined to go to sleep after lights out, complaining to their mother that they were being kept awake by the fact that both their beds were shaking and moving by themselves. Not surprisingly, Mrs Hodgson was unimpressed and, scolding both children for playing games, dismissed their continuing protests and went to bed herself. The following evening, much to her annoyance, events followed a similar pattern and Peggy Hodgson found herself again being called upstairs by what she considered to be her children's tedious bedtime pranks. This time both children claimed they could hear a shuffling sound, as though one of the bedroom chairs was moving by itself in the gap between their beds.

Determined to put a swift end to the continuing farce, Mrs Hodgon picked up the supposedly offending chair and took it downstairs, but as she returned and turned out the bedroom light, she herself heard an unusual shuffling sound which appeared to be coming from somewhere inside the room. This was immediately followed by four loud and heavy knocks as though their immediate neighbours, the Nottingham family, were banging on the party wall between the houses. As she stood in the doorway trying to work out what was going on, both Peggy and her two children saw a large chest of drawers on the opposite side of the room from the two single beds slide forward approximately eighteen inches towards the centre of the room. Mrs Hodgson's reaction was to push the chest of drawers back, but immediately it again moved forward away from the wall and, as she attempted to slide it back a second time, stuck fast as though being held there by an invisible force. Suddenly terrified by what was happening, Mrs Hodgson pulled both Peter and Janet out of bed and, summoning her two other children from the bedroom across the landing, decided to seek help from her brother John, who lived a few doors down on the same street. When it became clear that John Burcombe and his family were asleep, the frightened Hodgsons went round to the Nottingham house next door.

Vic Nottingham, a roofing contractor in his early forties, together with his twenty-year-old son Garry, went round to the Hodgsons' house. Both he and Peggy Hodgson were at first inclined to believe that someone was playing games on the family, but as they stood downstairs in the Hodgsons' living room, all heard the sound of heavy raps or loud hollow knocks coming at regular intervals from the walls of the house, almost as though, as Peggy Hodgson described it, someone was inside or behind the wall and trying to get in. Mr Nottingham and his son went over the house and checked all the rooms; they also looked inside the loft and went out into the garden, assuming that someone was fooling about and knocking on the outside walls. Nothing was amiss and, unnervingly, the sinister knocking continued despite there being no obvious cause or reason. By this time, Vic Nottingham's wife, also called Peggy, had joined them and, upset by what was happening, decided they ought to call the police.

Around 1 a.m., a patrol car from Enfield police station arrived at Green Street and WPC Carolyn Heeps together with a male colleague went into the Hodgsons' house. After listening to the accounts of both Peggy Hodgson and Vic Nottingham, they both carried out a thorough search of the house but again were unable to find anything out of place. As everyone stood in the ground-floor living room, the loud knocking began again and WPC Heeps later, at the request of the SPR investigators, signed a statement confirming that under full view of everyone in the room, one of the Hodgsons' armchairs suddenly slid approximately four feet across the floor towards the kitchen door: no one had moved and immediately afterwards, the policewoman inspected the chair and was unable to find any evidence of trickery. Unfortunately for Peggy Hodgson and her children, the two police officers were somewhat powerless – as no laws had been broken and as there was no actual demonstration of public disorder there seemed little point in them staying – and shortly afterwards they left, leaving both families still frightened and on edge. Fortunately, there were no further knocks or movement of furniture that night, but despite this, the Hodgsons all elected to sleep downstairs in the living room, an entire family afraid to go back upstairs to their beds.

Over the next five days, the Hodgsons' semi-detached house seemed to transform itself into a paranormal bedlam. Small objects, mostly children's toys – marbles and Lego bricks – began flying through the air, ricocheting off the walls and dropping down onto the floor. Janet, Peter, Rose and Jimmy denied throwing anything and it soon became clear to both Peggy Hodgson and the Nottinghams that this was somehow connected to the night-time disturbances earlier in the week. The marbles and plastic bricks seemed to appear out of nowhere and were propelled with incredible force. By the Sunday evening, desperate to get some help or explanation for what was happening, Vic Nottingham, like the Smiths at lonely Borley Rectory had done years before, decided to contact the *Daily Mirror* newspaper. The same evening, two pressmen, photographer Graham Morris and reporter Douglas Bence, a local man who knew the area, responded to a request by Tom Merrin, the *Daily Mirror*'s night news editor, and drove over to Enfield.

For some time after their arrival, nothing remotely unusual took place. Peggy Hodgson and her children had been staying next door in the Nottinghams' house and as the two *Daily Mirror* men waited around in the empty house it seemed as though the whole episode was nothing but a complete waste of time. However, as Bence and Morris prepared to leave, the Hodgsons came back into the house and suddenly, as if on cue, the barrage of toys and objects began again in earnest. Plastic Lego bricks shot across the living room and hit the walls: one struck photographer Graham Morris in the face as he stood next to Peggy Hodgson by the kitchen door. The Hodgson children began screaming and their mother also became extremely distressed. The two newspapermen eventually left in the early hours of the morning, both convinced that something exceedingly strange was taking place.

Back at the *Daily Mirror* offices, George Fallows, a senior reporter, listened to Douglas Bence and Graham Morris's story and decided to visit Green Street to see things for himself. After meeting with the Hodgsons and hearing their experiences and those of Vic and Peggy Nottingham first-hand, Fallows became extremely concerned for the wellbeing of Mrs Hodgson and her family; he was also convinced that there was a poltergeist at Green Street and decided that the only thing he could do was to call in the Society for Psychical Research. Fallows excused himself, walked down the road to the nearest telephone box and put a call through to the SPR's office at Adam and Eve Mews just off Kensington High Street. An hour later, Maurice Grosse was on his way to Enfield.

Peggy Hodgson's house in Green Street was to become a second home for both Grosse and subsequently fellow researcher Guy Playfair for the next fourteen months. Quickly conscious of the physical and mental strain the grim and frightening happenings were having on the Hodgsons, Grosse went out of his way to befriend the family. Three days after first visiting the house, Grosse experienced the phenomena first-hand. In the early hours of 8 August 1977, both he and three pressmen from the *Daily Mirror* were present at Green Street when a chair overturned, seemingly by itself, in Janet and Peter's bedroom. *Daily Mirror* photographer David Thorpe saw it move and come to rest, while all the time Janet Hodgson appeared to be in some strange cataleptic state that seemed outside of normal sleep. After attending the SPR lecture at Kensington Library, Grosse drove his E-Type Jaguar straight to Enfield, arriving just before 10 p.m. Soon afterwards eerie and alarming things began to happen: in the living room, a marble suddenly flew towards him and struck the wall; the doorbell chimes began moving by themselves and the kitchen door opened and closed by itself in full view of the fledgling researcher several times when all members of the family were accounted for; in the kitchen, a shirt lying on the kitchen table jumped by itself onto the floor, while Grosse was overcome by a sudden and intensely cold breeze which seemed to come up out of the floor at him and then quickly fade away.

Two days later, the strange happenings at Enfield made front page headlines in the *Daily Mirror* newspaper. This was quickly followed by both local and national radio interviews with Peggy Hodgon and Maurice Grosse, the effect of which, in the following weeks, was to precipitate both family and researcher into the midst of an intense and unwelcome media frenzy, throughout which frightening and ostensibly impossible things continued to take place inside the seemingly ordinary semi-detached North London house: continued raps and knocks on the walls as though some unseen presence was trying to communicate, objects thrown and moved unaccountably – Guy Playfair witnessed a large armchair slide along the floor and overturn by itself while Maurice Grosse was hit in the face by a cardboard box containing cushions and soft toys – while the equipment of both the psychical researchers and the journalists began to behave in odd and inexplicable ways – cassette tapes jammed while recordings were found to have been wiped and spoilt, fully charged camera flash-guns suddenly became drained of power, and an infra-red television camera inexplicably malfunctioned in the presence of specialist electronics experts from Cambridge. 'The atmosphere was one of absolute confusion, not knowing what on earth was going to happen next,' Guy Playfair recalled much later. 'The girls... were losing a lot of sleep, affecting their school work. It wasn't nice at all.' And there were even more disturbing things to come...

Throughout the weeks that followed, and with the intense and unnerving poltergeist activity showing no sign of alleviating or dying down, it became quite clear to both SPR investigators as well as other regular visitors to the house – Douglas Bence and Graham Morris spent a large amount of their spare time at Green Street in the hope of witnessing and photographing phenomena – that the focus of the strange disturbances was without doubt the younger daughter Janet Hodgson who, by December 1977, had celebrated her twelfth birthday. In her presence inexplicable incidents rapidly escalated

Front page of the *Daily Mirror* for 10 September 1977, the first published account of what is now regarded as one of the most important poltergeist hauntings to date. *(UKpressonline)*

and the young girl herself, on the threshold of puberty, appeared to be physically targeted and attacked by a malevolent and powerful invisible force. Sheets and bedclothes were pulled off her as she lay in her single bed; window curtains acting as though alive attempted to wrap themselves round her neck; on several occasions she was physically pulled out of bed by invisible hands, and once the bed's mattress was bodily dragged off the bedstead and dumped on top of her as she lay sprawled and exhausted on the floor. It seemed that the Enfield Poltergeist was following a classic pattern established by psychical researchers in previously reported cases covering many years and countries: that an adolescent child was nearly always present and through or about whom the phenomena was able to manifest.

In an attempt to obtain photographic evidence of the disturbances affecting the young Janet, Graham Morris set up a static camera in one corner of the back bedroom equipped with a motor drive and remote operation. Sequences of photographs taken using this remote camera seem to show pillows and bedclothes moving by themselves, as well as Janet Hodgson levitating and being thrown screaming across the bedroom. As a protective measure it became necessary to regularly sedate the child with valium, but despite the medication, dramatic and disturbing phenomena continued to take place. On one occasion, a sedated Janet was put to bed in her usual back bedroom, after which Mrs Hodgson and several visitors retired to the living room downstairs. Suddenly a loud crash from the first floor sent Peggy Hodgson's brother John and photographer Graham Morris rushing for the stairs. On entering Janet's bedroom they were shocked to find she was nowhere to be seen: following a search she was discovered in the far corner of the front bedroom, unconscious on top of a large radio set.

During the run-up to Christmas 1977, the Enfield poltergeist entered a new and seemingly even more incredible phase. Strange whistling and dog-like barking noises became audible in the house and both the Hodgsons together with Grosse and Playfair realised that they appeared to be coming from Janet Hodgson. By the second week of December, the barking noises had transformed themselves into a gruff male voice, a sinister personality over which Janet claimed she had no control. The voice answered questions posed by the researchers and was tape-recorded by Maurice Grosse on several occasions. At first it appeared that Janet was simply helping the haunting along by performing a bad attempt at ventriloquism. However, an experiment with a laryngograph showed that the voice was being produced by the vestibular fold or false vocal cords, and research by Guy Playfair at the SPR library showed that the phenomenon had been reported many times in cases of poltergeist haunting and 'diabolical possession' over the past 300 years.

The 'voice' of the Enfield Poltergeist has become one of the most well-known aspects of the case, but despite its familiarity, the researchers were never able to establish whether it was a secondary personality of Janet herself, or an independent or discarnate 'entity' speaking through her. At times several personalities appeared to be present, the most prominent of which, a man who called himself 'Bill', claimed to have been a former tenant of the house and imparted information that seemed highly unlikely Janet Hodgson would have known or been able to find out. 'Bill' described how he had gone blind and later, while sitting in a chair in the living room, had suffered a haemorrhage and died in the house. Following the publication of Guy Playfair's *This House is Haunted*, the author received a letter from the nephew of a previous Green Lane tenant confirming that a man named William Wilkins had in fact lived in the Hodgsons' house in the early 1960s and had died there under identical circumstances.

Perhaps the most controversial claims for astonishing phenomena connected with Janet Hodgson took place around the same time as the appearance of the voice of the ghostly 'Bill'. On 15 December 1977, a day that coincided with Janet's first period, David Robertson, a physicist from Birkbeck College at the University of London, who at Grosse and Playfair's request had moved temporarily into the house in order to carry out technical experiments into the haunting, attempted to induce under controlled conditions the startling levitation phenomena that had seemingly been captured previously by Graham Morris' remote camera. Robertson asked Janet if she could induce a levitation herself by bouncing up and down on her bed while he was present in the room. The eerie voice, which by now was a regular part of the phenomena, agreed to attempt an experiment but was adamant that Robertson had to leave the room. When the physicist was outside on the landing, Janet called out that she was floating in the air, but when Robertson attempted to go back into the bedroom he found that one of the beds had been pushed against the door, preventing it from opening, and the 'levitation' went un-witnessed. It seemed that Janet was simply playing games and fooling about in order, in a naïve and childish way, to impress her new visitor.

Robertson persisted in his attempt and Janet agreed to try a second time, again alone in the room. On this occasion she claimed to have floated up into the air and walked *through* the party wall of the house into Peggy Nottingham's bedroom next door; she went on to describe the room in detail and said she had also left something behind. When Mrs Nottingham went back to her own house she found a book belonging to Janet lying on the floor next to her bed that the young girl claimed she had taken there on purpose. Peggy Nottingham was adamant that Janet had never been upstairs in her house before and was unable to explain both the presence of the book on the floor and Janet's totally accurate description of the room.

Had Janet Hodgson defied all currently accepted laws of science, or was it, as sceptical commentators on the case have claimed, simply a combination of childish pranks and the fallibility of human memory, assisted by the will to believe on the part of the investigators? Later the same day, another of David Robertson's attempts to obtain hard evidence of paranormality at Green Street subsequently produced reports that are much more difficult to explain away so easily.

Continuing with the 'matter through matter' theme, Robertson asked Janet if she could make a large red plastic-covered chair cushion pass through the floor into the living room below while he waited downstairs. Soon after there was a commotion and Janet claimed that the cushion had suddenly disappeared. Robertson searched the room and confirmed that the cushion was nowhere to be seen. Soon afterwards he found it on the roof of the house in a position that Guy Playfair, who later retrieved the cushion by climbing with difficulty out of the window, claimed was impossible to have effected normally. Amazingly, a local baker who was walking along Green Street at the time, claimed that he saw the cushion suddenly appear out of nowhere directly in his line of vision, and was adamant that no one was leaning or throwing anything out of the front window of the house at the time. Sceptical of the stories that were rife in the area concerning the alleged haunting, as he walked past the front of the Hodgson house, the baker later claimed to have seen Janet floating horizontally past the window surrounded by what appeared to be a whirlwind of toys and books that moved and spun about as though suspended on lengths of elastic. The curtains in the room were also billowing inwards, despite the windows being firmly closed. This startling testimony was corroborated by Hazel Short, a lollipop lady who, around the same time, was on duty outside the school directly opposite the house. Mrs Short stated that she too witnessed Janet Hodgson suspended horizontally in front of the window and attempted unsuccessfully to replicate the effect by herself at home. It appears that a third witness to the same event, who Grosse contacted several weeks afterwards, was still so upset by what she had witnessed that she declined to make a statement.

Although the intensity of the phenomena at Green Street peaked in December 1977, the poltergeist continued to be active – with young Janet the centre of its activities. Concerned for both her safety and mental wellbeing, both Mrs Hodgson and the SPR researchers agreed that Janet should receive medical help, and in July 1978, she spent an extended period at the Maudsley Hospital in Denmark Hill, South London, where she underwent a series of professional psychiatric examinations. To the family's relief, as well as that of Playfair and Grosse, the doctors could find nothing wrong with the child and after a six-week stay Janet returned to Enfield.

Although Janet Hodgson was the focal point for the Enfield Poltergeist, eerie happenings still took place at Green Street in her absence. The nearby home of Peggy Hodgson's brother further along the street on occasion became a refuge when the haunted and hostile atmosphere of their own house became too much to bear. On one occasion when the family were staying overnight, John Burcombe was asked to go and fetch an alarm clock from his niece's bedroom. With the house empty and in darkness, Burcombe let himself in, switched on the hallway and landing lights and immediately went upstairs. As he approached the back bedroom, the handle on the door, which was closed, turned by itself and the door swung open. With some fortitude, Burcombe walked into the room and looked about for the alarm clock. As he stood in the centre of the room, the door swung shut behind him, again of its own accord. Locating the clock, he turned and, as he moved toward the bedroom door, it again opened by itself just enough to let him pass through. Not surprisingly, Burcombe made a hasty exit down the stairs and back to the relative safety of his own house. However, it was not the only time that Mrs Hodgson's brother was to experience phenomena at the Green Street house on his own and with the troubled Janet Hodgson absent.

Following Janet's return from the Maudsley Hospital, the Hodgsons took a well-needed break from both the media and paranormal circus and spent a week at the seaside at Clacton. While they were away, John Burcombe regularly visited the house to generally check on things and to take in the Hodgsons' mail; researcher Guy Playfair spent one night alone on the premises, although things were quiet and there were no disturbances. However, as with the incident of the alarm clock, some aspect or fragment of the mysterious force afflicting his young niece was still present at his sister's house, despite the entire family being over fifty miles away, and on this occasion it seemingly seemed to be able to make itself visible. After John Burcombe had again let himself in, he walked into the front room and was stunned to see the figure of a man sitting in one of the dining table chairs. The person was facing away with his back to him, but Burcombe was able to later describe a middle-aged man with thinning grey hair, dressed in a blue-and-white-striped shirt. Thinking that someone had broken into the house, Burcombe was about to challenge the man when he realised that the person had vanished and the chair was empty. In a recorded interview with Maurice Grosse, Burcombe recalled: 'I closed my eyes like a blink for a couple of seconds, opened my eyes – gone! I left the house like a rocket... I was scared.' For John Burcombe, this incident was the most disturbing out of all his experiences with the Enfield Poltergeist and he immediately left his sister's house vowing never to return on his own again. Had Burcombe in fact seen the ghost of the troubled and seemingly earthbound Bill Wilkins?

The appearance of apparitions at Green Street is unusual in that during traditional poltergeist cases they are absent or exceedingly rare and infrequently reported. In the closing days at Enfield other ghosts were allegedly seen: a small child, the figure of an old man, the legs of a man wearing blue trousers going up the stairs (witnessed by Mrs Hodgson), and, perhaps something unique in the history of ghost hunting, the apparition of one of the investigators himself, that of Maurice Grosse, which a visitor saw standing in the hall and then walk upstairs, when in fact the researcher had been upstairs for over half an hour and had not left the bedroom where he had been holding a solo vigil.

However, after over a year, in October 1978, the haunting finally ceased, coinciding with (and possibly even being brought about by) a visit to Enfield by Dono Gmelig-Meyling, a psychic medium from Holland brought to England by a Dutch journalist, who claimed to be able to bring peace to the Hodgsons' house. Several mediums had in fact visited the Hodgsons during the preceding fourteen months including Gerry Sherrick and Matthew Manning, whose book *The Link* (1974) describes the psychic's own experiences with poltergeist phenomena. These psychics had created brief intervals of calm in the Hodgson house, but on this occasion Gmelig-Meyling appeared to have instigated a permanent closure to the haunting. After sitting alone in one of the first-floor bedrooms for twenty minutes while Guy Playfair and journalist Peter Liefhebber waited in the living room, the Dutchman joined them downstairs and announced that the haunting presence had left and that the family would suffer no further disturbances. Apart from a brief resurgence of a very mild nature lasting only a few days in April 1979, this proved to be true.

Despite the attitude of some members of the SPR towards the Enfield case, Grosse remained a member for the rest of his life and served for several years as Chairman of its Spontaneous Phenomena Committee. He carried out several investigations of other poltergeist 'infestations' and alleged cases of haunting and was rewarded again with phenomena – at Charlton House in Greenwich he successfully recorded the sound of a piece of crockery which apparently materialised and smashed during the course of an investigative vigil and at another house in North London in the company of Mary Rose Barrington (who carried out a review of the Enfield Poltergeist for the SPR which concluded that as well as misrepresentation and some hoaxing, the case for genuine paranormality was high), Grosse succeeded in recording on videotape the sound of poltergeist knocking. Grosse also attended an experimental sitting with physical medium Rita Goold from Leicester, but the results of this were never published.

Shortly before his death from cancer in 2006, Maurice Grosse arranged for Dr Melvyn Willin to catalogue his collection of psychical research material including case histories, correspondence, cassette and videotapes, press cuttings, photographs and slides spanning thirty years of active investigation and this now forms part of the SPR archive held at the Cambridge University Library. His most famous investigation, however, continues to intrigue and fascinate over thirty years after its conclusion.

Consult: Matthew Manning, *The Link: The Extraordinary Gifts of a Teenage Psychic* (Colin Smythe, Gerrards Cross, 1974); Guy Lyon Playfair, *This House is Haunted: The Investigation of the Enfield Poltergeist* (Souvenir Press, London, 1980); Colin Wilson, *Poltergeist!: A Study in Destructive Haunting* (New English Library, London, 1981).

Fear in the North: The South Shields Poltergeist (2006)

Thirty years after the events at Enfield, North London, another major British poltergeist haunting became the subject of similar practical research, media scrutiny and controversy. For nearly twelve months, a small terraced house was the unlikely setting for an extraordinary confrontation between a frightened Tyneside family, two local ghost hunters, and a sinister invading entity involving an unprecedented level of physical and paranormal violence.

For our final case we return to the North East of England and the environs of the River Tyne, 160 years after the bizarre happenings in the home of the Procter family at Willington Mill, for a modern haunting that is perhaps the most extreme of all those that we have examined in this journey through two and a half centuries of British supernatural history. The case that has become known as the South Shields Poltergeist brings the experience of the paranormal firmly into the new millennium, mixing the age-old world of ghosts and psychic phenomena with our own technology-driven era of mobile communication, computerisation and the seemingly limitless possibilities of the Internet. It is, to date, a powerful twenty-first-century example of what has been described as 'one of the most bewildering phenomena we are ever likely to come across': the chilling, night-black world of the poltergeist.

In the early summer of 2006, Marianne Peterworth, a care home supervisor, and her partner, Marc Karlsonn, a caterer, both in their twenties, became convinced that their home on a South Tyneside housing estate was haunted. The house on Lock Street, built in the early 1980s, had no previous history of unusual happenings, but running up to the month of June, a continuing number of unexplainable incidents began to baffle and frighten the young couple: knocking and bumping noises, coats were found trailed up the staircase, ornaments and other items including a vase, a set of stepladders and a chair appeared to move about the house by themselves, a bedroom blind was continually taken down despite being firmly replaced a number of times, cups appeared to jump from the kitchen worktops, while on one occasion as Marianne and her father were standing by the open back door, a cup appeared to drop from an upstairs window which, on investigation, was found to be closed and the blind drawn. A number of incidents appeared to take place in and around their three-year-old son Robert's bedroom: furniture in the room was found moved out onto the first-floor landing and toy cars were thrown at the couple as they walked down the stairs; on each occasion their son was playing in another part of the house. When her brother found a toy rocking horse hanging by its reins from the loft hatch, Marianne, who had already visited a local spiritualist church in the hope of finding a solution to the problem, asked a priest to visit the house and carry out a blessing. However, despite the religious ceremony, the disturbances continued.

On 9 July 2006, the family spent the afternoon away from the house. On their return, furniture was found to be moved and the rocking horse had been transported from Robert's bedroom into another room. Following the visit of the priest, there was a period of calm, but a short time afterwards, the familiar happenings began again and there were the first inklings of the threatening atmosphere and violence that was to pervade much of the later haunting. One evening after their son had been put to bed, a large toy rabbit was found moved onto the upstairs landing with one of Marc's box cutter blades placed in its hand; while a short time later, as Marianne sat in the kitchen, the chair seemed to be pulled out from under her as if by an invisible hand.

Around this time, the happenings at Lock Street, in a similar way to the disturbances at Enfield, came to the attention of two regional researchers who we have already briefly met in connection with their retrospective investigation of the Willington Mill case: Darren W. Ritson, a ghost hunter from Newcastle, and Michael Hallowell, a free-lance journalist and writer who columns for the local *Shields Gazette*. On 17 July 2006, they visited the house and interviewed the family, during which time both men were rewarded with incidents of apparent phenomena. During a period upstairs in Robert's bedroom, a plastic nut from a toy workbench appeared to fly across the room and strike the door of a cupboard with a loud cracking sound: both Marianne and Marc were in full view of the investigators at the time. A short while afterwards, on the opposite side of the room to where the adults were standing and totally out of reach, the same plastic nut jumped off the top of a chest of drawers, followed a minute later by a toy car which slid off a shelf into a wastepaper bin. Suitably intrigued, the researchers agreed to return to the house later on in the week, while at the same time requesting that Marianne keep a diary of any further happenings.

Over the next few days, the activity in the house on Lock Street continued. Knocks and banging sounds came from the empty upper floor while the family were down-stairs in the living room; toys were thrown about, either seemingly appearing from nowhere or flicking up off of shelves and pieces of furniture, striking the windows and walls of Robert's bedroom with startling force – on one occasion a plastic toy struck the bathroom door with a tremendous bang while Marianne was alone upstairs, while the following afternoon, a wooden train struck Marc on the head as plastic nuts and screws flew about the room. Furniture and other items were found moved or thrown about and doors appeared to open by themselves. Around Thursday lunchtime, 20 July, two chairs were discovered stacked on top of one another on a table in one of the upstairs bedrooms, and a short time later, on entering the main bedroom, Marianne saw the vacuum cleaner shaking and vibrating by itself despite being switched off and unplugged from the wall. Later, while the couple were downstairs in the kitchen, Marianne was partially successful in filming the movement of one of the dining room chairs which was seen to pull itself away from the table, using her mobile phone.

Worryingly for the young couple, whatever strange forces were at work in the unassuming terraced house appeared to be becoming increasingly focused on their three-year-old son Robert. One evening, a short time after he had been put to bed, Marianne looked into his bedroom and was horrified to find the child lying with his eyes wide open underneath the table in his room with his quilt wrapped around him, as though he had been lifted off the bed and crammed into the small space. Robert himself claimed on several occasions to see a man inside the house, sitting on the living room sofa, standing inside the cupboard under the stairs, and floating in the air over his bed. During periods when the house was empty, the family found items of furniture, including the chest of drawers from Robert's bedroom, pulled out onto the upstairs landing on their return, while crayons and other items known to be in the room appeared to drop onto the back patio, despite the bedroom window being closed and the blind drawn.

On Friday, 21 July 2006, Michael Hallowell and Darren Ritson returned to Lock Street and again interviewed the family. After discussing the happenings that had taken place since their previous visit, Hallowell, of Native American heritage, suggested that the activities of the poltergeist might be restricted by the performance of an Indian 'smudging' ritual, a symbolic ceremony designed to achieve specific goals on a spiritual path known as 'The Medicine Way'. With the couple's agreement, the 'smudging' ceremony was carried out, but despite a slight alleviation following the investigators' visit, the disturbances in the house continued to occur. Words and messages, seemingly from the ghost, nicknamed 'Sammy', began to appear on one of Robert's erasable doodle-boards, and the movement of objects and the sound of an invisible person moving about inside the house continued to plague the household. One evening, as Marianne lay in the bath, the bathroom door suddenly swung open by itself with incredible force. Sitting up, the young mother could clearly see that the landing beyond was empty, but further along the hallway, shadows cast by a night light were moving about on the open bedroom door of her son's room where the child lay sleeping, accompanied by shuffling noises and the distinct sound of footsteps creaking the floorboards. Frightened, but assuming that it was Marc looking for something in the bedroom, she called out twice but there was no answer, although the sounds of movement and the flickering shadows on the bedroom door continued. In answer to her second call, Marc, who had been downstairs all the time, came up from the kitchen, at which point the disturbances instantly ceased. When the couple checked the room, they found Robert fast asleep in his bed and the only sound was his steady rhythmic breathing.

During the course of the South Shields investigation, a number of other investigators were invited to visit the house by the two principal researchers. Jill Butler, a psychic medium and friend of Michael Hallowell, was the first to spend time at Lock Street and it was during her initial visit on Friday 25 August that a particularly sinister incident that became a hallmark of much of the later phenomena to occur around both the young family and the researchers took place. After a period spent discussing the recent happenings, Marianne, accompanied by Ritson and Hallowell, took Jill for a tour around the house. As the group entered Robert's bedroom, they were confronted by a strange and disturbing sight: a bizarre tableau created by two of the child's soft toys which had been positioned on a low plastic table together with one of the carving knives from the kitchen downstairs. What astonished all the onlookers was that the knife had been arranged so that one toy, a rabbit, appeared to be holding the blade against the throat of the second toy, a soft duck which lay upside down on the table top.

A short time later, as Robert played in the garden and the adults gathered in the living room, two large plastic bricks that had been stored in a box in the child's bedroom dropped with a loud clatter onto the patio outside, as though they had passed through the closed and shuttered window. At the time, the investigators were controlling the bedroom and a locked-off video camera set up by Darren Ritson showed that during the period that the incident took place, no one had entered or left the bedroom. However, unknown to both Marc and Marianne, as well as the three investigators, the South Shields Poltergeist was keeping its most powerful phenomenon of the day in reserve for later. After the three ghost hunters had left, the couple took their son to a local nursery, leaving the house locked and empty. On their return, Robert's bedroom was found to be in complete chaos, as though a 'psychic storm' similar to the forces summoned by the Black Monk of Pontefract had torn through it: furniture was overturned, bedclothes strewn over the floor, toys pulled from shelves and cupboards, while the child's bed had been bodily dragged out into the middle of the room.

The disturbances at Lock Street were to last throughout September 2006 and during that time other witnesses testified to experiencing strange and frightening phenomena. Bob and Marrisse Whittaker, husband and wife broadcasters from Orion TV, at the invitation of Michael Hallowell, interviewed Marc and Marianne at the house and were witnesses to apparent phenomena. During the course of her interview with Marianne, one of Robert's electronic toys began turning itself on and

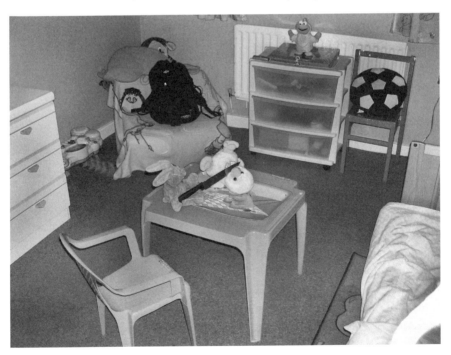

The sinister manipulation of ordinary children's toys was a chilling manifestation of the South Shields Poltergeist. *(Michael Hallowell/Darren W. Ritson)*

off and uttering the phrase *Can you find me?* that was later found not to be part of its ordinary programming. Both Michael Hallowell's father Peter, and his wife Jackie, claimed to have seen the figure of a man wearing a beige-coloured T-shirt standing next to the family and the investigators when no one matching the description was present in the house. Several members of Ritson's North East Ghost Research Team (NEGRT) spent time with the family and confirmed several incidents: objects being thrown around and manipulated in strange ways, messages – *Stop it now* and *Go now* – appearing on Robert's doodle-board, as well as a twenty-first-century interpretation of the writing phenomenon that has accompanied other poltergeist cases from the past including Enfield: the appearance of anomalous text messages addressed to Marianne on mobile phones, at times when the devices were either switched off or completely deactivated. These in themselves have become chilling taglines: on one occasion a message read *the bitch will die today*, while another proclaimed *going to die today going to get you.*

As the investigation progressed, it became clear that the focus of the Lock Street Poltergeist was twenty-two-year-old Marc Karlsonn. This became dramatically apparent on what has been called the 'Night of Terror', subsequently one of the most controversial aspects of the case. Around twenty minutes to midnight on the evening of 26 August 2006, as he was watching television in his South Tyneside home, Michael Hallowell received a frantic telephone call from an hysterical Marianne Peterworth asking him to come to the house. Ordering a taxi, Hallowell improvised a makeshift bag of equipment including a stills camera, and arrived at Lock Street just after midnight. About an hour before, shortly after the couple had retired for the night, objects began to be thrown at them as they lay in their bed, and the quilt itself became animated as though something was trying to drag it off the bed. At the same time, Marc, like Janet Hodgson at Enfield and Diane Pritchard at Pontefract, suddenly seemed to be at the centre of a frightening physical assault. As his body was overcome by a fierce burning sensation, vicious scratches began to appear across his

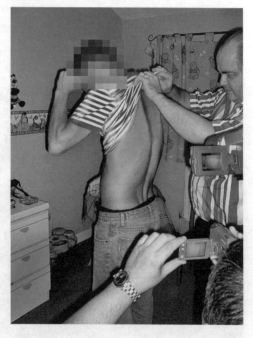

Over a dozen marks were inflicted on Marc Karlsonn during the 'Night of Terror'. *(Michael Hallowell/Darren W. Ritson)*

torso: on his arrival, Hallowell was able to observe and photograph over a dozen marks that were still visible on the skin.

A short time later, as Michael Hallowell and Marianne explored the house, Robert's bedroom was again found in complete disarray. As he surveyed the mess, Hallowell made a bizarre and evidential discovery: a blue plastic table had become completely distorted as though subjected to a strong heat source which had caused the material to warp and buckle before setting again in its new shape. An hour later, the table was found to be back in its original unaltered form. It was at this point, as Hallowell stood taking photographs of the wrecked bedroom and the table, that both he and Marianne had another unnerving experience. Through the open bedroom door, the couple both saw a tall black figure slowly walk from the bathroom across the landing directly outside and pass out of sight into the main bedroom. As it crossed the door and headed towards the bathroom, the figure, which the researcher later described as looking like a man dressed in a jet-black body stocking 'which covered him from the top of his head to the soles of his feet', appeared to pause momentarily and stare in at them before moving away. This sinister apparition, witnessed by both Hallowell and Marianne, appeared to personify the malicious and violent nature of the entire South Shields case, and as such remains one of the most chilling aspects of the Lock Street haunting.

The 'Night of Terror' concluded with another physical assault on the troubled Marc Karlsonn, one that was witnessed and filmed by an incredulous and horrified Michael Hallowell. As the investigator kept a vigil in their bedroom while the couple attempted to get some rest, the caterer began to complain of the hot burning sensation that had preceded the earlier incident. At the investigator's request, Marc pulled off his T-shirt and Hallowell could see that the marks made earlier in the evening had virtually disappeared, but as he watched, more marks and scratches suddenly began to appear. In their subsequent book, *The South Shields Poltergeist* (2008), Hallowell recalled the incident in vivid detail:

> You could actually watch the scratches forming… First an elongated red patch, then sharply defined scratches within it. Shortly afterwards, cuts started to appear on the right-hand facing side of his back; they immediately bled. Then his skin started to change colour. It went dark, almost as if it was sunburnt. At one point, there was more red, angry, discoloured, cut and scratched flesh than ordinary… You'd have thought he'd been given the cat o' nine tails. It was horrendous.

As before, the marks lasted for a short time and then began to fade. For what remained of the night, Marc and Marianne attempted to get some sleep and Hallowell retired to the kitchen, where he made notes on the evening's dramatic activities. It was during this period that he was able to capture what has become one of the case's most iconic

A bottle of mineral water seemingly balanced on edge by supernatural forces, from videotaped footage recorded by paranormal researcher Michael Hallowell. *(Michael Hallowell/ Darren W. Ritson)*

images: a plastic bottle of mineral water leaning at a crazy, seemingly impossible angle on the kitchen tabletop.

> I couldn't believe what I was seeing. Instead of standing flat on its base, the bottle was tipped sharply at an angle. I could see no way that the position could be explained by the conventional laws of physics. In scientific terms, the position the bottle had adopted seemed to be impossible.

Over the weekend of 2-3 September 2006, Ritson and Hallowell organised a night-long vigil at Lock Street accompanied by several members of the NEGRT group, during which another more elaborate 'smudging' ritual was carried out in an attempt to cleanse the house of the haunting presence. In much the same way that the presence of the Dutch psychic Dono Gmelig-Meyling appeared to bring the Enfield Poltergeist case to a conclusion, this ceremony, now firmly focused on Marc Karlsonn, was the pivotal moment (although phenomena continued in the house for some time afterwards) in bringing twelve months of unhappiness and fear for the young Tyneside family to a close. Now the researchers were able to return fire on a psychic level and bring the fight into the camp of the haunter itself. Throughout the night, all of the investigators claimed to have experienced unusual happenings: the movement of objects, knocks and bangs, messages appearing on Robert's doodle-board and on Marianne Peterworth's mobile phone. For most of September, the house on Lock Street was quiet. Following a brief resurgence of activity which lasted a week towards the end of the month, the haunting finally came to a conclusion in the early autumn of 2006.

Although a common thread or pattern runs through all of these extreme poltergeist hauntings, the case at South Shields has the closest parallels with that of Enfield: modern ghosts for a modern age. As well as the violent movement of objects, apparitions and apports, the vicious attacks on Marc Karlsson mirrored the dramatic levitations and other physical phenomena centred on the young Janet Hodgson. The attitude of the principal investigators, like Guy Playfair and Maurice Grosse, was not one of dispassionate observation: both researchers felt a duty to help the terrified family through their extraordinary ordeal, at the same time attempting to obtain and preserve for posterity as much evidence as possible of paranormal activity under what were at times intensely difficult and demanding conditions. Like the Enfield Poltergeist, the case has polarised opinions and in many ways demonstrates the difficulty that psychical researchers face in both investigating cases of haunting and afterwards presenting the evidence to a public audience in a post-*Amityville Horror* world.

Early in October 2009, three years after the cessation of activity at Lock Street, and following the publication of a full-length account of the haunting, Alan Murdie, Chairman of the Ghost Club and an experienced researcher, appraised the case for the Society for Psychical Research. As well as interviewing both Michael Hallowell and Darren Ritson, Murdie spent a day examining the mass of evidence collected and now preserved at Hallowell's South Tyneside home. Writing subsequently in the SPR *Journal* about both the haunting itself and the investigative approach of the researchers, Murdie commented:

> Certainly, if events happened as alleged, it was reasoned there would be a considerable quantity of documentary, photographic and other evidence available that would be consistent with the claims… This proved to be the case. I was able to inspect over 450 original photographs, and make copies of many of them. Some of these provide a measure of corroboration to specific incidents… such as the claimed distortion of a plastic table and its apparent restoration to its original shape. There are also films, documents and witness statements… The authors revealed in confidence a number of details and contacts not disclosed in their book, so the opportunity is available for further detailed study of this case. As a consequence, I am of the opinion the South Shields Poltergeist joins a small but significant collection of spontaneous cases where credible evidence has been obtained by investigators whilst disturbances were still occurring.

In 1979, researcher Michael Goss demonstrated that over 1,000 poltergeist cases had been recorded in nearly a century, between 1880 and 1975, two years before the explosion of activity at Green Street, Enfield. There is no doubt that as old hauntings fade away, new ones appear to take their place. We can only imagine what the rest of the twenty-first century will reveal to the researchers, both of today and tomorrow, who are brave enough to seek out the future extreme hauntings of Britain.

[*N.B. In order to protect the identity of the family involved in the South Shields case, their names together with that of the address of the house involved have not been made public. For this commentary we have adopted the pseudonyms used by the original investigators.*]

Consult: Michael Goss, *Poltergeists: An Annotated Bibliography of Works in English, circa 1880-1975* (Scarecrow Press, New York, 1979); Michael J. Hallowell & Darren W. Ritson, *The South Shields Poltergeist: One Family's Fight Against an Invisible Intruder* (Sutton Publishing, Stroud, 2008); *Darren W. Ritson, Supernatural North: True Ghost Stories* (Amberley Publishing, Stroud, 2009)

ABOUT THE AUTHORS

PAUL ADAMS was born in Epsom, Surrey in 1966 and has been interested in the paranormal since the mid-1970s. Employed as a draughtsman in the UK construction industry for nearly thirty years, he has worked in three haunted buildings but has yet to see a true ghost. As well as the history of psychical research, his main interests at present are in materialisation mediumship and the physical phenomena of Spiritualism. He has contributed articles to several specialist paranormal periodicals and acted as editor and publisher for *Two Haunted Counties* (2010), the memoirs of Luton ghost hunter, Tony Broughall. Adams is the co-author, with Peter Underwood and Eddie Brazil, of *The Borley Rectory Companion* (2009) and *Shadows in the Nave* (2011), and has written *Ghosts & Gallows* (2012), a study of British true crime cases with paranormal connections, and *Haunted Luton* (2012) where he has lived since 2006. He is also an amateur mycologist and viola-player.

EDDIE BRAZIL was born in Dublin in 1956 and was later raised in London. His first encounter with the paranormal occurred at the age of ten when, at his family home in Stockwell, the sound of disembodied footsteps made him flee the house in terror. It was an experience which led to a lifelong fascination with the supernormal, in particular the haunting of Borley Rectory, about which he has co-authored a definitive study, and has also written for magazines and the media. Aside from ghost hunting, his other interests include photography, church architecture, exploring the sites of former battlefields, and the classic ghost stories of M.R. James. He is also a guitarist and composer, and in 1983 wrote the theme music to the British comedy movie, *Expresso Splasho*. He is currently working on a book of original photographic interpretations of the ghosts of M.R. James. Eddie lives with his wife and daughter in Hazlemere, Buckinghamshire.

The authors at St Lawrence's Church, West Wycombe. *(Rebecca Brazil)*

The world of the paranormal is in constant interaction with our everyday lives and the authors are always interested in collecting and hearing about accounts of new and original hauntings, poltergeist phenomena and mediumship. If you have had an experience you would be willing to share with us, please get in touch. We can be reached by e-mail at info@limburypress.co.uk, or alternatively write to us c/o The History Press, The Mill, Brimscombe Port, Stroud, Gloucestershire, GL5 2QG. All information will be treated in confidence.

BIBLIOGRAPHY & FURTHER READING

History of Psychical Research

Beloff, John, *Parapsychology: A Concise History* (The Athlone Press, London, 1993)

Berger, Arthur S. & Berger, Joyce, *The Encyclopedia of Parapsychology and Psychical Research* (Paragon House, New York, 1991)

Fielding, Yvette & O'Keeffe, Ciarán, *Ghost Hunters: A Guide to Investigating the Paranormal* (Hodder & Stoughton, London, 2006)

Underwood, Peter, *The Ghost Hunter's Guide* (Blandford Press, Poole, 1986)

National & Regional Guides

Adams, Norman, *Haunted Scotland* (Mainstream Publishing, Edinburgh, 1998)

Broughall, Tony & Adams, Paul, *Two Haunted Counties: A Ghost Hunter's Companion to Bedfordshire & Hertfordshire* (The Limbury Press, Luton, 2010)

Haunted Series, The History Press: Wide-ranging collection of paranormal guides covering towns and cities throughout the UK. A full list of titles can be found at *www.thehistorypress.co.uk*

Haining, Peter (Ed.), *The Mammoth Book of True Hauntings* (Constable & Robinson Ltd, London, 2008)

Jones, Richard, *Haunted Britain and Ireland* (New Holland Publishers Ltd, London, 2007)

Puttick, Betty (Ed.), *Supernatural England* (Countryside Books, Newbury, 2002)

Underwood, Peter, *A Gazetteer of British Ghosts* (Souvenir Press, London, 1971)

National Paranormal Organisations

For anyone involved in serious research into the paranormal, membership of the following three British societies should be considered. They are the Ghost Club: (www.ghostclub.org.uk), founded in 1862; *ASSAP*, the Association for the Scientific Study of Anomalous Phenomena: (www.assap.ac.uk), founded in 1981: and the *SPR*, the Society for Psychical Research: (www.spr.ac.uk), established in 1882. Their publications and archives contain invaluable information and resource material, much of which is now being made available online.

INDEX